The Development of the Financial Sector
in Southeast Europe

Springer
Berlin
Heidelberg
New York
Hong Kong
London
Milan
Paris
Tokyo

Ingrid Matthäus-Maier
J. D. von Pischke
Editors

The Development
of the Financial Sector
in Southeast Europe

Innovative Approaches
in Volatile Environments

With 40 Figures
and 29 Tables

 Springer

Ingrid Matthäus-Maier
KfW
Palmengartenstraße 5–9
60325 Frankfurt
Germany
ingrid.matthaeus-maier@kfw.de

Dr. J. D. von Pischke
2529 Trophy Lane
Reston
VA 20191-2126
USA
vonpischke@frontierfinance.com

ISBN 3-540-20327-3 Springer-Verlag Berlin Heidelberg New York

Cataloging-in-Publication Data applied for
A catalog record for this book is available from the Library of Congress.
Bibliographic information published by Die Deutsche Bibliothek
Die Deutsche Bibliothek lists this publication in the Deutsche Nationalbibliografie; detailed bibliographic
data is available in the Internet at <http://dnb.ddb.de>.

Springer-Verlag Berlin Heidelberg New York
a member of BertelsmannSpringer Science+Business Media GmbH

http://www.springer.de

© Springer-Verlag Berlin · Heidelberg 2004
Printed in Germany

Hardcover-Design: Erich Kirchner, Heidelberg

SPIN 10967133   43/3130/DK-5 4 3 2 1 0 – Printed on acid-free paper

The Contribution of the German Government to the Reconstruction of Southeast Europe

Michael Bohnet

Formerly Director General at the Federal Ministry for Economic Cooperation and Development, Bonn, Germany

Just a few years ago we witnessed tremendous upheavals, unspeakable crimes against humanity and massive armed strife throughout the territory of the former Yugoslavia. Enormous progress has been made since that time towards achieving stability in the entire region. Where people were displaced and subjected to violence, it has now become possible in some places to live peacefully together and to engage in economic activity, albeit on a modest scale in many cases. Where governmental institutions had been destroyed or had never existed, new structures are now able to grow. Where companies and markets had been destroyed, production and growth have once more taken hold.

The German Government Position on Political Developments in Southeast Europe

The prime goal of the German government's activities in Southeast Europe has been to restore and safeguard political stability. Only political stability can provide a basis for peaceful development, for economic recovery and for securing a reliable social framework. We know from experience in Western Europe that political stability and prospects for peaceful development can best be reached through cooperation among peoples and countries. Southeast Europe is prone to conflict and continues to harbour explosive potential. In this situation, integration and cooperation are not only relevant, but of equal importance for ensuring domestic stability. The international community has reached agreement with representatives of the countries in Southeast Europe on current territorial borders. Now it is vital for the different ethnic groups living within those borders to achieve a balance of interests, to be given equal opportunities for participation in the political process and for sharing the benefits of economic progress.

Some success is already evident, as shown by the transparent local elections in Kosovo in 2002, whereas other developments, such as the tragic death of Serbia's

Prime Minister Zoran Djindjic, demonstrate that important challenges remain. We are following the processes of democratisation with a critical eye but not without optimism, although it cannot yet be taken for granted that political tensions in these countries will ease for good. Progress requires continued and determined action. The German government, in particular through the activities of Federal Ministry for Economic Cooperation and Development (BMZ), is fully committed to these goals.

As neighbours of Southeast Europe, we bear special responsibility for stable political and economic development in the region. We also have a special interest in peaceful and democratic development, which is of tremendous importance for security and stability throughout Europe. Moreover, the stabilisation of Southeast Europe will create an attractive location for economic activity and an attractive market in our immediate neighbourhood comprising more than 55 million people. These prospects must play a role and guide the debate on how intensively, and based on what responsibilities, cooperation with the countries of Southeast Europe should be continued.

Prospects for Southeast Europe

German and international activities in Southeast Europe have long since moved beyond emergency or humanitarian aid to cooperation that has a sustained impact and is geared towards bringing about lasting structural change. In certain cases, we have succeeded in achieving self-sustaining processes of reconstruction that provide a basis for stakeholders to consider their integration into Europe at large, which can foster peaceful development throughout the entire region and making it permanent.

The European Union stabilisation and association agreements are making a vital contribution in this respect. Two such agreements have been concluded, with Albania and Croatia, and at the time of writing a third was under negotiation with Macedonia. It is encouraging that a date has been specified for the possible accession of Bulgaria and Romania in 2007. The prospect of EU accession is no doubt partly due to our sustained efforts to promote the modernisation of government and society (with the participation of the ethnic minorities) in these two countries. In turn, this should provide an incentive for the other countries in Southeast Europe to undertake the major efforts required to create similar prospects for themselves. BMZ is doing its share to help with the transition process on which this depends.

German Government Activities in Southeast Europe

At Germany's initiative, the Stability Pact for Southeast Europe was established in June 1999 through an enormous effort by the international community. First, it mobilises new funds for development in Southeast Europe. Second, the Stability Pact has been an important political tool for fostering mutual cooperation between the countries in question and especially their integration into overall European structures. The Pact has been called a milestone in the history of cooperation. In the focal areas of the Stability Pact, participating countries make concrete commitments to domestic reform, peaceful coexistence, the peaceful and cooperative resolution of diverging interests and constructive approaches to important regional problems. The donor nations of Western Europe, in turn, share their experience and financial resources to enable the countries of Southeast Europe to pursue their own path of self-reliant, ownership-based development.

Evidence of the commitment by the German government is the funding we provide. Within the scope of the Stability Pact alone, the German government has made available about € 615 million of special funds. In addition, resources are made available from BMZ's budget: commitments over the past ten years or so have totalled approximately € 1.6 billion. In 2001, the volume of BMZ commitments for the countries of Southeast Europe was about € 150 million.

The German government's overall strategy for the utilisation of these funds foresees coordinated action by various ministries, using their specific expertise on a case-by-case basis to contribute to a comprehensive and coherent approach. The Federal Ministry of Economics and Labour (BMWA) supports the involvement of German enterprises (for example through grants for market studies) while contributions by the Federal Foreign Office are mainly for democratisation, human rights, support to the media, assistance in moving closer to the EU, humanitarian aid, disarmament and arms control.

Priority Areas of BMZ Involvement

BMZ is the lead agency for economic cooperation and development tasks of high political significance. Priority areas comprise a vast range of tasks. In its cooperation with Southeast Europe, BMZ uses all its tried-and-tested instruments, adapted to each of the different countries of the region. This applies, in particular, to financial cooperation programmes, which have developed innovative instruments within the framework of the Stability Pact.

Reforming State and Society

Many Southeast European countries need to reform and modernise their government administrative structures. A high degree of political, economic and social uncertainty hampers the democratic and peaceful development of society and has a negative impact on investment and financing. Of decisive importance is a stable and transparent political situation and the further development of popular participation. It is important to build strong government structures for efficient administration and a functioning legal and institutional environment. In Southeast Europe, unresolved property disputes, outdated tax systems and inefficient administrative procedures continue to hamper the dynamism of small and medium-sized enterprises.

For these reasons, BMZ strengthens governmental institutions through legal and structural reform, promotes the development, effectiveness and integrity of administrative bodies, and supports democratic forces. BMZ addresses this concern through official development cooperation, nongovernmental organisations and political foundations.

Strengthening the Financial Sector and Promoting the Private Sector

We are particularly committed to strengthening the financial sectors in the region. The KfW Group is the lead German government agency implementing these programmes. A functioning financial sector is especially important for mobilising domestic resources for development. Sustained economic growth and increases in employment are possible only if we succeed in raising the level of investment. The financial sector plays a key role in this regard: the loans it provides enable people to make investments.

As in many developing and transition countries, the financial sector in Southeast Europe often fails to fulfil this task. Small and medium-sized enterprises (SMEs) are largely denied access to financial services, but sustained investment is impossible without these companies. Southeast Europe has taken the first important steps in this regard: most newly created jobs and sources of income in the region are a result of the activities of SMEs. The decisive question is: how can we ensure that financial sector potential is used to the full?

Strong financial sector institutions are essential in order to protect the economy from destabilising financial transactions. We need to ensure that efficient supervisory institutions and appropriate financial standards are in place and that these institutions are strengthened in the transition process. Germany has made important contributions in this regard. For instance, we provide advice via Deutsche Gesellschaft für Technische Zusammenarbeit (GTZ) to Serbia's national bank on legal, structural and management issues. A further focus of our efforts is on the rehabilitation and reform of state banks.

We have taken innovative action to develop the financial sector in the region. In Kosovo, for instance, Micro Enterprise Bank – which we were instrumental in setting up and have subsequently supported – is just one success story. Its credit services are tailored primarily to SMEs and microenterprises. This concept was developed with substantial input from KfW. Revolving funds were also set up to increase the effectiveness of the resources deployed. We are exploring how this mode of operation can be made permanent. A decisive indicator of our success is whether we succeed in building local institutions and capacities that are indispensable for sustainability.

We include Germany's private sector in our cooperation. One example of Public-Private Partnership (PPP) in Southeast Europe is the rehabilitation of the water supply in Elbasan, Albania. Berlinwasser worked with local utilities to create a modern system. In Albania, until recently Europe's poorest country, there was very little experience on which to base such a project. Initial difficulties were overcome successfully, producing a model project that provides a wealth of experience for projects in similar sectors elsewhere.

Summary and Outlook

Europe is a shared continent in which all its people should be able to live in peace and make autonomous decisions about their own lives without fear of hunger, poverty, or war. In brief, we want to form a continent in which all citizens can feel at home.

I believe that we can safely claim that BMZ is making an important contribution toward this objective – one that goes well beyond the scope of traditional development cooperation. BMZ's involvement in Southeast Europe has become a core task. This can be seen in its enormous contributions to the Stability Pact for Southeast Europe and the considerable funding it has provided for Southeast Europe. This commitment, this remarkable effort, is worthwhile: a great deal of political and economic progress has been made, progress that can be witnessed by everyone everywhere.

Far-reaching reform, prevention of social upheaval, and adjustment to Euro-Atlantic structures remain on the agenda. An unprecedented political dynamism has emerged in relations among Western, Eastern and Southeast Europe. This dynamism will lead to the accession of ten states to the European Union in the near future, giving BMZ partner countries an incentive to pursue domestic reform, adjust their social and legal systems, and create scope for economic activity while protecting social equity. A positive economic outlook also means promising prospects for civil society in general.

The international community expects a commitment to ownership, readiness to pursue far-reaching reforms in all sectors, a clear commitment to the development of democratic institutions, an active willingness to build a social market system, respect for human rights, and the establishment of a domestic environment that enables people to take their lives into their own hands. We must not forget that the basis of our work and motivation are the people; the outlook ultimately depends upon whether people have faith in the processes of reform and development. This is the big challenge for policymakers.

BMZ will continue to adapt its outreach to the challenges in the region. Southeast Europe can count on the political and economic support of the German government and of BMZ. We will continue to focus our efforts on the development and consolidation of democratic structures, the reorientation towards a social market system, environmental stewardship and on achieving a pluralistic society. The financial sector will continue to play a central role in this regard. We welcome KfW's initiative to publish an assessment of this dynamic progress complete with an exploration of the key issues involved. It is our hope that this work can serve as an example for similar developments in other regions.

Table of Contents

List of Abbreviations

AIMS	Assessing the Impact of Microenterprise Services
AFRICAP	AfriCap Microfinance Fund
ATM	automatic teller machine
BCC	Banca Commerciale Carpatica, Romania
BiH	Bosnia and Herzegovina
BIO	Belgian Investment Corporation for Developing Countries
BMWA	German Federal Ministry of Economics and Labour
BMZ	German Federal Ministry for Economic Cooperation and Development
CBM	Central Bank of Montenegro
CEC	Romanian Savings Bank
CEE	Central and Eastern Europe
CEECs	Central and Eastern European countries
CEPS	Centre for Population, Poverty and Public Policy Studies
CGAP	Consultative Group to Assist the Poorest
CGF	Credit Guarantee Fund
CIS	Commonwealth of Independent States
CKB	Crnogorska Komercijalna Banka, Montenegro
DEFCO	development finance corporation
DEG	Deutsche Investitions- und Entwicklungsgesellschaft mbH
DFID	Department for International Development, United Kingdom
DOEN	Stichting Duurzame Ontwikkeling En Natuurbescherming (Foundation for sustainable development and nature conservation, Netherlands)
EAR	European Agency for Reconstruction
EBRD	European Bank for Reconstruction and Development
EDAIS	Enterprise Development Impact Assessment Information Service
EDP	Electronic Data Processing
EFBH	European Fund for Bosnia and Herzegovina
EFK	European Fund for Kosovo

EFM	European Fund for Montenegro
EFS	European Fund for Serbia
EMB	Euro Market Bank
EU	European Union
EURIBOR	Euro Interbank Offered Rate
FBiH	Federation of Bosnia and Herzegovina
FDI	foreign direct investment
FEFAD	FEFAD Bank, Albania
FIE	Centro de Fomento a Iniciativas Economicas, Bolivia
FINCA International	Foundation for International Community Assistance
FFP	private financial fund
FMO	Netherlands Development Finance Company
GDP	gross domestic product
GDRs	German depository receipts
GRF	German-Romanian Fund
GTZ	Deutsche Gesellschaft für Technische Zusammenarbeit
HCLP	Housing Construction Loan Programme
IAS	International Accounting Standards
IFC	International Finance Corporation
IFI	international financial institution
IFPRI	International Food Policy Research Institute
IMF	International Monetary Fund
IMI	Internationale Micro Investitionen
Imp-Act	Improving the Impact of Microfinance on Poverty: Action Research
IPC	Internationale Projekt Consult
IRR	internal rate of return
ISSP	International Social Survey Programme
IT	information technology
KCIS	Kosovo Credit Information Service
LFS	LFS Financial Systems GmbH, Berlin
LIP	Loan Initiatives Projects
LSMS	Living Standards Measurement Surveys
MCR	Microcredit Romania

MEB	microenterprise bank
MEB BiH	Microenterprise Bank of Bosnia and Herzegovina
MEB Kosovo	Microenterprise Bank of Kosovo
MEC	Microenterprise Credit, Moldova
MFB	micro-finance bank
MFB	Microfinance Bank of Serbia
MFC	Microfinance Centre in Poland
MFI	microfinance institution
MIS	management information systems
MSE	micro and small enterprise
NGO	non-governmental organisation
OECD	Organisation for Economic Cooperation and Development
PB	partner bank
PPP	Public-Private Partnership
RBYU	Raiffeisenbank Yugoslavia
RLP	Rural Loan Programme
ROA	return on assets
ROI	return on investment
RS	Republika Srpska
RSBF	Russia Small Business Fund
RZB	Raiffeisen Zentralbank Östereich
SDC	Swiss Agency for Development and Cooperation
SEE	Southeast Europe
SKB	SKB Banka AD, Slovenian commercial bank
SME	small and medium-sized enterprise
SMEF	Small and Medium-sized Enterprise Facility
SWIFT	Society for Worldwide Interbank Financial Telecommunication
TA	technical assistance
TC	technical cooperation
USAID	United States Agency for International Development
WB	World Bank
ZOP	Central Clearing Bank, Yugoslavia

CHAPTER 1

Introduction

Ingrid Matthäus-Maier* and J. D. von Pischke**

* Member of the Board of Managing Directors, KfW, Frankfurt, Germany
** President of Frontier Finance International, Inc., Washington DC, USA

The promotion of micro and small and medium-sized enterprise (SME) finance has been one of the most promising initiatives in the reconstruction of Southeast Europe (SEE). The approaches to financial sector development that have been taken by KfW and its partners have fostered sound institutions and reached growing numbers of low-income people and disadvantaged groups. These remarkable achievements have contributed to the stabilisation of the financial sectors in the region, which promotes economic growth and fights poverty. These successes are all the more astounding in view of the fact that only a short time ago the region was engaged in the bloodiest conflict in Europe since World War II.

KfW's Approach to Financial Sector Reform in Southeast Europe

KfW's approach to financial sector development effectively addresses the structural weaknesses of the financial sectors in the region. Each of our projects must operate according to sound banking principles, which is what KfW stands for. Yet, our task is not merely to implement isolated projects, even if they are successful. Rather, our initiatives are designed to build technically sound and operationally efficient financial sectors in Southeast Europe. Competition is the most important principle on which our strategy is based. As in any other market, effective competition provides incentives for banks to offer market-based and demand-oriented financial services. Competition encourages the development of better products and services at lower cost.

The promotion of competition distinguishes our initiatives from those of private sector players that want to maximise their financial return on individual projects. As a public institution, KfW has the capacity and a mandate to implement projects that create externalities in high-risk environments, as follows:

- we work to create externalities, an economic term that refers to benefits that are enjoyed by many but for which we as sponsors and innovators are not directly rewarded. Externalities can be achieved, for example, by demonstrating that financial services for low-income groups can be provided on a for-profit basis, and by developing financial products which are then adapted by local banks with which we have no project relationships.

- KfW's goal of reforming financial sectors requires us to assume risks beyond those generally accepted by the private sector. The quality of our projects demonstrates that it is indeed possible to manage these risks wisely and to minimise any adverse financial consequences that materialise. For example, we have always invested a lot of effort in selecting the likely winners among the banks interested in participating in our programmes.

Supporting Our Target Groups

The justification for donors' involvement in financial sector development in Southeast Europe lies in the important role of small and medium-sized enterprises (SMEs). SMEs constitute the most important driving force in the economic recovery of Southeast Europe. They account for the majority of newly created jobs; small and frequently family-run businesses often provide the sole source of income for people who became unemployed when state-owned enterprises were forced to close due to their inefficiency. Without intervention by the donor community, many microentrepreneurs[1] and SMEs would not be able to grow and create additional jobs. Most local banks are not sufficiently liquid to serve the large numbers of potential clients and do not offer financial services adapted to small and medium-sized enterprises. Many local banks are agent or pocket banks, characterised by close personal and financial ties to individual companies to the detriment of portfolio quality. Others have focused on lending to state-owned enterprises, many of which are unable to repay their loans.

But it is not only SMEs that lack access to financial services. Particularly in Bosnia and Herzegovina and in Kosovo, large quantities of private housing were destroyed during the civil wars. Homeowners wishing to rebuild their houses are often unable to obtain sufficient long-term credit for reconstruction.

---

[1] The boundary between microenterprise and small business is always arbitrary, and no definition is entirely satisfactory. On this basis, KfW makes no overall official distinction between micro and small enterprise. By international standards, many firms that may be considered microenterprises in the transition economies of Southeast Europe would be classified as small businesses in the developing world. KfW's primary target group in Southeast Europe can also be defined initially as businesses that have not previously received credit from formal financial institutions during the transition process.

A Twofold Strategy

KfW employs a twofold strategy to address these unsatisfactory conditions and to make finance available to micro and small enterprises and to homeowners.

KfW, together with other development institutions, has established micro and SME banks that cater specifically to low-income people. On behalf of the German government, KfW has stakes in such banks in Kosovo and Serbia and in Albania, Bosnia and Herzegovina (BiH), Bulgaria, Romania, and most recently Macedonia. The Micro Enterprise Bank (MEB) of Kosovo was founded in 2000 and for a while was Kosovo's only bank. By late 2002, the bank had over 3,200 outstanding loans totalling almost € 17 million. For the first time in a decade, many small enterprises in Kosovo now have access to a bank and to financial services in general. MEB also offers savings facilities and money transfer services within Kosovo and abroad. The British journal *The Economist* rated MEB as the most profitable bank in Southeast Europe in 2002. Sufficient revenues are a precondition for serving the poorer sections of society in a sustainable way. The bank's results demonstrate that its clients often have better repayment profiles than many companies in Western Europe. MEB also contributes to creating opportunities for women: over 80% of its loan officers are women.

Second, KfW cooperates with the best among the local commercial banks through a downscaling approach that is designed to enable these banks to lend to a new clientele consisting of low-income people. The funds for this initiative have been provided by the German government in partnership with other bilateral and multilateral donors: the EU, the governments of Austria and Switzerland and the Dutch development finance institution FMO. These funds are loaned to the partner banks for on-lending to final borrowers. Potential partner banks undergo a strict selection process and loan officers are trained to manage the credits properly. Hardware and software systems may have to be installed at the banks in order for the programme to be run professionally. These measures help partner banks attract significant credit business that is characterised by sound investments and reliable borrowers, rather than political considerations or personal relationships.

Both approaches, downscaling and the microbank initiative, are designed to tackle structural weaknesses in financial sectors. The projects provide financial resources that the troubled banking sectors so urgently lack, and systematically address staffing, technical and administrative bottlenecks at the partner banks.

Encouraging Results

KfW programmes in our partner countries are having an impact on the target groups of small entrepreneurs, refugees, other underprivileged groups and also on the development of the financial sector. By the end of 2002, local partner banks in the downscaling programme had issued 6,300 loans to small entrepreneurs and home owners, amounting to more than € 53 million, while the seven microbanks with which KfW cooperates in Southeast Europe had issued 40,000 loans totalling €230 million.

Our development mandate is to reach the poorer strata of society with credit programmes. The refinancing fund we established in BiH on behalf of several donors is a good example of the effectiveness of our approach. We have commissioned independent experts to evaluate the achievements of this fund and its two windows, the Housing Construction Loan Programme and the SME Loan Programme, as reported in this book.

The impact assessment of the Housing Construction Loan Programme indicates that it contributes significantly to improving the housing situation in Bosnia and Herzegovina. Loans have primarily been used for basic renovation and rehabilitation (75%) and for enlarging existing structures (25%). The programme reaches low-income groups and refugees and creates substantial secondary effects, such as employment: it creates new jobs and preserves many others, primarily at SMEs in the local construction industry.

The impact assessment of the SME loan programme reveals interesting results. A broad variety of SMEs in all sectors have gained access to credit, with the majority of the funds flowing to the production sector. Notwithstanding the stringent requirements of the lending process, one-quarter of the loans were made to start-ups and re-start-ups, that is, enterprises resuming activities after having been shut down during war or because of economic crises. The programme was successful in reaching microenterprises, 90% of which have fewer than 20 employees. It has also been shown that many enterprises considerably increased the number of their staff.

Besides contributing to the development of SMEs and to the improvement of housing, the programme has also had positive effects on the partner banks. The institutional capacity of the banks has been strengthened considerably through staff training, management consultancy inputs and the installation of software. Five of the six banks have started to make housing loans from their own resources. KfW has every reason to believe that the SME programmes are institutionally sustainable.

KfW as an Agent of Bilateral and Multilateral Donors

The German government has contributed significantly to these successes. The Federal Ministry for Economic Cooperation and Development (BMZ) mandated KfW to implement public infrastructure projects in developing and transition countries, including Southeast Europe. The German government provided €322 million for financial cooperation with Stability Pact countries in Southeast Europe from 2000 to 2002. Financial sector promotion is a focal area of German bilateral cooperation: 22% of the funds have been committed to this purpose.

KfW is increasingly active on behalf of multilateral and other bilateral donors. From 2000 to 2002 alone, we concluded agreements totalling almost €70 million with other donors. Financial sector projects account for the bulk of these funds.

KfW is pleased to share a commitment with the EU, the Austrian and Swiss governments and the Dutch FMO to foster the development of the financial sectors in Southeast Europe and to enhance cooperation in the banking sector. Our financial sector portfolio in the region totalled about € 150 million at the end of 2002, which enabled our projects to achieve the critical mass required to make an impact on our target groups.

Drawing a Balance

These successes give us cause for optimism. However, we still have a long way to go before the financial landscape of the region is thoroughly reformed. The banking sectors will continue to depend on sustained commitment by donors for some time to come.

In 2002, a Symposium on Financial Sector Development in Southeast Europe was organised by KfW to draw an interim balance and assessment of results and to analyse the reasons for the successes as well as the potential for further improvement. This meeting, held in November 2002 in Berlin, examined these issues in more detail. The aim was to bring together key players, i.e. institutions and individuals involved in our initiatives.

This book is based on presentations at the conference and focuses on the following topics:

- the link between the development of the financial sector and economic development in selected countries in Southeast Europe;

- the components of successful and innovative financial sector approaches;

- the impact of financial sector projects at the household, institutional and financial sector levels;

- the potential for more private sector leadership in institutional development and commercialisation, and options for the eventual exit of public donors.

Finally, this book addresses the current nature of these themes in at least four important ways:

- the trouble spots in Southeast Europe have received far less public attention since the wars in Bosnia and Kosovo ended in 1995 and 1999 respectively. Positive news has started to trickle in but often goes unnoticed. The encouraging achievements in small and medium-sized enterprise development make good news. This is important in itself, but also because it demonstrates that the taxpayers' money spent on SME promotion is being spent wisely.

- it is very useful to record lessons learnt using KfW's approaches and to generate options for further improvements and fine-tuning as SEE financial sectors mature.

- financial sector development in Southeast Europe is characterised by close donor coordination, which is all too infrequent. Synergies are created through joint efforts by like-minded development agencies.

- the promotion of financial sector development in Southeast Europe offers a model for other regions in crisis. The case of Southeast Europe demonstrates that sound banking is possible in volatile environments when the right approaches are applied.

Finally, the efforts of those who have contributed to this book also deserve acknowledgement. We include the authors and also the many others who have provided time and effort to gather and present data, to share experiences and to offer advice and criticism. Their efforts and commitment have made it possible to document the important elements of a dynamic and socially useful process of reconstruction and development.

The Symposium was funded by FEFAD Foundation, an entity established by the Albanian government and KfW almost a decade ago to support microenterprise and SME development in Albania. FEFAD Foundation was the pioneer financial institution that spawned a bank dedicated to providing services at the small end of the financial market. The six other microfinance banks that KfW has supported in Southeast Europe are structured along the lines of the FEFAD model.

The editors are grateful to Klaus Glaubitt, Doris Köhn and Hanns-Peter Neuhoff of KfW for their consistent and unflagging promotion of the commercial approach to micro and SME development which is featured in this book. Their vision has prevailed and is now widely shared. We also provide our profound thanks to Wolfram Erhardt and Haje Schütte, who conceptualised the Symposium, coordinated the thematic inputs and devoted countless hours of professional energy to advising the editors of this book. Tina Butterbach's outstanding organisational work was invaluable throughout.

The chapters that follow are grouped into four thematic areas. The first part provides an overview of the economic transition of the region. Subsequent parts are devoted to the innovative approaches to building financial sectors in Southeast Europe, to the pioneering banks and bankers in SEE, and to research and impact analysis for accountability and management. The book concludes with an editorial summary that identifies further steps in policy, research and implementation that could build upon the good results already achieved.

PART I:

The Evolution of Financial Sector and Economic Development in Southeast Europe

Introduction to Part I

Recent research based on a large sample of countries has established a positive historical relationship between financial sector development and economic growth. This lends support to the strategy of stimulating financial sector development in order to boost economic performance over the long run.

In the short run, this positive relationship does not necessarily apply. Arnaud Mehl and Adalbert Winkler discuss the performance of financial sectors in Southeast Europe (SEE) since the start of the transition process around 1990. They note that ill-conceived financial sector reforms led to financial crises and ultimately to devastating losses in output. The financial sector was an impediment to growth in SEE during much of this period.

With tightened regulatory and supervisory regimes and the opening up of domestic financial sectors to foreign investors, finance has recently begun to play a positive role in economic development in SEE. However, these financial sectors do not yet function in a fully satisfactory manner and are not yet strong sources of overall economic growth. One reason is that lending to businesses remains low in response to exogenous risks and to supply and demand factors. Many financial institutions have served primarily as safekeepers of money and have not yet contributed strongly to the growth-creating intermediation of funds that characterise active credit markets. An important challenge for policy makers is to manage the growth of domestic credit in a noninflationary way.

CHAPTER 2

The Financial Sector and Economic Development: Evidence from Southeast Europe

Arnaud Mehl* and Adalbert Winkler**[1]

* Economist, ECB, Frankfurt, Germany
** Senior Economist, ECB, Frankfurt, Germany

Introduction

The turn of the century witnessed a significant renewal of interest in Southeast Europe.[2] The international community, notably the European Union (EU), took steps to bring lasting peace and stability to the region under the auspices of the Stability Pact and the Stabilisation and Association Process. These steps have coincided with considerable progress in the countries of Southeast Europe. All of them are now democracies and are forging ahead with political, economic and administrative reforms. International investors have started to identify the oppor-

---

[1] Dr. Arnaud Mehl and Dr. Adalbert Winkler are grateful to Oscar Calvo-Gonzalez, Nikolaus Siegfried, Franziska Schobert and Andrea Wölfel for helpful comments. The views expressed in the paper do not necessarily represent those of the European Central Bank.

[2] There is no consensus on the exact delimitation of the region. The EU's relations with Southeast Europe in the framework of the Stability and Association Process refer only to the western Balkans, namely Albania, Bosnia and Herzegovina, Croatia, the Former Yugoslav Republic of Macedonia (FYR Macedonia) and the Federal Republic of Yugoslavia (FR Yugoslavia), today known as Serbia and Montenegro. This paper uses a larger definition, that of the Regional Strategy Paper of the European Commission – World Bank joint office for Southeast Europe, adding Bulgaria, Romania (which are also EU accession countries) and Moldova (see http://www.seerecon.org). The case of Kosovo and Montenegro, two territories within FR Yugoslavia, is also briefly considered. All countries share a communist or socialist past and are a fairly heterogeneous group. Bosnia and Herzegovina, Croatia, Kosovo, FYR Macedonia, Montenegro and Serbia were republics or provinces of former Yugoslavia, whereas Moldova was a republic of the former Soviet Union. Only Albania, Bulgaria and Romania had been independent states since the end of World War II. In the cold war era, Bulgaria and Romania were members of the Warsaw Pact, while former Yugoslavia was an active promoter of the non-aligned movement and Albania chose a policy of almost complete isolation.

tunities brought about by these changes. Nevertheless, the region has still a very long road ahead before it reaches EU standards of living and economic development. To address this challenge, it is essential to design relevant economic policies and to ensure the appropriate involvement of the private sector. In both respects, the potential contribution of the financial system to economic growth is of particular relevance.

All Southeast European countries inherited a financial sector that played no role in the market-based allocation of resources across time and agents. Central banks and state-owned commercial banks[3] passively accommodated and monitored payment flows between enterprises, as directed by central planners or, in the case of former Yugoslavia, by socially-owned enterprises.[4] In view of these significant distortions, there was widespread consensus in the early 1990s that financial sector reform could contribute importantly to the transition from plan to market and ultimately foster growth (Blommestein and Spencer, 1993; Fries and Lane, 1994).

It is still too early to draw definitive conclusions, but the information available suggests that performance in recent years in Southeast Europe has been mixed, despite the positive and causal link between financial development and economic growth over the long term that has been historically established for a large sample of countries. In the first half of the decade, ill-conceived financial sector reforms led to financial crises in many countries of the region and ultimately to large output losses, thereby making finance an impediment rather than a promoter of growth. Thanks to tightened regulation and supervision and to the opening of domestic banking sectors to foreign investors, Southeast European countries have recently reached a stage where the financial sector has ceased to be detrimental to growth. However, these sectors do not yet perform their functions in a fully satisfactory manner and still fail to support growth actively. In particular, lending to businesses remains dismal, owing to idiosyncratic supply factors and demand factors. This needs to be properly addressed.

The remainder of the paper is set out as follows: Section 2 highlights the main lessons drawn from academic research on the link between finance and growth. It focuses on the banking sector, as capital markets are severely underdeveloped and in some countries non-existent. Section 3 summarises the major macroeconomic trends in Southeast Europe in the last decade. The evolution of the region's financial sectors and their originally negative and now currently limited impact on economic growth is discussed in Sections 4 and 5. Bottlenecks to lending to busi-

---

[3] With the exception of former Yugoslavia, these banks were created with the break-up of the monobank system in the late 1980s and early 1990s. But at the beginning of the reform period they were "little more than an accounting construction and were run by segments of the old bureaucratic network and staff." (Berglof and Bolton, 2002).

[4] Former Yugoslavia had created a two-tier banking system in the 1960s. However, this reform softened budget constraints by *de facto* making captive a large number of banks that lent money to their socially-owned enterprise owners on non-commercial terms (Gomel, 2002).

nesses must be drastically reduced if the conditions necessary for boosting economic growth are to be improved; this issue is discussed in Section 6. Section 7 summarises the results and draws some tentative policy conclusions.

Finance and Growth: International Evidence over the Long Run

The relation between financial development and economic growth has been debated for over a century. As early as 1912, Schumpeter argued that banks actively spurred technological progress by selecting and financing those entrepreneurs with the best chances of successfully implementing innovative products and production processes. Conversely, Robinson (1952) claimed that the financial system responded passively to economic growth as economic development creates demand for particular types of financial arrangements. More recently, Lucas (1988) went even further by asserting that the role of the financial factors had been greatly over-emphasised and might not be decisively relevant for economic growth. Indeed, new growth theory in the mid-1980s and early 1990s did not offer much guidance on how to introduce finance in growth models. The few attempts that included growth-supporting effects of the financial system (Bencivenga and Smith 1991; Greenwood and Jovanovic, 1992; King and Levine, 1993a) initially derived their insights from finance theory and transplanted them into a growth model, which is why the theoretical link between financial development and economic growth remains controversial. These models basically assume that "financial development leads to economic growth, without showing the mechanics behind this supply-leading relationship" (Hermes, 1994).

Generally speaking, financial systems arise to overcome information and transaction frictions and to facilitate the allocation of resources across space and time in an uncertain environment (Merton and Bodie, 1995). In theory, they can affect growth by promoting capital accumulation and/or by exerting a positive impact on the pace of productivity growth (Levine, 1997). Specifically, financial systems[5] serve a wide array of functions:

- savings pooled from disparate depositors have a direct effect on productivity: without access to a range of investors many manufacturing processes would be condemned to operate at inefficient scales of production;

- allocating resources according to information acquired about investment projects permits the selection of the most promising prospects, allowing capital to flow to its highest value use. Identifying entrepreneurs with the best chances of successfully creating innovative goods and production processes positively affects the rate of technological progress;

---

[5] Additional functions or other classifications can be found in the literature; see, for instance, Merton and Bodie, 1995 or Levine, 1997.

- managing liquidity and idiosyncratic risks through aggregation and transferring these risks to those most willing and able to bear them improves resource allocation and the savings rate by inducing a portfolio shift towards projects with higher expected returns. This further allows innovative projects characterised by high yield and risk to be financed and it accelerates technological change;

- the monitoring of managers helps to ensure that funds allocated are spent as envisaged. Financial institutions and markets act as "delegated monitors" (Diamond, 1984), which facilitates the separation of management and ownership, reduces verification costs, helps harden budget constraints and enforces market discipline.

Recent empirical work tends to suggest that financial development has indeed been a significant and inextricable part of the growth process. In a seminal paper, King and Levine (1993b) study long-run growth in 80 countries from 1960 to 1989. Controlling for other factors that affect long-run growth[6], they find that real GDP per-capita growth is significantly correlated with financial sector depth and with the extent to which loans are directed to the private sector.[7] The magnitude of the relation is large: according to some of their estimates, increasing financial sector depth from 20% of GDP to 60% of GDP increases GDP per capita growth by 1% per annum.[8]

Association does not prove causality. Nevertheless, the hypothesis that the relation is causal and that financial development tends to precede and contribute to long-run economic growth seems to survive a battery of econometric probes. King and Levine (1993b) find evidence that the initial level of financial development is a good predictor of future rates of economic growth, capital accumulation and technological change. Converging results emerge from studies conducted at the

---

[6] These factors include initial income, educational attainment, political stability and measures of monetary, trade and fiscal policy.

[7] These indicators are defined respectively as (i) the ratio of broad money to GDP (monetisation ratio) and (ii) credit to private enterprises to GDP (financial intermediation ratio). Both ratios measure the extent to which resources are intermediated across time periods and agents via the banking system. The monetisation ratio measures the transfer of financial resources from the non-financial sector to the financial sector in terms of a monetary aggregate (broad money), while the financial intermediation ratio measures the extent of financial resource flowback to the non-financial sector.

[8] While not as extensive as the body of work on the banking sector, certain studies on the stock market also suggest a positive link with economic growth. Theory indicates for instance that well-developed stock markets strengthen corporate control by facilitating takeovers or making it easier to tie managerial compensation to performance. This enhances managerial incentives and improves resource allocation (see Levine, 2001, for an overview). Empirical studies (e.g. Levine and Zervos, 1998) confirm that stock market liquidity is positively and significantly correlated with current and future rates of economic growth, capital accumulation and productivity growth.

firm level (e.g. Demirgüç-Kunt and Maksimovic, 1998)[9], industry level (e.g. Rajan and Zingales, 1998)[10] or time-series-based analysis (e.g. Rousseau and Wachtel, 1998).[11] Moreover, Levine, Loaza and Beck (2000) showed that countries with legal systems that give high priority to secured creditor rights, rigorous contract enforcement and high-quality accounting standards tend to have better developed financial intermediaries, which is especially the case for systems inspired by the German legal tradition.[12] Their research, using national legal origin as an instrument for financial development, shows that this exogenous component of the latter is positively correlated with economic growth, a result that by construction is not affected by reverse causality bias.[13]

Turning to the channels through which finance contributes to long-term growth, Beck, Levine and Loayza (2000) find that financial development is significantly correlated with total factor productivity but not robustly correlated with either private savings rates or capital accumulation.[14] Therefore, the contribution of finance to long-term growth is to improve the economy's productivity rather than to increase the quantity of physical capital.

The downside of the positive correlation between finance and growth is that financial crises, in particular banking crises, are associated with significant output losses, at least in the short run (Caprio, 1997). In general, banking crises entail three types of costs (World Bank, 2001a): a) the stock of unrecoverable loans that were wasted for unproductive purposes as revealed by banks' insolvency; b) the public finance cost of bailing out banks and c) real output losses triggered by a further drop in investment from either a general loss of confidence or restricted access to credit. Moreover, while financial crises are to a certain extent triggered by macroeconomic shocks, there is incontrovertible evidence that "poor banking" causes financial crises and subsequent economic downturns (Sundararajan and Balino, 1991; Caprio and Klingebiel, 1996; Caprio 1998).

In light of this, there can be two different scenarios characterising the link between finance and growth. In the first, a poorly functioning financial sector leads to financial crises and ultimately to large output losses. In this case, finance im-

---

[9] According to this study, firms in countries that have active stock markets and comply with legal norms are able to obtain external funds and grow faster than predicted by their individual characteristics.

[10] This paper finds that industrial sectors that obtain finance external to the firm or sector grow faster in countries with more-developed financial markets.

[11] In this study, the authors show that financial intermediation leads real sector activity.

[12] As opposed in particular to systems inspired by the French legal tradition. The authors recall that legal scholars use a classification that consists of four major European legal systems: English, French, German and Scandinavian.

[13] The national origin of a legal system can be regarded as exogenous to economic growth because the English, French and German systems spread to other countries mainly through conquest and colonialism. They can be considered as an endowment for these countries.

[14] See also the evidence presented by De Gregorio and Guidotti (1992).

pedes rather than promotes economic growth. In the second scenario, the financial sector performs its functions well, thereby fuelling economic growth. In the following sections, this distinction will be used to analyse the link between the financial sector and economic development in Southeast Europe.

Macroeconomic Performance in Southeast Europe in the Last Decade

In common with all transition economies, those in Southeast Europe also experienced a sharp output decline in the first half of the 1990s, with recessions ranging from minus 3% per annum on average in Albania and Romania to minus 23% in Bosnia and Herzegovina (Figure 1). The severity of the initial output collapse can be explained, inter alia, by the transition from a command to a market economy, the break-up of the Yugoslav federation and the subsequent wars, as well as by inadequate macroeconomic and structural policies. Output started to recover in the second half of the decade, with growth reaching 3% per annum or above in Albania, Croatia and Bulgaria.[15] Only in the most recent period (1999 to 2001) did all countries post positive real growth rates, with the exception of FR Yugoslavia.

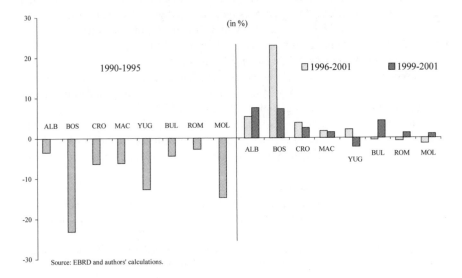

Figure 1.   Average real GDP growth

---

[15] The very high real output growth between 1996 and 2001 in Bosnia and Herzegovina (above 20% per annum) is mainly the outcome of a base effect originating in the production collapse triggered by war in the first half of the decade. In the period 1999–2001, the average annual growth rate was lower, at 7.1% per annum.

Output losses are far from being overcome. Compared to the pre-transition situation in 1989, figures for real output in 2001 were back to between 75% and 85% of their former levels in Bulgaria, Croatia, FRY Macedonia and Romania, but stood at only 50% or below in FR Yugoslavia and Moldova (Figure 2). Albania was the only country which had caught up with and surpassed its 1989 real output level: since 1993 it has posted real GDP growth rates in excess of 7% per annum (except for 1997).

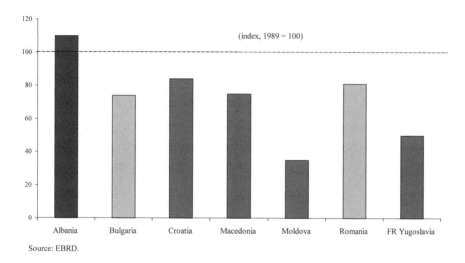

Source: EBRD.

Figure 2. Estimated level of real GDP in 2001

Investment trends mirrored the evolution of real output, but displayed even larger swings (Table 1). For example, investment in Bulgaria collapsed in 1996/1997, falling initially by about half and subsequently by almost a further 25%. In Croatia, investment declined in 1999 and 2000 by 1% and 3% respectively, whereas output decreased in 1999 by only 0.4%.

Turning to inflation dynamics, in the first half of the 1990s, all countries experienced high inflation or hyperinflation crises triggered by the lifting of administrative prices, disruptions related to the wars in former Yugoslavia and excessive money printing (Table 2). In the second half of the decade, prices stabilised in Albania, Bulgaria[16], Croatia and FYR Macedonia, with average annual inflation capped at around 10% per annum. Conversely, in Moldova, Romania and FR Yugoslavia, inflation rates remained high.

---

[16] The 83% average annual inflation rate reported for Bulgaria in Table 2 is somewhat misleading as it includes the 1996-1997 hyperinflation episode that ultimately led to the adoption of a currency board in 1997. From 1998 to 2001, average inflation was 9.4% per annum.

Table 1. Gross fixed real investment in selected Southeast European countries (% change)

	Bulgaria	Croatia	Moldova	Romania
1993	−17.5	n.a.	n.a.	8.3
1994	1.1	n.a.	n.a.	20.7
1995	8.8	n.a.	−16.0	6.9
1996	−52.8	n.a.	−8.0	5.7
1997	−23.9	n.a.	−8.0	−3.0
1998	16.4	2.5	10.0	−18.1
1999	25.3	−1.1	−22.0	−5.1
2000	8.2	−3.5	−15.0	5.5
2001	16.0	9.7	−2.0	6.6

Source: EBRD for all countries, except Moldova (National Bank of Moldova).

Table 2. Average annual inflation rates in Southeast European countries (%)

	1990-1995	1996-2001
Albania	49	11
Bosnia and Herzegovina	n.a.	−0.6 / 8.2[1]
Bulgaria	95	83[2]
Croatia	298	5
FRY Macedonia	282	3
FR Yugoslavia	271[3]	53
Moldova	235	20
Romania	115	59

Source: EBRD and authors' own calculations.

Notes: [1] In the Croat-Muslim Federation/in the Republika Srpska;
            [2] Including hyperinflation crisis in 1996-97;
            [3] Excluding 1,100,000,000,000 % inflation rate in 1993 (larger than a million million percent).

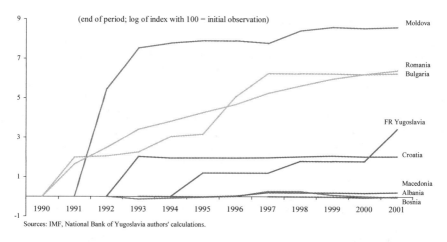

Sources: IMF, National Bank of Yugoslavia authors' calculations.

Figure 3. Exchange rate against the Euro

In the first half of the 1990s, high inflation led to and was fostered by sharp exchange rate depreciation, in particular against the euro, although varying from country to country (Figure 3). The domestic currencies of Croatia, Bulgaria, Moldova, Romania and FR Yugoslavia experienced the largest depreciation throughout the decade, ranging from 600% to more than 500,000%. This greatly lowered confidence in domestic currencies as a store of value and has had long-lasting consequences on household portfolio choices. The Macedonian denar lost roughly one-quarter of its value. Only the Albanian lek and the Bosnian convertible mark remained stable vis-à-vis the euro but depreciated by about 30% and 20% respectively against the US dollar. In the second half of the 1990s, almost all countries managed to stabilise their exchange rates, mainly by anchoring their domestic currency to the euro under a currency board (Bosnia and Herzegovina and Bulgaria), a conventional peg (FR Yugoslavia and FYR Macedonia) or a managed float (Croatia).

To sum up, macroeconomic developments in the first half of the 1990s were characterised by high monetary instability and substantial output losses in Southeast Europe. In the second half of the 1990s most countries moved closer to a path of stability and growth, albeit with considerable differences in timing and degree. The next step is to examine whether financial sector trends help to explain this macroeconomic record.

The Evolution of Financial Sectors in Southeast Europe

Early 1990s: Inadequate Financial Sector Reform Has an Adverse Impact on Economic Activity

Notwithstanding the heterogeneous macroeconomic developments in the countries of Southeast Europe, their financial sector development has displayed a degree of similarity. When political changes led to the first economic reforms in the early 1990s, there was widespread consensus that restructuring and privatising state-owned commercial banks was a priority. However, mainly due to reasons of political economy (Bokros, 2002) these efforts were either delayed or failed because they did not address deeply-rooted corporate governance problems (Keren and Ofer, 2002). Moreover, newly founded private banks also suffered from severe corporate governance problems. Indeed many of them proved to be "agent" or "pocket" banks (World Bank, 1989 and 1993), i.e. banks that granted bad loans to the companies of their owners.[17] This entailed two types of costs: a) inefficiency costs related to resource misallocation; b) reputation costs as pocket banks severely undermined private sector confidence in the banking system. Finally, banks in general were not accustomed to assessing credit risk and dealing with risk management. Loan security, credit monitoring and other key elements pertaining to financial intermediation were also weak (Gelb and Honohan, 1991; Caprio, 1995). Many countries in the region, notably Bulgaria, experienced relatively stable lending activity in the early 1990s, but this was due more to the persistence of soft budget constraints than financial development (Berglof and Bolton, 2002).

These deficiencies went largely unnoticed as long as inflation soared or even turned into hyperinflation as in Bulgaria, Croatia, Macedonia and Yugoslavia. Inflation eased the repayment burden of insolvent borrowers and led to highly negative real interest rates. However, when the first attempts at macroeconomic stabilisation took hold, "false credit" – in the form of loans to counterparts who are known to be unlikely to pay back in real terms – triggered an increase in non-performing loans (McKinnon, 1992). Banking supervision and regulation that initially supported the founding of new agent and pocket banks with a fairly liberal licensing regime proved largely unable to address these unprecedented difficulties. As a result, some countries such as Bulgaria in 1997 and Croatia in 1998/1999 faced banking crises as banks became illiquid and insolvent and were eventually closed or sold (Gomel, 2002).

Other countries, such as Romania and Serbia under the Milosevic regime, managed to avoid outright crises thanks to high inflation rates fuelled by central bank and government interventions.[18] Somewhat differently, the 1997 financial crisis in Albania was triggered by the non-bank financial sector, in particular by collapsing pyramid schemes which affected enterprises and households.[19] In Moldova, the impact of the Russian crisis was strongly felt by domestic

---

[17] In FYR Macedonia, for example, as late as end-September 1999, six banks had exposures to a single shareholder in excess of the country's prudential legal limit (Drummond, 2000).

[18] In Romania, for example, the intervention in Bancorex, the largest state-owned bank, was based on concerns about systemic risk (IMF 2001b).

[19] In the 1990s, pyramid schemes also caused financial turbulence in Bulgaria, Romania and FYR Macedonia (Gomel, 2002). However, the systemic impact was nowhere as large as in Albania (Jarvis, 2000).

banks. In early 1999, 14 out of a total of 22 banks were assigned to the National Bank's Bank Resolution Unit (IMF, 2001a).

In line with past evidence, these financial crises were associated with substantial output losses and a large decline in investment.[20] Real GDP plummeted in the crisis in Albania by 7% in 1997 and in Bulgaria by 11% and 7% in 1996/97 respectively. Croatia's output losses in 1999 were more limited at 0.4 %. Interestingly, the recession that year was the only one since the end of the war in the mid-1990s. Likewise, from 1997 to 1999 Romania went through three years of recession, while struggling with several bank failures and crises. After experiencing its first year of positive growth in the transition period, Moldova posted two years of real output losses in 1998 and 1999. Although there was no outright crisis, major weaknesses in the banking sector have been identified as a cause of slow growth in FYR Macedonia (Drummond, 2000).

In a nutshell, during the first decade of financial development in Southeast Europe, the financial sector in general performed inefficiently and this had a negative impact on economic growth. Of course, poor macroeconomic performance was also impeded by the break-up of Yugoslavia and the subsequent wars, the swings in EU economic activity and their impact on trade as well as the inherent difficulties of the transition process in other policy areas. Nevertheless, it is fair to say that inadequate financial sector reform probably played a part.

The Late 1990s: Harder Budget Constraints, More Stringent Supervision and Allowing Foreign Investor Participation

In the late 1990s, the authorities started to press ahead with reforms to reduce the risk of financial sector crises and their potential adverse impact on economic activity. To this end, central banks hardened budget constraints on commercial banks as they reduced or ceased lending to them. Moreover, the authorities took a considerably more rigorous approach to banking supervision and regulation, endeavouring to adopt international standards or even more stringent requirements in some cases (Talley, Giugale and Polastri, 1998). And finally, they opened up the domestic banking sectors to foreign investors in order to enforce the harder budget constraints on the real sector and improve the reputation of the banking system.

In the second half of the 1990s, several central banks in the region reconsidered their position toward domestic banks and drastically reduced their loans to them (Figure 4). At the end of 2001, central bank lending to commercial banks in all countries of the region was virtually nil.

Rather than lending to domestic banks, central banks have accumulated foreign assets. Indeed, by the end of 2001, only the central banks of Albania and Moldova

---

[20] As already noted, investment reacted to financial crises even more strongly than to output.

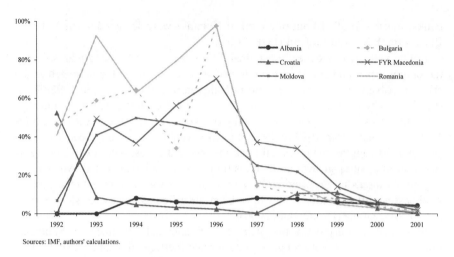

Sources: IMF, authors' calculations.

Figure 4. Monetary authorities' claims on banks as a share of reserve money

were not covering outstanding reserve money with an equal or larger amount of net foreign assets.

The regulatory and supervisory reforms made themselves felt in many areas, but the main focus has been to strengthen capital adequacy requirements. The authorities consolidated and improved banking sector capitalisation with the expectation that bank owners and managers would be encouraged to invest on a more commercial basis. The amount of capital needed to obtain a banking licence increased quite substantially, and some countries raised capital adequacy ratios even above the 8%-Cooke reference value (Table 3).[21]

Financial crises and higher capital adequacy ratios led to consolidation: since the middle of the 1990s, the number of banks in countries with a comparatively large number of licensed banks (e.g. Bosnia and Herzegovina, Croatia and Bulgaria), has dropped significantly (Figure 5).

Tighter capital requirements serve their purpose only if accounting regulations, especially those pertaining to the valuation of assets, are appropriate (Dziobek, Frecaut and Nieto, 1995). Moreover, compliance with such regulations has to be closely monitored. Hence, many countries have tightened their regulations on loan classification and loan loss provisioning. International accounting standards have been introduced in several countries to improve transparency. Finally, on-site and off-site inspection has been strengthened.

The other response to the financial crises of the late 1990s was the fundamental dismantling of the barriers to foreign investors. At the end of 2001, foreign banks accounted for an important and in some countries a dominant share of total banking-sector assets (Figure 6).[22]

---

[21] See also the respective country assessments in EBRD (2001).

[22] An exception is Montenegro (see Box).

Table 3. Minimum capital requirements in Southeast Europe, 2001-2002

Country	Minimum capital requirement (as specified)	Minimum capital require-ment (in EUR million)	Minimum required capital adequacy ratio (in %)
Albania	ALL 700 million	≈5.5	12
Bosnia and Herzegovina	BAM 15 million	≈7.7	10
Bulgaria	BGN 10 million	≈5.1	12
Croatia	HRK 40 million	≈5.4	10[1]
FR Yugoslavia	USD 5 million	≈5.6	8
FYR Macedonia	EUR 9 million	9.0	8
Moldova	MDL 32 million	≈2.8	12
Romania	ROL 250 billion	≈9.6	12

Source: World Bank database on bank regulation and supervision, respective national authorities.

Note: [1] raised from 8 in December 1998.

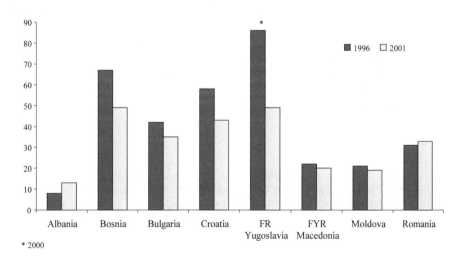

* 2000

Sources: EBRD, IMF, national authorities.

Figure 5. Number of banks in Southeast European countries

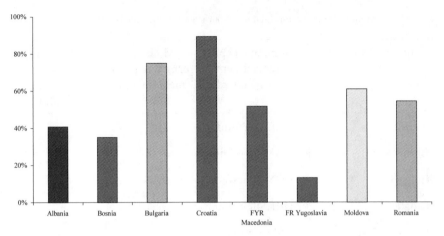

Sources: National central banks, World Bank.

Figure 6.   Share of foreign banks in total assets (2001)

In fact, opening banking to foreign investors has occurred in EU accession countries generally (Caviglia et al. 2002) as governments realised that bank failures
incur substantial fiscal costs (Brixi et al. 1999; Tang et al. 2000).[23] Admitting
foreign institutions and ownership was a measure of last resort to improve the
corporate governance of domestic banks and harden budget constraints.

In most countries of Southeast Europe, the majority of state-owned banks were
sold to foreign investors, bringing about a pronounced change in the nationality of
ownership over a period of less than three years.[24] For example, between 1997 and
2000 the number of foreign-owned banks operating in Croatia increased from 7 to
20, and their share of total assets from 4% to 84%. Similar developments took
place in Bulgaria, Romania and at a somewhat slower pace in Bosnia and Herzegovina. Serbia is the country where foreign investors reacted most quickly when a
new reform-oriented government took office early in 2001. The opening up of the
financial sector took off in Kosovo with the founding of the foreign-owned Micro
Enterprise Bank (Box).

---

[23] In Croatia in 1998 and the first half of 1999, for example, the Croatian National Bank
intervened to address the difficulties of 17 distressed banks, accounting for 17% of bank
assets. About 80% of deposits in the bankrupt banks (about 5.5% of broad money and 2%
of GDP) were covered by deposit insurance funded by the budget (IMF, 2000; Gomel,
2002).

[24] An exception is Albania, where foreign investors mainly entered the market via greenfield
investments as, at the start of transition, the banking sector comprised only three state-
owned banks. One of them was sold to foreign investors in 2000, the second was liquidated
in the late 1990s, while the Savings Bank is still state-owned. A detailed overview of financial sector developments in Albania is provided in Winkler (2000).

Foreign investment is characterised by a clear regional pattern. With the exception of Moldova, most investors are banks based in the euro zone. These banks originate from Austria (Bank Austria Creditanstalt, Raiffeisen Zentralbank, Volksbank), France (Société Générale, Crédit Lyonnais), Germany (Commerzbank, as an investor in microfinance banks), Greece (National Bank of Greece) and Italy (UniCredito Italiano, Banca di Roma).[25]

Box: Banking Sector Development in Montenegro and Kosovo

Montenegro's financial system during the socialist and post-socialist Yugoslav era consisted primarily of banks founded by socially-owned enterprises to provide inexpensive financial services, especially credit, to their parent companies. With the liberalisation of the financial sector in 1989, many enterprises that did not have access (or at least, privileged access) to existing banks, founded banks of their own.

With euroisation in 2000, the banking sector was subjected to hard budgetary constraints. As in other countries, the immediate effect was that banks were unable to hide their huge bad-loan portfolios in an environment of lower inflation. To address this problem and protect deposits, the Central Bank of Montenegro (CBM) strictly regulated banks' lending activities. CBM specified that loans could be provided only if they were funded by the bank's own resources or by term deposits of the same maturity. Since the banks' capital base was very small and term deposits practically non-existent, lending was reduced. Only very short-term loans were allowed. In April 2001, CBM took control of the largest bank in the country because its loan portfolio was deteriorating. In addition, CBM obliged all local banks to re-register under the Central Bank Law. In late 2002, only one bank, with foreign participation, was still operating.

Hence, the banking sector in Montenegro continues to be very small. Deposits are mainly from legal entities. The Montenegrin economy continues to be cash-dominated, with banknotes and coins in circulation (c. EUR 310 million) estimated to be three times larger than the volume of bank deposits. In contrast to other countries in the region, Montenegrin banks played only a limited role in the conversion to the euro (ISSP and CEPS, 2002). Although deposits increased somewhat, the changeover to the euro failed to persuade Montenegrins to deposit their legacy currency banknotes with banks. In contrast, in Croatia, Bosnia and Herzegovina, Kosovo, FYR Macedonia and FR Yugoslavia, deposits soared at the end of 2001.

---

[25] See Bank Austria Creditanstalt (2002) and Witte and Zeitinger (2002) in this book.

Kosovo's financial sector had a history similar to Montenegro's until 1989, when the autonomous provincial status of Kosovo was discontinued. The situation deteriorated steadily in the 1990s, leading to the final collapse of the financial sector during the 1999 war (World Bank, 2001b). In January 2000 the opening of Micro-Enterprise Bank (MEB), a foreign-owned institution, marked a new start. By the end of 2001, the Bank and Payment Authority of Kosovo had issued full licences to seven commercial banks, most of them local. Total assets amounted to roughly EUR 500 million, mainly funded by local deposits. Foreign banks dominated the system, with more than 70% of total deposits held at MEB.

The banking sector's main activity is to place local deposits and other liquid assets with banks abroad. Lending to the local private sector is still in its infancy, representing less than 10% of total assets. However, the portfolio is considered to be rather healthy (IMF, 2001d).

Finance and Growth in the Shorter Run: Evidence from Southeast Europe

Monetisation and Intermediation Trends

Against a background of significant changes in the regulatory set-up and owner-ship structure of the banking sectors, monetisation and financial intermediation ratios may be used as yardsticks for financial development. The monetisation ratio, defined as the ratio of broad money to GDP, measures the extent to which private agents use banks to make payments and store value by making deposits. The financial intermediation ratio compares credit extended by banks to the pri-vate sector with GDP, and shows the extent to which the banking sector actively supports the economy.

The following features can be observed in Southeast Europe (Charts 7 and 8):

- with the exception of Albania (monetisation), financial development lags behind that of the EU accession countries from Central and Eastern Europe and is very much lower than in industrialised economies.

- monetisation ratios are almost twice as high as intermediation ratios, with the exception of Albania, where the margin is even larger. This contrasts with industrialised economies where both indicators tend to be of comparable magnitude.

- monetisation has gradually increased over time, while intermediation has declined significantly in the regions that were previously part of Yugoslavia. In the other countries, the monetisation ratio has remained largely stable, but at low levels.

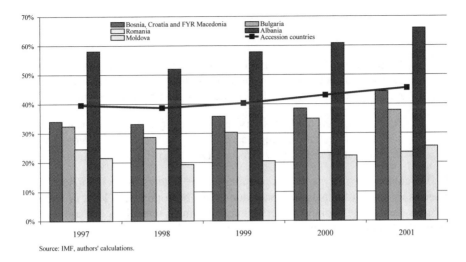

Source: IMF, authors' calculations.

Figure 7. Broad Money to GDP (1997–2001)

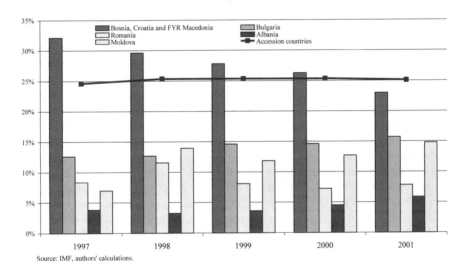

Source: IMF, authors' calculations.

Figure 8. Claims on private sector to GDP (1997–2001)

The country-specific developments can be summarised as follows:

- The areas which formerly belonged to Yugoslavia display similar develop-ment patterns: monetisation increasing slightly from comparatively high levels, whereas credit to the private sector dropped from more than 30% of GDP in 1997 to less than 25% in 2001;

- Bulgaria has recovered steadily from the 1996/1997 crisis, both in terms of monetisation and intermediation;

- Romania and Moldova have basically continued to post low and erratic levels of financial development (around 20% of GDP for the monetisation ratio and between 5% and 15% of GDP for the intermediation ratio);

- Albania exhibits the largest discrepancy between the two indicators, with a monetisation ratio as high as 60%, the highest in the region, and an intermediation ratio below 10% of GDP, the lowest in the region.

To conclude, the reform efforts seem to have fostered overall monetisation, whereas effects on financial intermediation have been mixed, at least in terms of volume. Hence, the banking sectors conduct payment operations and are used as safety vaults but contribute to a lesser extent to the financing of the economy.

Initial Monetisation and Intermediation as Predictors of Future Economic Growth

Against this background, evidence of a positive role of finance for growth in the region is mixed. Further to King and Levine (1993b), who argue that finance has a causal impact on growth if initial financial development is a good predictor of future economic growth, charts 9 and 10 plot countries' financial development in 1997 (measured by the monetisation or the intermediation ratio) against average real GDP growth between 1997 and 2001.[26]

The results are inconclusive. At first glance, initial monetisation seems to be a poor predictor of future economic growth, whereas initial intermediation stands out as a fairly good one, suggesting that the latter has a much stronger causal impact on growth than the former.

However, as the data sample is very small, the results are at best illustrative. Moreover, other relevant variables that determine economic growth are omitted.[27] Finally, the results are sensitive to outliers. For example, if Bosnia and Herzegovina are excluded from figure 9, the correlation coefficient increases to 0.73, while excluding it from figure 10 would lower the correlation coefficient to 0.30.

---

[26] The choice of the initial period is tricky. Ideally, one would want it to be as far back as possible to capture the long-term effects of financial development on growth. However, it seems advisable to exclude the first half of the 1990s which was characterised by many distortions that would blur the results. 1997 (the last year of Bulgaria's banking crisis, and the year of the collapse of the pyramid schemes in Albania) is considered the optimal choice in this respect. It has to be acknowledged that results are sensitive to the choice of initial period.

[27] In particular, small sample size and lack of data prevent the use of more rigorous panel-modelling techniques adopted by King and Levine (1993b) and which could lead to different conclusions.

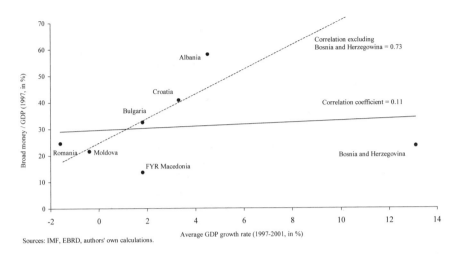

Figure 9. Initial financial development (monetisation) and subsequent economic growth

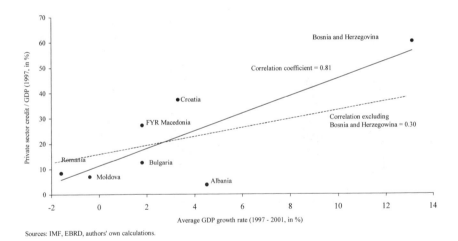

Figure 10. Initial financial development (intermediation) and subsequent economic growth

Financial Intermediation: Quantity Subordinated to Quality

The absence of conclusive results is probably due to the fact that most countries' authorities endeavoured in the second half of the 1990s to put their crisis-prone financial sectors on a more stable footing. In other words, the challenge was to ensure that a poorly organised financial sector would not again become an obstacle to growth. The impetus was more on stability than efficiency. And indeed, the overall increases in the monetisation ratio indicate that this strategy has been successful, reflecting growing confidence by private-sector players in their banking sectors.

However, insofar as the financial crises of the 1990s were largely the outcome of extending loans to non-creditworthy borrowers, the authorities' policies uncompromisingly focused on measures that put lending quality first, and quantity second.[28] The evidence available suggests that this goal has been reached at the cost of a lower volume of credit to the economy, in particular to the business sector. Five features emerge:

First, and most importantly, the quality of loan portfolios improved significantly in the late 1990s and/or remained at comparatively high levels (Figure 11). Of course, a substantial part of the improvement merely reflects the recapitalisation of banks, with governments taking over bad loan portfolios by issuing bonds. Moreover, the 1999–2001 period is one of relative expansion, so that portfolios have yet to pass the stress test of an economic downturn, while budget constraints enforced by the banking system seem to have hardened somewhat in most countries.

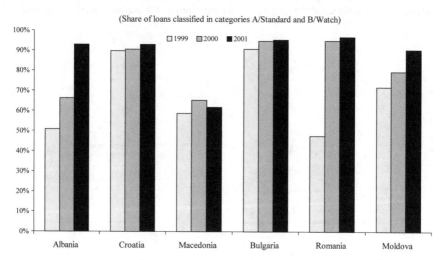

(Share of loans classified in categories A/Standard and B/Watch)

Source: National central banks.

Figure 11. Loan portfolio quality

---

[28] The increase in minimum capital requirements in absolute terms and as a percentage of risk-weighted assets; the tightening of supervision and regulation including loan classification and provisioning; and the consolidation of banking and its opening to foreign investors can be interpreted as attempts to create incentives for prudent lending and to punish the granting of "false credit".

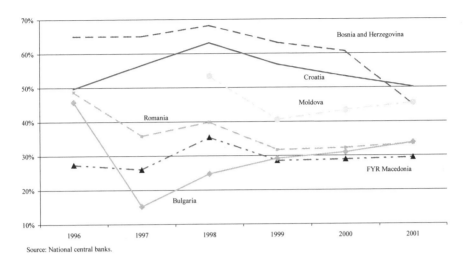

Source: National central banks.

Figure 12. Loans as a share of total banks' assets (1996–2001)

Second, while banks stopped lending to old, non-creditworthy borrowers, the share of credit to the private sector as a proportion of total banking sector assets declined substantially in Bosnia and Herzegovina, Croatia and Romania (Figure 12). In Bulgaria and Moldova, credit volumes recovered after the financial crises in 1997 and 1998, but remain below pre-crisis levels.

Rather than making loans, banks have purchased safe and liquid assets, either by depositing funds at foreign banks or – if available – buying domestic liquid assets, i.e. treasury bills (Gomel, 2002).[29] The increasing share of liquid assets explains to a large extent the high capital adequacy ratios that currently prevail in the region, for example in Albania and Moldova (Table 4), largely surpassing the statutory requirements (Table 3).[30]

Third, in many countries the composition of loan portfolios seems to have changed significantly as banks increased their consumer and mortgage lending, while credit to businesses stagnated or was less dynamic. In Croatia, for example, lending to businesses remained subdued for almost two years before rebounding in the first half of 2001. Hence, in mid-2001, loans to businesses accounted for only 44% of total loans, while loans to households ranked second, at 42% (Croatian National Bank, 2001). In Bulgaria, the share of consumer credit and residential mortgages in bank loan portfolios increased substantially, from 2% at the end of 1995 to 20% in March 2002 (IMF, 2002a). In Romania, the share of loans to households is still marginal, but has increased from about 6% to 7% (National Bank of

---

[29] Again, this behaviour is typical of most transition countries in a post-crisis period. See OECD (1997), EBRD (1998) and Berglof and Bolton (2001).

[30] Of course, higher minimum capital requirements, recapitalisation efforts and foreign involvement in the banking sector have also contributed to the high degree of capitalisation.

Table 4. Capital adequacy ratios[1] in Southeast Europe, 1998–2001

Country	1998	1999	2000	2001
Albania	−1.8%	8.2%	42.0%[2]	35.3%
Bosnia				32.0%
Bulgaria	37.0%[3]	43.0%	35.5%	31.1%
Croatia	12.7%	20.6%	21.3%	18.4%
FYR Macedonia	25.9%	28.7%	36.7%	34.3%
Yugoslavia, FR			0.7%	21.9%
Moldova			48.5%	43.4%
Romania	10.3%	17.9%	23.8%	28.8%

Sources: National central banks and IMF country reports.

[1] Risk-weighted assets to capital.

[2] The increase in 1999 partly reflects the capitalisation of the Savings Bank by the government.

[3] 1996: 5.7%, 1997: 28.9%.

Romania, 2002). Only in FYR Macedonia are bank credits primarily directed to corporations (Drummond, 2000; National Bank of Macedonia, 2002), although the proportion of good-quality loans (classified as "standard" or "watch") remains low (Figure 11).

Fourth, in many countries, the majority of loans have short maturities, i.e. less than one year, ranging from roughly 50% in Bulgaria to about 80% in Moldova. In Albania and FYR Macedonia, the share of short-term loans even increased in 2001. One exception is Croatia, where the share of long-term loans stood at about 65% in 2001, an increase of approximately ten percentage points compared to the year-end figure for 2000.

Finally, central bank data for Bulgaria indicate that the supply of credit to small and medium-sized enterprises is especially limited. According to the Credit Regis-ter, "almost 50% of all credits in the banking system … were concentrated on some 250 borrowers." (National Bank of Bulgaria, 2002). Hence, SMEs have to rely primarily on cash and informal sources (IMF, 2002a). Similar conclusions have been drawn for other countries in the region (Pissarides, 2001).

Bottlenecks to Further Financial Intermediation

Low levels of financial development, as reflected by low intermediation, prevent the banking system from contributing positively to economic growth. Rather than performing their standard functions, as outlined in Section 2, banking sectors in

Southeast Europe pool savings, but then invest them in low-risk and liquid assets. Moreover, the allocation of resources is highly concentrated, excluding many potential borrowers with productive investment projects. Although foreign ownership has reached very high levels in most countries and banking supervision and regulation have improved, financial development has materialised mainly through monetisation rather than intermediation. This can be explained by a number of factors: [31]

1. *Idiosyncratic Shocks*

   - Many countries in the region are still subject to exogenous shocks, usually of a political nature. The most prominent recent examples are the Kosovo war in 1999, the collapse of the Milosevic regime in 2000 and the crisis in Macedonia in 2001. Albania suffered from a severe energy crisis in 2001, which affected most parts of the economy.

   - The legal and institutional environment in the region remains weak. For example, corporate financial accounts are still largely unreliable. The legal indicators relating to commercial law and financial regulation applied by EBRD place countries in this region last among the transition countries (EBRD, 2001).

2. *Supply Factors*

   - Risk aversion is typical of banks in a post-crisis period before the necessary but time-consuming changes in procedures and risk management are implemented.

   - There is lack of adequately trained staff with experience in selecting, analysing and monitoring clients. This is a legacy of the socialist era and the "pocket banking" practices adopted in the early 1990s. Under the old governance and ownership structures, these skills were not needed. Many banks, even if they are now privatised and operating under new and appropriate governance structures, are still unable to provide financial intermediation services effectively.

   - There is anecdotal evidence that "foreign-owned banks are more likely to cherry-pick the best borrowers available on the market (especially those from their own countries of origin)" (Grigoriana and Manole, 2002).[32] Moreover, at least initially, they seem to restrict themselves to wholesale banking, focusing on areas that generate fees and commissions, such as international payment transactions, short-

---

[31] The list is based on information from Bank of Albania (2002), IMF (2001c), National Bank of Bulgaria (2002), IMF (2002a and b), IMF (2001b).

[32] See also Buch (1996).

term trade credits and the issuance of securities (Buch, 2002).[33] So far, the key contribution of foreign-owned banks seems to have been to create a level of stability based on the track record and reputation of powerful parent institutions (Keren and Ofer, 2002; Grigorian and Manole, 2002). Looking ahead, it will be interesting to monitor whether and when foreign banks will perform as true intermediaries in the local financial systems.[34]

- The deposit base of many banking sectors is mainly characterised by short-term funds, often denominated in foreign currency (Figure 13). This severely restricts lending, both in terms of absolute volume and maturity, as banks are eager and required by regulation to avoid large maturity and/or currency mismatches.[35]

(January 2002)

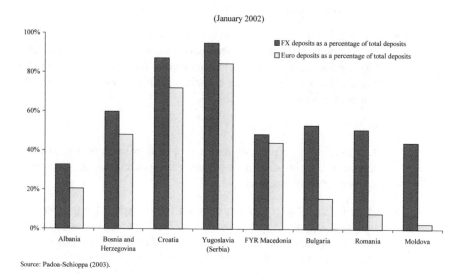

Source: Padoa-Schioppa (2003).

Figure 13. Foreign exchange deposits in total deposits

---

[33] Of course, there are exceptions both in terms of institutions and countries, with foreign banks being increasingly engaged in retail operations. Moreover, Fries and Taci (2002) find that banks under foreign ownership in transition economies seem to be associated with neither stronger nor weaker real growth in customer loans compared to domestically-owned banks.

[34] Since foreign banks historically have had limited operations in third countries' markets, any forecast would be highly speculative (for an attempt, see Pomerleano and Vojta, 2001).

[35] In Romania, for example, IMF staff expressed concerns about the rapid expansion of foreign-currency-denominated credit, as it exposes banks to higher credit risks (IMF 2002c). Similar concerns have been expressed by Drummond (2000).

3. *Demand Factors*

- Private sector development is characterised by a large number of micro, small and medium-sized enterprises that are fairly young, fragile and often without a credit history. Hence, most banks do not consider them creditworthy and deny them access to credit. The most prominent example in this regard is Albania, where almost the entire enterprise sector is composed of micro and small businesses (Muent, Pissarides and Sanfey, 2000).

- Many small borrowers are unfamiliar with normal bank credit approval procedures. Hence, they face substantial difficulties in obtaining credit from the formal financial sector.

Summary and Conclusions

While the positive and causal link between financial development and economic growth is firmly established for a large sample of countries over the long run, the evidence in recent years for Southeast Europe is mixed. During a large part of the 1990s, the malfunctioning financial sector in the region was an impediment rather than a promoter of economic growth, leading to financial crises and ultimately large output losses. At the end of 2002, the financial sector could not be considered to be performing its functions well and to be fuelling economic growth. Describing the financial sector as stable and crisis-free would be more apt, while pointing out that it was failing to support growth actively. There are several reasons for this:

1. As a consequence of the severe crises, the authorities tightened regulation and supervision, and opened up the domestic banking sector to foreign investors. By the end of 2001, the financial sectors in the region were characterised by a more stringent regulatory environment with the ownership majority in foreign hands.

2. Tighter supervision and foreign ownership contributed to a rise in deposits as public confidence in the banks strengthened. Conversely, lending to the private sector relative to GDP stagnated or declined as increasing regulatory pressure shifted emphasis to the provision of high-quality lending and as banks became more risk averse.

3. The cautious behaviour of the banks can be explained by a number of additional factors: exogenous risks are still widespread; there is no tradition of high-quality lending and a lack of know-how to support it; most potential borrowers are micro, small and medium-sized enterprises that are rather fragile and without an adequate track record. They are usually unable to deal or comply with standard lending requirements or to offer collateral acceptable to commercial banks.

Of course, finance will not be the only key determinant of economic growth in the region. Other factors, such as sound macroeconomic conditions, institution building and governance, to mention only a few, are obviously important. Given the low level of financial intermediation, it is understandable that domestic policy makers and international institutions are keen to promote lending, in particular to micro, small and medium-sized businesses. But several caveats apply. As emphasised by the World Bank (2001a), financial development is not a policy choice variable. Attempts to boost it artificially by engineering excessively rapid growth in domestic credit contribute to inflation, exchange depreciation, doubtful loans and insolvent banks. The expansion of lending must not be accompanied by a return to bad credit practices.

For this reason, policy should focus on alleviating the bottlenecks to financial intermediation identified above, by

- creating a stable macroeconomic framework and a sound institutional and legal environment, conducive to financial transactions;

- helping banks train staff and management to design and implement procedures which promote high-quality lending;

- paying due attention to the lending environment in the respective countries, in particular to potential clients in the business and corporate sector.

Experience from other regions indicates that this is easier said than done (Von Pischke, 1991; Webster et al., 1996). There have been many attempts of this sort in transition countries as well, with mixed results (EU 2000; Schmidt and Zeitinger, 2001). Hence, innovative approaches to foster financial development in volatile environments are particularly warranted.

References

Bank of Albania (2002). Report on Supervision 2001, Tirana.

Bank Austria Creditanstalt (2002). Comparison of banks, Central and Eastern Europe, 2001, mimeo.

Beck, T., R. Levine and N. Loayza (2000). 'Finance and the Sources of Growth', Journal of Financial Economics, 58, pp. 261-300.

Bencivenga, V.R. and B.D. Smith (1991). 'Financial Intermediation and Endogenous Growth', Review of Economic Studies, 58(2), pp. 195-209.

Berglof, E. and P. Bolton (2002). 'The Great Divide and Beyond. Financial Architecture in Transition', Journal of Economic Perspectives, 16 (1), pp. 77-100.

Blommestein, H.J. and M.G. Spencer (1993). 'The Role of Financial Institutions in the Transition to a Market Economy', IMF Working Paper, Washington D.C.

Bokros, L. (2002). Financial Sector Development in Central and Eastern Europe, in Winkler, A. (ed.), Banking and Monetary Policy in Eastern Europe. The First Ten Years. Houndmills and New York: Palgrave Publishing, pp. 11-42.

Brixi, H.P., H. Ghanem and R. Islam (1999). 'Fiscal Adjustment and Contingent Government Liabilities. Case studies of the Czech Republic and Macedonia', World Bank Policy Research Working Paper, No. 2177, Washington D.C.

Buch, C. (1996). 'Opening up for Foreign Banks – Why Central and Eastern Europe Can Benefit', Kiel Working Paper No. 763, The Kiel Institute of World Economics.

Buch, C. (2002). 'Governance and Restructuring of Commercial Banks', in Winkler, A. (ed.), Banking and Monetary Policy in Eastern Europe. The First Ten Years. Houndmills and New York: Palgrave Publishing, pp. 43-71.

Cavigila, G., G. Krause and C. Thimann (2002). 'Financial Sectors in Accession Countries. some Key Features', in Thimann, C. (ed.), Financial Sectors in EU Accession Countries, European Central Bank, Frankfurt am Main, pp. 15-30.

Caprio, G. (1997). 'Safe and Sound Banking in Developing Countries – We're Not in Kansas Anymore', World Bank Working Paper, No. 1739, Washington D.C.

Caprio, G. and D. Klingebiel (1996). 'Bank Insolvencies – Cross Country Experience', World Bank Policy Research Paper, No. 1620, Washington D.C.

Caprio, G. (1998). 'Banking on Crises, Expensive Lessons from Recent Financial Crises', World Bank Working Paper, No. 1979, Washington D.C.

Croatian National Bank (2001). 'Indicators of Banking Institution Operations', Banks Bulletin, 1(3), Zagreb.

De Gregorio, J. and P.E. Guidotti (1992). 'Financial Development and Economic Growth', IMF Working Paper, WP/92/101, Washington D.C.

Demirgüç-Kunt, A. and V. Maksimovic (1998). 'Law, Finance, and Firm Growth', Journal of Finance, 53(6), December 1998, pp. 2107-2137.

Diamond, D. (1984). 'Financial Intermediation and Delegated Monitoring', Review of Economic Studies, 51, pp. 393-414.

Drummond, P. (2000). 'Former Yugoslav Republic of Macedonia – Banking Soundness and Recent Lessons', IMF Working paper, WP/00/145, Washington D.C.

Dziobek, C., O. Frecaut and M. Nieto (1995). 'Non-G-10 Countries and the Basle Capital Rules. How Tough a Challenge is it to Join the Basle Club?' IMF Paper on Policy Analysis and Assessment, No. 95/5, Washington D.C.

EBRD (1998). Transition Report, London.

EBRD (2001). Transition Report, London.

European Union Commission (2000). PHARE – An Evaluation of Phare-financed programmes in support of SMEs, Final Synthesis Report, Brussels.

Fries, S.M. and T.D. Lane (1994). 'Financial and Enterprise Restructuring in Emerging Market Economies', IMF-Working Paper, Washington D.C.

Fries, S.M. and A. Taci (2002). 'Banking Reform and Development in Transition Economies', EBRD Working Paper, No. 71, London.

Gelb, A. and P. Honohan (1991). 'Financial Sector Reform', in. Thomas, V. et al. (eds.), Restructuring Economies in Distress, Policy Reform and the World Bank, Washington D.C.

Gomel, Giorgio (2002). 'Banking and Financial Sector in Transition Countries and Convergence towards European Integration', mimeo, http.//eaces.gelso.unitn.it/ Eaces/work/Papers/Gomel-eaces_080502-rev.pdf

Greenwood, J. and B. Jovanovic (1990). 'Financial Development, Growth, and the Distribution of Income', Journal of Political Economy, 98(5), pp. 1076-1107.

Grigorian, D.A. and V. Manole (2002). 'Determinants of Commercial Bank Performance in Transition. An Application of Data Envelopment Analysis', IMF Working Paper, WP/02/146, Washington D.C.

Hermes, N. (1994). 'Financial Development and Economic Growth. A Survey of the Literature', International Journal of Development Banking, 12(1), pp. 3-22.

IMF (2000). IMF Concludes Article IV Consultation with Croatia, Public Information Notice (PIN) No. 00/4, http.//www.imf.org/external/np/sec/pn/2000/ pn0004.htm.

IMF (2001a). Republic of Moldova. Recent Economic Developments, CR 01/22, Washington D.C.

IMF (2001b). Romania. Selected Issues and Statistical Appendix, CR 01/16, Washington D.C.

IMF (2001c). Bosnia and Herzegovina. Sixth and Seventh Review Under the Stand-By Arrangement and Request for Waiver of Performance Criterion, Staff Statement, and News Brief, CR 01/106, Washington D.C.

IMF (2001d). Kosovo – Progress in Institution-Building and Economic Policy Challenges Ahead, Washington D.C.

IMF (2002a). Bulgaria, Financial System Stability Assessment, CR 02/188, Washington D.C.

IMF (2002b). Bulgaria. Selected Issues and Statistical Appendix, CR 02/173, Washington D.C.

IMF (2002c). Romania. First and Second Reviews Under the Stand-By Arrangement, Request for Waivers, and Modification of Performance Criterion – Staff Report; Staff Statement; News Brief on the Executive Board Discussion; and Statement by the Executive Director for Romania, CR 02/194, Washington D.C.

ISSP and CEPS (2002). Montenegro Economic Trends, July 2002, Podgorica and Brussels.

Jarvis, C. (2000). 'The Rise and Fall of Albania's Pyramid Schemes', Finance and Development, 37(1), pp. 46-49.

Keren, M. and G. Ofer (2002). 'Globalization and the Role of Foreign Banks in Economies in Transition', mimeo, http.//eaces.gelso.unitn.it/Eaces/work/Papers/Globalization%20and%20the%20Role.pdf.

King, R.G. and R. Levine (1993a). 'Finance, Entrepreneurship and Growth', Journal of Monetary Economics, 32, pp. 513-542.

King, R. and R. Levine (1993b). 'Finance and Growth. Schumpeter Might Be Right', Quarterly Journal of Economics, August 1993, 108(3), pp. 717-37.

Levine, R. (1997). 'Financial Development and Economic Growth. Views and Agenda', Journal of Economic Literature, 35, June 1997, pp. 688-726.

Levine, R. (2001). 'International Financial Liberalisation and Economic Growth', Review of International Economics, 9(4), pp. 688-702.

Levine, R. and S. Zervos (1998). 'Stock markets, Banks and Economic Growth', American Economic Review, 88(3), pp. 537-558.

Levine, R., N. Loayza and T. Beck (2000). 'Financial Intermediation and Growth. Causality and Causes', Journal of Monetary Economics, 46, pp. 31-77.

Lucas, R. (1988). 'On the Mechanics of Economic Growth', Journal of Monetary Economics, July 1988, 22(1), pp. 3-42.

McKinnon, R.I. (1992). The Order of Economic Liberalization, Financial Control in the Transition to a Market Economy. Baltimore and London: Johns Hopkins University Press.

Merton, R. and Z. Bodie (1995). 'A Conceptual Framework for Analysing the Financial Environment', in Crane, D.B. (ed.), The Global Financial System: a Functional Perspective. Boston: Harvard Business School Press.

Muent, H., F. Pissarides and P. Sanfey (2000). 'Taxes, Competition and Finance for Albanian Enterprises. Evidence from a Field Study', EBRD Working Paper, No. 54, London.

National Bank of Bulgaria (2002). Annual Report 2001, Sofia.

National Bank of Macedonia (2002). Annual Report 2001, Skopje.

National Bank of Romania (2002). Annual Report 2001, Bucarest.

Neuhauss, W. (2002). 'Refinancing Banks in an Unstable Financial Environment', in Winkler, A. (ed.), Banking and Monetary Policy in Eastern Europe. The First Ten Years. Houndmills and New York: Palgrave Publishing, pp. 72-87.

OECD (1997), Economic Survey. Hungary 1996-97, Paris.

Padoa-Schioppa, T. (2002). 'The Euro Goes East', Lecture delivered at the 8th Dubrovnik Economic Conference, 29 June 2002, http.//www.ecb.int.

Pissarides, F. (2001). 'Financial Structures to Promote Private Sector Development in South-Eastern Europe', EBRD Working Paper, No. 64, London.

Pomerleano, M. and G.J. Vojta (2001). 'What Do Foreign Banks Do in Emerging Markets? An Institutional Study', Paper presented at the 3rd Annual Financial Markets and Development Conference on 'Open Doors. Foreign Participation in Financial Systems in Developing Countries' organised by the World Bank, IMF and Brookings Institution.

Rajan, R. and L. Zingales (1998). 'Financial Dependence and Growth', American Economic Review, 88(3), pp. 559-586.

Robinson, J. (1952). 'The Generalisation of the General Theory', in The rate of interest and other essays, London: Macmillan, pp. 67-142.

Rousseau, P. and P. Wachtel (1998). 'Financial Intermediation and Economic Performance. Historical Evidence from Five Industrialised Countries', Journal of Money, Credit and Banking, 30(4), November 1998, pp. 657-678.

Schmidt, R.H. and C.-P. Zeitinger (2001). 'Micro-Finance Banks. Building New Institutions Instead of Remodelling Existing Ones', Small Enterprise Development, 11 (2), pp. 32-43.

Schumpeter, J. (1912). Theorie der Wirtschaftlichen Entwicklung, Leipzig: Dunker & Humblot.

Sundararajan, V. and T.J.T. Balino (1991). 'Issues in Recent Banking Crises', in. Sundararajan, V. and T.J.T. Balino (eds.), Banking Crises. Cases and Issues, Washington D.C.: International Monetary Fund, pp. 1-57.

Talley, S., M. Giugale and R. Polastri (1998). 'Capital Inflow Reversals, Banking Stability, and Prudential Regulation in Eastern Europe', World Bank Policy Research Paper, No. 2023, Washington D.C.

Tang, H. E. Zoli and I. Klytchnikova (2000). 'Banking Crises in Transition Countries. Fiscal Costs and Related Issues', World Bank Policy Research Paper, No. 2484, Washington D.C.

Von Pischke (1991). Finance at the Frontier, World Bank: Washington D.C.

Webster, L., R. Riopelle and A.-M. Chidzero (1996). 'World Bank lending for small enterprises, 1989-1993', World Bank technical paper, No. 311, Washington D.C.

Winkler, A. (2000). 'Financial Sector Development and Financial Institution Building in Albania', Südosteuropa Zeitschrift für Gegenwartsforschung, Heft 9-10, pp. 474-502.

World Bank (1989). World Development Report, Washington D.C.

World Bank (1993). Russia – The Banking System in Transition, Washington D.C.

World Bank (2001a). Finance for Growth, Policy Research Report, Oxford University Press.

World Bank (2001b). Kosovo – Economic and Social Reforms for Peace and Reconciliation, http://www.seerecon.org.

Zeitinger, C.-P. (2002). 'Sustainable Microfinance Banks – Problems and Perspectives', Paper prepared for the KfW symposium on 'Innovative approaches to financial sector development in volatile environments', Berlin 7-8 November 2002.

PART II:

Innovative Approaches to Building Financial Sectors in Southeast Europe

Introduction to Part II

How can a capital base be created in transition economies when financial markets are insufficiently capitalised, unable to correlate risk and yield efficiently, hampered by conflicts of interest, or if they fail to seize market potential? This challenge has been addressed by the KfW Group, IFC and EBRD and is the subject of Part II. In order to tackle these shortcomings, funds for financial sector development and institution building – especially those invested as equity in banks and other financial intermediaries – must be employed in a meaningful way. Investors, however, have varying time horizons depending on their corporate missions and objectives. And official donor organisations have exit strategies, as their role is inconsistent with permanent equity participation in commercial institutions that operate efficiently in the private sector.

KfW Offers Comprehensive Solutions to Regional and Sectoral Challenges

Doris Köhn and Wolfram Erhardt illustrate KfW's comprehensive approach to financial sector development in Southeast Europe. These authors argue that even if individual projects are successful and viable, a project-centred approach is insufficient to reform the region's financial sectors. A broader, sectoral view is required, with carefully selected, complementary initiatives that have a catalytic effect. Accordingly, KfW's approach to financial sector development is based on four important principles.

First, project design is adapted to local conditions. Interventions are fine-tuned within the context of a broader and robust structural framework. Second, target-group orientation emphasises micro and small and medium-sized enterprises because of their capacity to weather crises, create employment and help alleviate poverty. The third principle is competition and market orientation. KfW works with a set of financial institutions selected because of their potential to use resources wisely in commercial transactions and in a socially beneficial manner. The aim is to foster competition and consolidation in the banking industry. To this end, the refinancing and technical assistance provided by the downscaling programme described here and in Part III are complemented by the greenfield approach – establishing new, target-group oriented banks. Market orientation includes donors' provision of funds at rates and with maturities more favourable than those prevailing in the distorted SEE markets in order to facilitate the achievement of clear development objectives. These objectives include rational pricing achieved through building competitive markets. Fourth, KfW seeks a strong element of donor coordination and policy dialogue.

Klaus Glaubitt and Haje Schütte describe the merits of and challenges facing the European funds set up to support the downscaling programmes that KfW implements on behalf of the European Commission and the governments of Austria,

Germany, the Netherlands (FMO) and Switzerland. Since 1998, these programmes have stimulated private commercial banks to provide SME and housing loans to enterprises and private citizens in Bosnia and Herzegovina, Kosovo, Montenegro and Serbia. These funds were independently established for fixed periods of operation in each recipient country by some or all of the donors noted above. They promote an essential element of financial sector development – lengthening the term structure. By providing long-term funding, these funds enable local commercial and microfinance banks to offer term loans to clients for investment in productive fixed assets and housing. This instrument is especially important, as the general lack of confidence in banks impedes savings mobilisation and makes depositors reluctant to make time deposits.

The authors argue that these funds could deliver benefits more efficiently and achieve greater impact if they were institutionalised through a proposed European Development Foundation for Southeast Europe, an approach that is consistent with efforts to construct entities with a regional focus. The process of institutionalisation would entail pooling the funds' resources and managing them through a foundation established for this purpose and having a long or unlimited corporate life. In this form, these funds could a) further assist private financial institutions to reach a greater number of potential clients currently regarded too risky and costly to accommodate, and b) continue to enable private financial institutions to spearhead financial sector development by launching innovative services and techniques that reduce transaction costs, lengthen term structures and refine valuation processes.

IFC Links Financial Market Efficiency to Poverty Alleviation

Since the 1990s, the International Finance Corporation (IFC) has linked its investment strategy to poverty reduction, turning its attention also to the bottom end of the market. Aftab Ahmed cites IFC's three major priorities in transition countries over the last dozen years: to develop the legal and regulatory framework for the financial sector, to transfer state-owned assets to private ownership, and to develop private financial institutional infrastructure. These priorities have enabled IFC to achieve a positive development impact in "the first wave of privatisation and building institutional infrastructure." IFC has helped to frame laws and regulations, started new stock exchanges and participated in the design and implementation of voucher systems for the distribution of state-owned assets.

A major factor complicating transition was the devastating loss of employment. Support for new enterprises from traditional commercial banks did not translate into rapid job creation. New lending vehicles oriented toward firms or the creation of firms at the bottom end of the market were essential. This led IFC to support the formation of specialised microenterprise banks based on a common business model and supported by a strong, like-minded shareholder group focused on good corporate governance.

IFC was instrumental in establishing such a shareholder group in 1996 by insisting that the technical partner of the MicroEnterprise Bank (MEB) in Bosnia and Herzegovina also provide equity. IPC was selected as the technical partner and, in 1998, took the innovative step of forming IMI (Internationale Micro Investitionen AG). IMI is a specialised microfinance investment company whose major shareholders, in addition to IFC and IPC, are currently the KfW Group, BIO, Commerzbank, DOEN Foundation, FMO and others. IMI invests in new microfinance banks (MEBs) managed by IPC, as described by the paper by Zeitinger in Part III below.

The success of this model, according to Ahmed, is due to cooperation among the investors and their commitment to sustainability and impact; the provision of international financing until a domestic deposit base is developed; appropriate, low-cost lending technology; good management; and equity participation by IPC, the technical assistance provider. Ahmed cites the importance IFC attaches to the rapid expansion of this successful model, including linking the MEBs to local funding sources.

EBRD's Investments in Financial Institution Building

Elizabeth Wallace of the European Bank for Reconstruction and Development (EBRD) summarises the achievements of EBRD-sponsored financial institutions in 24 countries. Their target group consists of micro, small and medium-sized enterprises that would otherwise not have been able to obtain formal credit. By the end of 2002, more than 106,000 loans had been made in Russia, and the total for the region was 250,000 loans since the first pilot project was launched in 1994. The portfolio at risk (the total balance of loans on which any portion is in arrears for more than 30 days) was less than 1%. EBRD provides subsidised funding and technical assistance (TA) for these operations, which are designed to become sustainable within a few years.

Two types of projects have been implemented. The first is downscaling, moving existing commercial banks down market to serve the target group of micro and small entrepreneurs. Downscaling was initiated in Russia and has also proved quite successful in Kazakstan. EBRD experience indicates that the business environment is not an obstacle to downscaling – the key is having a receptive partner bank. Risks can be high, especially those associated with financial instability, changes in management and the integrity of a bank's operations and its commitment to the target group. It takes time for a participating bank to adjust its operations to and become comfortable with micro and small clients and the techniques through which they can be served. Portfolio growth is correspondingly slow. And, the advisors or consultants can make or break a downscaling effort. Despite the positive results achieved in many cases, doubt remains about the extent to which downscaling will be retained after EBRD funding expires. Wallace gives a number of reasons why bankers may resist the procedures that are appropriate for lending at the small end, even where these produce very good results.

The second type of project focuses on establishing greenfield banks (newly formed banks started from scratch), which include the microenterprise banks (MEBs). Compared to downscalers, they tend to be more efficient, they provide more loans more quickly and can cover their costs and reach profitability within two or three years. The MEBs are discussed here and in Part III by their owners, who each provide a slightly different description of basically the same entity depending on their individual ownership and functional roles.

Options for the Eventual Exit of Public Sector Donors

Volker Neuschütz of Deutsche Investitions- und Entwicklungsgesellschaft (DEG – part of the KfW Group) reviews development finance and how it operates or could operate in SEE. He emphasises the importance of permanent equity capital as a stabilising influence in volatile environments and as a catalyst for the growth of small and medium-sized enterprises. He addresses two central questions: how long to stay and in what capacity. DEG invests directly in enterprises, including banks, and began incorporating exit expectations in its participations in the late 1980s. It has made successful exits from banks in Bosnia and Slovenia and elsewhere that include privatisations of state-owned development finance institutions. In certain cases, DEG has been able to use floatations on stock exchanges to exit from banks in which it has had an equity interest. Exits are planned for banks in Montenegro, Romania and Yugoslavia.

DEG uses its board presence to prepare for exit. It actively solicits and enlarges its network of business contacts in order to identify and engage potential future investors who could take over its ownership stake and seats on the board.

Neuschütz defines two elements of a successful exit strategy, which requires balancing overall objectives: first, to achieve an internal rate of return reflecting the risk taken by DEG in making its developmental contribution. Second, to achieve the development goals that originally motivated the investment, thereby enabling DEG to fulfil its institutional and social missions. "Best execution" at the outset, followed by the strategic alignment of interests and diligent control when operations are underway lead to the desired exit. The process may require up to eight years.

Neuschütz notes that donors allocate funds according to political and ideological criteria, and that they should not attempt to play independent entrepreneurial roles, as they are not in fact entrepreneurs. Entrepreneurship is brought in through a "strategic investor" who has the experience and incentive to take risks and engage in ventures that would be regarded as too challenging in the absence of donor collaboration. Identifying and recruiting strategic investors is an important function of donors that provide equity capital.

The chapters in Part II illustrate different modes of exit. DEG and IFC, for example, exit from a commercial investment by selling their shares and relinquishing their seat on the supervisory board. In the case of the proposed European Development Foundation for Southeast Europe, exit consists of transforming limited-life project funds into permanent capital for the new foundation, with continued donor involvement through seats on the foundation's supervisory board for as long as they wish to remain involved.

Resilience in Crises

Microfinance on a commercial basis in SEE began in difficult circumstances. The overall situation has gradually improved, but the region has not passed the point beyond which peace and prosperity are assured. How well could microfinance weather a downturn? If crisis occurs, is the micro, small and medium-sized enterprise sector more or less vulnerable than large firms? There are no facts about the future, but Bolivian experience offers hope that microfinance can stand up well in national crises, as documented by Elisabeth Rhyne of ACCION International.

Bolivia is one of the poorest nations in the western hemisphere, but has the region's most dynamic microfinance market. Regulated microfinance institutions in Bolivia weathered the crisis that began in the late 1990s. In 1998, about 400,000 Bolivian microentrepreneurs were using micro credit. The aggregate portfolio of microfinance institutions had tripled since 1994. Four major lenders serving about 170,000 clients dominated the market, their portfolio quality was good and they reported healthy returns on equity. Consumer lending, subject to less stringent credit criteria than those applied by microlenders, had mushroomed. Lenders competed ever more fiercely for good clients.

In 1999, several events disrupted external trade and unemployment levels rose, creating a national crisis of major proportions. It was not until 2002 that the situation had stabilised. Demand fell and competition increased as markets became saturated. Repayment problems multiplied as debt service capacity evaporated. Microlenders discovered that many of their clients also had debts outstanding to other microlenders. Consumer lending institutions collapsed. A movement formed demanding debt relief, and protest ultimately culminated in violence and tense, potentially explosive stand-offs.

While the entire financial system suffered, the large regulated microlenders suffered less because they managed delinquency well. Four of the largest five reported profits in 2002 and two were among the most profitable of Bolivia's financial institutions. Rhyne suggests that informal businesses adapt quickly to crises. FIE and Caja Los Andes, issuing only individual loans, actually grew during the crisis and remained profitable throughout. Two large microlenders that offered group loans were able to break even during these tough times. It appears that group lending performs less well in a crisis because the strongest group members have already migrated to individual lenders and because a default by one member of a group may trigger default by all other members, who are unwilling to cover the arrears of the original defaulter. Rhyne concludes that a crisis leads to better practices within and among lending institutions and also highlights the importance of better regulatory oversight.

CHAPTER 3:

Competition and Complementarity: KfW's Approach to Financial Sector Development in Southeast Europe

Doris Köhn* and Wolfram Erhardt**

* First Vice President Europe, KfW, Frankfurt, Germany
** Project Manager, KfW, Frankfurt, Germany

The Challenge of Economic Reconstruction in Southeast Europe

A few years ago, KfW was mandated by the German government, the European Commission and other bilateral and multilateral donors to design an appropriate approach to support financial sector development in Southeast Europe. In view of the extent of the social and economic crises in the region, it is particularly remarkable that the KfW-managed financial sector programmes have yielded such significant results in such a short period of time.

Obviously, lasting success will only materialise in high-risk environments if projects are professionally designed and managed. Since the Southeast European countries began their reforms only recently, we were able to design successful interventions in the region on the basis of experience gained elsewhere, taking advantage of the lessons learnt while avoiding many of the mistakes of the past.

In the following, we briefly review KfW's mission to contribute to financial sector reform in the region before going on to describe how our interventions have been based on state-of-the-art small and medium-sized enterprise (SME) finance. Yet, the "state of the art" by no means implies taking a static approach. Maturing financial sectors and growing SME demand for more sophisticated financial products, as well as political interference and unexpected failures of partner banks are only some of the challenges our project management has had to confront. This has required and stimulated the continuous improvement and fine-tuning of our approaches.

The Legacy of War

The economic crisis in the region is the result of two major impacts. The transition process which got underway in the early 1990s led to double-digit negative growth rates. Later, the violent conflict accompanying the disintegration of Yugoslavia dealt another blow to economic growth. In Bosnia and Herzegovina (BiH), for instance, GDP fell by 40% in 1993 and again in 1994. In addition, in the countries where fighting occurred, significant infrastructure, including roads, railways and bridges, was destroyed – and with it the prerequisites for economic growth. And the extent of the humanitarian crisis far exceeds the imagination. Many lost their lives, and in Bosnia and Herzegovina alone over two million people, or half the population, were driven from their homes. In Kosovo, the numbers of refugees and displaced persons exceeded one million. Even if most of the refugees have since returned from foreign countries, the number of displaced persons continues to grow as many are discriminated against when they return to their homeland.

In this environment, the resumption of economic activity is of high priority. Most of the state-owned enterprises have long ceased to operate, leaving thousands jobless. High unemployment persists across the region, with official figures reaching 40% in Bosnia and Herzegovina.

Promotion of Small and Medium-Sized Enterprises

As in other developing and transition countries, the small and medium-sized enterprise sector has the potential to provide urgently needed employment and income opportunities in Southeast Europe. SMEs account for over 60% of the GDP of Bosnia and Herzegovina, for instance, and they make up an even larger share of overall employment. The financial sector in the region, however, has been unable to offer SMEs sufficient finance and it faces a number of constraints:

- the banking system in most SEE countries has been misused by non-financial interests. Loans were issued on the basis of political considerations and personal relationships (usually to related companies) to the detriment of SMEs and the quality of loan portfolios.

- banking supervision has been weak, offering no comfort to the "ordinary client" in terms of transparency, safety and the soundness of the banking sector.

- local banks have failed to develop demand-oriented credit technologies, i.e. credit products and procedures that are responsive to the credit demands of SMEs.

- the lack of refinancing sources also limits the availability of SME credit. The mobilisation of domestic savings is seriously hampered by a deep distrust of local banks. Perceived country risks add to the difficulties facing local banks seeking funds in international capital markets.

It is against this background that KfW was mandated by various European donors to identify and address the most critical obstacles to the revival of the region's financial sectors. The aim is to provide demand-oriented financial services particularly to small and medium-sized enterprises, thus contributing to the development of the financial sector and the economy as a whole.

Complementarity and Competition: The Strategy of KfW-Managed Projects in Southeast Europe

In the context of international development cooperation, SME finance in particular is one area where the successful and synergistic interaction between theory and practice is making itself felt. In the course of the last two decades, state-of-the-art principles have evolved that enable micro and SME finance projects to be successful.

The creation of sustainable institutions now ranks among the most important aims of financial sector initiatives. In fact, sustainability is much more than a modern buzzword; it has tangible consequences and it implies that all efforts have to be directed towards creating institutions capable of serving low income entrepreneurs on a long term basis. This calls for the implementation of credit technologies and loan-pricing practices tailored to lenders, enabling them to cover their risk and transaction costs and generate reasonable profits.

SME finance has long stopped being regarded as a tool for channelling social welfare services to the needy. Yet, it was unthinkable only a couple of years ago that the commercialisation of SME finance would proceed so quickly. If financial sector projects are to be successful, a market and marketing perspective is required: "the poor" must be regarded as self-reliant customers who have freedom of choice in increasingly competitive markets. Low-income groups, too, require diversified financial products: It is not only credit services, but savings, money transfer and insurance products, designed specifically for these customer segments which are being developed and offered.

Drawing on these insights, KfW's approach to financial sector development incorporates four important principles: project design tailored to relevant objectives; target-group orientation; adherence to the principles of competition and market orientation; and a strong element of donor coordination and policy dialogue.

Tailored Project Design

Our projects address two important structural weaknesses that confront the region's financial sectors:

- the lack of medium and long-term refinancing funds fundamentally restricts the ability of banks to issue loans to SMEs and homeowners at sufficiently long maturities.

- institutional weaknesses and unsuitable credit technologies make it difficult for local banks to deal with the risk and administrative costs related to SME lending.

The projects, consequently, provide refinancing lines to local financial institutions, which in turn on-lend the funds to the target groups. The second component relates to institution-building measures aiming at creating professional, profitable and thereby sustainable credit departments in local banks.

Target-Group Orientation

According to KfW's development mandate, the programmes are oriented towards the poorer strata of society. This calls for the development of credit products and procedures that are in line with the specific demands of these target groups.

Competition and Market Orientation

In Southeast Europe, KfW is pursuing a *comprehensive* approach to financial sector development. Obviously, individual projects must aim to be successful and viable in the long run. Yet, no purely project-centred approach will succeed even over the long term in reforming the region's troubled financial sectors. In addition to strengthening individual financial intermediaries, positive structural developments need to be created at the sectoral level. Promoting a competitive financial sector environment is particularly important in this context. Insufficient competition often permits banks to keep interest margins high, thus nurturing institutional and procedural inefficiencies. Competitive financial sectors, on the contrary, create powerful incentives for local banks to develop institutional and product innovations which benefit the small-entrepreneur target group.

The design of our initiatives in Southeast Europe is based on the following considerations:

- our interventions are guided by the overarching principle of subsidiarity; in other words, we believe that donor activities are justified and necessary only if financial markets do not adequately cater to low income entrepreneurs' demand for financial services. Therefore, our projects aim at strengthening *local financial intermediaries* instead of supporting parallel delivery structures. Parallel structures, such as project centred implementation units, come into being when, for instance, highly subsidised and primarily donor-run institutions are created which compete with the local banks for retail clients. Such institutions have often ceased operating altogether shortly after external assistance was discontinued. The partner institutions in KfW-managed projects, therefore, are strategically positioned to build profitable and lasting business relationships with the target groups. This precondition is important to ensure that the new lending activities continue after donor assistance is phased out. Technical assistance packages are offered according to the requirements of each individual partner institution: this enables our partner banks to strengthen their position in an increasingly competitive environment.

- focus must be placed on *private* financial intermediaries which have demonstrated their commitment to sound banking. Credit decisions must be taken exclusively according to the quality of borrowers and the soundness of their investments. Public banks or other state agencies, in contrast, are often subject to political interference: credit decisions are then likely to be influenced by political considerations and personal relationships, to the detriment of portfolio quality.

- in order not to create monopolies in emerging financial sectors, KfW promotes a *variety of promising institutions* simultaneously. Our refinancing lines are open to all interested local banks with the requisite level of expertise. This facilitates competition among banks, benefiting customers. The microbanks play an important role in this context by demonstrating to local banks that micro and small enterprises, too, can be profitably served by credit technologies which are tailored to their situations.

- *productive incentive mechanisms* have to be established at all relevant levels. In order to achieve sustainability, a refinancing scheme requires appropriate incentives at the level of the refinancing fund, the partner banks and the final borrowers. The prospect of long-term cooperation with the refinancing funds on a commercial basis is a powerful stimulus for local banks to manage funds wisely and to make repayments on time.

- the principle of market orientation implies that funds be provided in conformity with *market conditions*. First and foremost this refers to the refinancing rates at which local banks draw on the programmes' funds. The cost of funds must be low enough to provide banks with a sufficient incentive to venture into the low-income market segment and high enough to avoid causing market distortions – making the mobilisation of domestic savings a viable option for the banks while encouraging international investors and lenders to resume business with the region. Admittedly, it is difficult to determine efficient market rates in practice: long-term SME-financing is still mostly provided by donors that refinance local banks in "high risk" SEE countries.

These important considerations, derived from the principle of market orientation, are designed to prevent donor-sponsored initiatives from crowding out the private sector and for-profit initiatives. Because public funds for development cooperation are relatively limited, the aim of KfW-managed projects is to motivate the private sector to play an increasingly important role in micro and SME finance. We work on the assumption that donor-financed investments pay off to the degree that private sector players adopt and adapt our pioneering activities in order to provide financial services to small entrepreneurs and homeowners – the target groups.

Policy Dialogue and Donor Coordination

A thorough reform of the institutional and legal environment is a precondition for greater involvement by the private sector. The reform agenda is long throughout Southeast Europe. Serbia, for instance, has adopted ambitious reforms, taking many painful decisions in an extremely short period of time. The closure of several state-owned banks significantly contributed to cleaning up the sector. But much more remains to be done. Many rules and regulations that have persisted since the pre-war era are inconsistent with OECD supervisory and regulatory standards. Excessive reporting requirements, for instance, lead to high transaction costs and have deterred many potential investors.

It is crucial to engage SEE authorities in a policy dialogue on the reasoning behind and approaches to financial sector development. The simple fact of donors being involved has often been as important as the financial contributions themselves. Discussions help to encourage local policymakers to take necessary but painful decisions that ensure the effectiveness and sustainability of donor-sponsored initiatives. Additional financial contributions should therefore always be linked to visible improvements in the framework conditions.

By taking a coordinated approach in SEE, donors contribute to the effectiveness of the policy dialogue and – through the pooling of resources – achieve substantial economies of scale.

Financial Sector Innovations in Southeast Europe

The design of the financial sector innovations in Southeast Europe is based on the strategies and activities described above and can be grouped into four main areas:

- the German government together with other European donors provides the financial resources for the European funds for Bosnia and Herzegovina, Kosovo, Montenegro and Serbia. These funds employ the downscaling approach: they provide refinancing lines to local commercial banks and capacity-building inputs through technical assistance. Framework agreements are concluded with local commercial banks and, as a recent development, also with nonbank microfinance institutions with the required level of expertise. The funds have become key providers of long-term finance to the region's banks.

- KfW holds equity stakes in seven microbanks across the region. The establishment of microbanks uses the greenfield approach to institutional development: microbanks are set up from scratch for the specific purpose of serving poor and low-income groups, particularly microenterprises and SMEs, by providing demand-oriented financial services. The microbanks also serve as powerful demonstration vehicles, showing that lending to the target groups can be profitable. The combination of downscaling and greenfield approaches has a structural impact on the financial sector overall, especially by promoting competition and consolidation among banks.

- Credit Guarantee Facilities (CGF) back transactions between international commercial banks and local partner banks. They provide guarantees against default by financial institutions (but not for their clients' failure to repay loans) on a first loss basis. In this way, local partner banks can acquire additional resources from the international capital market in the form of medium and long-term refinancing loans. The partner banks then on-lend the funds at their own risk to the target groups.

- the capitalisation of deposit insurance agencies contributes to mobilising savings in the domestic financial markets. In most SEE countries, citizens have little trust in the banking sector and prefer to keep their savings abroad or outside the banking system – often literally "under the mattress". Deposit insurance systems establish a national safety net for deposits, building trust in the banking sector, which mobilises more domestic capital.

Subsequent chapters in this book describe these innovations and their effects in more detail.

Outlook

The single most important conclusion we have drawn from our experiences is that sound banking is possible even in unstable economic and social environments such as those found in Southeast Europe. Our activities provide important demonstration effects that motivate domestic and foreign banks to resume business, even at the lower end of the market.

Our initiatives are not intended to create mere islands of stability, however. KfW promotes a comprehensive approach to financial sector development. We focus on structuring the financial sector so that competition and consolidation occur within the banking industry. The refinancing and technical assistance provided by our downscaling programme, complemented by the greenfield approach, aim at building the institutional capacity of local commercial banks. The Credit Guarantee Facility initiates and supports new business relationships with international banks, and the deposit insurance mechanism fosters the mobilisation of local resources.

KfW's support is tailored to the characteristics of the financial sector in each country. The approach is sufficiently flexible to change with the financial sector as it develops. We continuously fine-tune our programmes and diversify the financial services offered. Thanks to the commitment of donors, our activities have constantly gained in scale as well as in scope.

Our programmes have proven positive benefits for SMEs, as demonstrated in various impact studies (see also Part IV). SMEs and other customers at the lower end of the financial market today enjoy much easier access to financial services, which helps the growth of their economic activities.

However, important challenges remain to be addressed in order to ensure that our programmes continue to make an impact on financial-sector development as a whole and to ensure its orientation towards poor and low-income target groups:

- experience shows that it is easier and more lucrative for banks to serve urban areas. In the beginning, our initiatives focused mainly on cities. Rural areas in Southeast Europe remain largely untouched by commercial banks, although these areas often can benefit most from assistance. This is why we have expanded our activities into rural areas in Bosnia and Herzegovina, Kosovo, Montenegro and Serbia.

- another challenge is to reach out to even poorer borrowers who may nevertheless represent a viable target group for the financial institutions. In close coordination with the donors, substantial progress has already been made. In Bosnia and Herzegovina, Kosovo and Montenegro, cooperation arrangements have been set up with professionally managed non-governmental microfinance organisations. Our credit lines help these NGOs reach growing numbers of customers who are often "smaller" and "poorer" than the average customer reached at present.

- other innovations we are developing include micro insurance products and micro pension schemes tailored to low-income groups in Southeast Europe. These services will provide access to long-term savings programmes, enabling people to make provisions for their old age and serving as a cushion in times of hardship.

- further initiatives must be undertaken to promote the development of the local capital markets, particularly since the revised equity requirements envisaged under the new Basel II regulations will further complicate local financial intermediaries' access to international capital markets. Securitisation of our partner banks' loan portfolios is one of the possibilities we are currently exploring as a means of mobilising additional funds for target-group oriented programmes.

The remainder of this book illustrates the successes achieved by the various interventions described above; it will also outline the important challenges that confront financial sectors today and those they are likely to face in the near future. Yet, financial sector promotion is no panacea for the structural problems of the region's economies. Institution-building efforts have to be complemented by measures that create an environment conducive to sound banking. This entails reforming banking legislation and bringing banking regulation and supervision into line with OECD standards. The countries themselves will have to increasingly adopt economic policies that are conducive to the development of SMEs. Minimising and streamlining bureaucratic procedures for small entrepreneurs and simplifying tax and other regulations are some of the challenges that SEE governments should address. KfW remains committed to complementing these policies with programmes that help to support the small-entrepreneur target group through demand-oriented financial services and which contribute to creating safe and sound banking sectors throughout the region.

CHAPTER 4:

Providing Long-Term Funds to Local Financial Institutions – The European Refinancing Funds in Southeast Europe

Klaus Glaubitt* and Haje Schütte**

* Vice President, KfW, Frankfurt, Germany
** Principal Project Manager, KfW, Frankfurt, Germany

Banks without Money: Starting from Scratch

The reason behind KfW's support for financial sector development in Southeast Europe is well illustrated by a reference to Willie Sutton's famous quote. When asked why he robbed banks, he is said to have replied "because that's where the money is". However, this definitely did not reflect Albanian banking reality back in 1994. Robbing a bank in Albania at that time would have been a largely unrewarding undertaking, as a sectoral study initiated by KfW revealed. Albania had a non-functioning banking system that was very short of funds.

This has changed dramatically, both in Albania and in the other countries in Southeast Europe. To the delight of entrepreneurs, traders and other clients who did not previously have access to the services offered by the formal banking sector, there is now considerable money in the banking system.

An Answer: The European Funds

The European Funds operate in Bosnia and Herzegovina, Kosovo, Montenegro and in Serbia. They are funded by the European Commission, the German, Swiss, and Austrian governments and the Dutch FMO. They were created by KfW between 1998 and 2002 in order to alleviate the difficulties that SMEs had in raising long-term finance. In the aftermath of civil conflict, the situation in Bosnia and Herzegovina, Kosovo, Montenegro and Serbia were broadly similar: an unstable political and economic environment inhibited private sector development, banks' services to SMEs and other private clients were inadequate, and donors' support and policies were largely uncoordinated.

The European Funds share a common structure, as illustrated by the following example for Montenegro. Donors appointed KfW as their agent to lend funds to

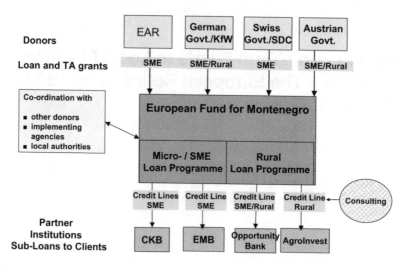

Abbreviations: CKB: Crnogorska Komercijalna Banka
EAR: European Agency for Reconstruction
EMB: Euro Market Bank
SDC: Swiss Agency for Development and Co-operation

Figure 1.   European Fund for Montenegro

local financial institutions carefully selected by KfW. The commercial banks, micro-finance banks and microfinance institutions (MFIs) on-lend these funds at their own risk to their clients. Technical assistance provided by consulting firms helps these financial institutions to increase their capacity. Each of the funds provides refinancing to a number of institutions in each country in order to foster competition.

The Development of the European Funds in 2002

This approach has successfully induced local commercial banks to offer financial services to SMEs and other clients whom they would otherwise consider too costly or too risky to serve. This is illustrated by the following overview of the European Funds in 2002.[1]

The European Fund for Kosovo (EFK): from the Fund's inception in 2000 up to the end of 2002, some €9.2 million had been committed by donors, of which €8.5 million was disbursed to partner institutions. In spite of the difficult lending environment, outstanding loans to clients in 2002 rose sharply from €4 million in the first quarter to more than €7 million during the fourth quarter. This development

---

[1] Further details on specific funds are found at the conclusion of the paper by Addai and Nienborg in this book.

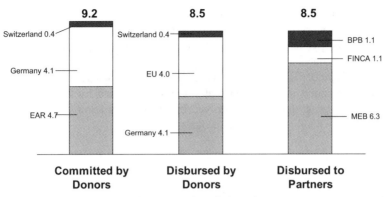

Source: partner financial institution information, including audited annual reports

Figure 2. European Fund for Kosovo: Loans Outstanding (as of December 31, 2002; € million)

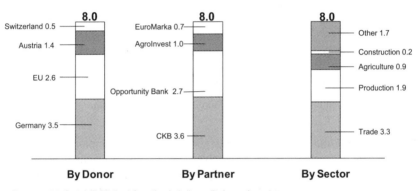

Source: partner financial institution information, including audited annual reports

Figure 3. European Fund for Montenegro: Loans Outstanding (as of December 31, 2002; € million)

was a result of the expansion of the SME programme to include two new partner institutions: the Bank for Private Business, a local commercial bank, and Finca Kosovo, an MFI. In addition, the EFK initiated housing loans by providing funds to the Microenterprise Bank of Kosovo (MEB Kosovo). With considerable new donor funding, the EFK has grown steadily in 2003.

The European Fund for Montenegro (EFM): at the end of 2002, loans worth € 8 million were outstanding to four partner institutions; the funding for these loans was provided by three donors – Switzerland, Germany and the EU's European Agency for Reconstruction (EAR). With a € 1.2 million portfolio in the first quarter, the overall rate of growth for the year was very considerable. In 2002, two new institutions, Opportunity Bank and AgroInvest, came on board and a rural loan programme was introduced. Most of the loans were relatively small and primarily used to finance working capital investments (80%); the average loan amount was €6,000 and the average maturity eight months. Portfolio at risk remained below 1% throughout the year.

This development is noteworthy; when the EFM was inaugurated in 1999 there was only one sound private bank that was unencumbered by the socialist past. Confidence in banks had been destroyed by the expropriation of deposits. Consolidation of the banking sector was progressing slowly.

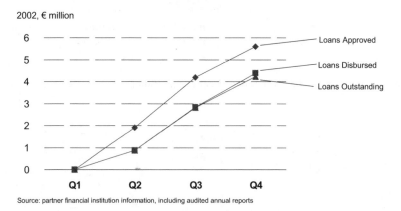

Source: partner financial institution information, including audited annual reports

Figure 4.   European Fund for Serbia: Portfolio Development by Partner Banks

The European Fund for Serbia (EFS): the EFS started operations in 2002. Initially, the banking sector was in a deplorable state, a result of having to serve political purposes. The National Bank of Yugoslavia has withdrawn licences from more than 20 failing banks and initiated major restructuring in the sector. However, the consolidation process will take time before its full impact is felt. Against this background, KfW was mandated by three donors – Switzerland, Germany and EAR – to provide refinancing funds for SME loans via three existing commercial banks specifically selected for this purpose. This funding was complemented by technical assistance for training, institution building and the supervision of the partner banks.

Altogether, 163 loans worth a total of €5.6 million had been approved by the end of 2002, of which €4.1 million had been disbursed. Sixty percent of the loans were issued to the production sector and 80% of these were invested in fixed assets; the average loan amount was €35,700 with an average maturity of 37 months. In addition, refinancing loans and technical assistance were provided to the Microfinance Bank of Serbia.

The European Fund for Bosnia and Herzegovina (EFBH): EFBH, which started operating in 1998, is the oldest and largest Fund. At the end of 2002, loans totalling more than €32 million were outstanding. The EU, Germany, FMO (the Netherlands), Austria and Switzerland contributed to the EFBH. Funds are being loaned

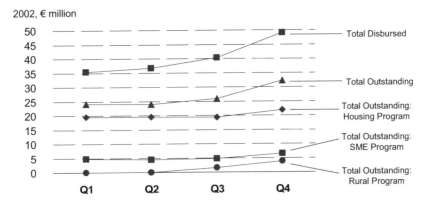

Source: partner financial institution information, including audited annual reports

Figure 5. European Fund for Bosnia and Herzegovina: Development of Loans Disbursed and Outstanding

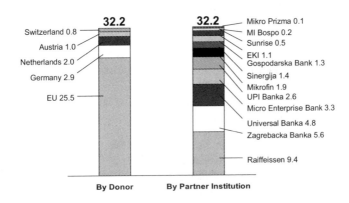

Source: partner financial institution information, including audited annual reports

Figure 6. European Fund for Bosnia and Herzegovina: Loans Outstanding (as of December 31, 2002; € million)

to six commercial banks and – as a new development – to six microfinance institutions. In 2002, the retail lenders used these funds to provide SME, housing and rural SME loans. Technical assistance to the partner institutions was phased out in 2002. To keep pace with operational growth, institutional capacities in local fund management are being strengthened and business operations further streamlined.

The process of consolidation is advancing steadily throughout the banking sector. In 2002, the market became more competitive due to the increased presence of foreign banks, primarily Austrian. With €24 million in additional funds pledged, the EFBH is poised to grow strongly in 2003.

In summary, the results presented here show that the European Funds are effectively meeting the considerable demand for long-term refinancing by local financial institutions. In 2002, the European Funds experienced strong operational growth, and new funding supplemented amounts already revolving through partner institutions. Increasing diversification within the European Funds was observed with the addition of new products, such as rural SME loans and housing loans, and the participation of new partner institutions.

Through the provision of long-term refinancing and technical assistance, the European Funds support the development of the financial sector, be it through downscaling commercial banks, the financing of microfinance banks or the upgrading of micro credit organisations. The close coordination of these multi-donor programmes in SME, housing finance and financial sector development enhances the assistance provided by the European Union and by leading bilateral donors. These Funds are doubtless one of the key development policy successes in Southeast Europe.

Success Brings New Challenges

The progress achieved to date has required continuous operational adjustments, while revealing new institutional challenges. To maintain and foster the successful development of the European Funds, these challenges will have to be met by further joint action on the part KfW and its partners in the region.

Several structural issues should be addressed in order to perpetuate and extend the impact of the European Funds:

1. the funding agreements between KfW and other donors give KfW a mandate to propose exit strategies for donors, and these could institutionalise the European Funds. Currently, the Funds are set up by donors on a contractual basis for a limited period in each beneficiary country.

2. the targeting and reporting requirements that were so critical in determining priorities in the Funds' early operations emerge as administrative and operational burdens when their original purposes are achieved. Limited flexibility in the way the funds are used combined with complex reporting procedures impede effective management, reduce the rate at which funds revolve, and raise administrative costs.

3. the complex governance structure inhibits KfW and the other donors from proactively tackling problems as they arise.

4. the involvement of local partners other than the partner banks has been limited to informal and ad hoc consultations and exchanges of information with central banks and local authorities.

5. each Fund was set up for a specific country without a regional focus, and this slows the development of new services. Moreover, political stability and economic prosperity call for close intraregional cooperation rather than emphasising the individual state.

These shortcomings could be met by institutionalising the European Funds. This would entail establishing a unified and long-term, if not permanent, corporate entity. This would enable the European Funds to address the challenges that the financial sectors in Southeast Europe are soon likely to face.

KfW believes that the provision of long-term refinancing at market-driven, though favourable, conditions will remain warranted in Southeast Europe for a considerable period in order to promote enterprises which are not adequately served at present. One example in this respect is micro and small enterprises in rural areas. Long-term funding will help microenterprises and SMEs to recreate a vibrant private sector, thereby creating jobs and income for many people. Long-term refinancing on favourable terms and conditions is also warranted to finance housing and investments in public services, such as municipal infrastructure or environmental protection measures. However, long-term refinancing is not the only financial service that will benefit private sector development in the region: new services such as guarantees and venture capital will stimulate private sector growth in Southeast Europe.

Relying on private commercial banks to achieve these benefits will not be sufficient. Financial intermediation within the region is low compared to the levels found in the East European transition countries, and even under the best circumstances change takes time. In fact, the prospects are not too favourable: Basel II will require banks to allocate equity according to the risks of their loan portfolios. The perceived high risks in Southeast Europe will retard international lending to commercial banks in the region, which in turn is likely to restrict lending to micro and SME clients.

An institutionalised fund could also help to mitigate the severe maturity mismatches that are common in banks in Southeast Europe. The legacy of bank defaults, fraud and expropriation causes people to distrust banks. This, combined with historically high levels of inflation, explains why savings are generally in the form of sight or short-term deposits. Even in countries where short-term deposits may be plentiful, such as Bosnia and Herzegovina, they do not offer a prudent basis for creating large portfolios with the long maturities required to finance SMEs and housing finance. Bank supervisors in the region tend to tolerate this unsustainable situation and intervene only in extreme cases. Support for the development of capital markets, for example by introducing guaranteed savings certificates, could help to remedy this situation. Institutionalised European Funds could lengthen maturities and reduce mismatches by providing long-term refinancing, helping broaden the banks' outreach to yet unserved clients, and by promoting financial sector innovations through the co-financing of development and risk costs.

Potential Options for Institutionalising the European Funds

The major benefit of institutionalisation would be to facilitate long-term finance by providing a legal structure for pooling funds, for obtaining new funds, and for improving the efficiency of re-flows across donor and sector lines. Institutionalisation does not require a "bricks and mortar" institution for cost-effective wholesale fund management.

There are several ways to approach institutionalisation, the most important being "on-shore", "off-shore/country-specific" and "offshore/regional focus". The legal form would be the same in each case: a foundation would be set up as owner of the funds. Donors would continue guiding the use of their funds indirectly through the foundation's decision-making and advisory bodies. Institutionalisation offers donors an ideal exit by allowing them to dispense with their project monitoring functions while permitting them to continue to guide fund management as long as they wish to remain involved.

Studies indicate that "on-shore" institutionalisation with a legal presence in each of the respective countries is likely to require a greenfield structure. This is because no suitable exit option is available in the form of an existing institution that is sufficiently mature to manage the fund. In addition, laws governing foundations in the countries concerned are not compatible with the commercial nature of the European Funds' activities. On-shore institutionalisation entails significant currency and tax risks, the lack of an efficient and transparent legal system, and the danger of undue local political and administrative interference. In addition, local know-how with respect to foundations and fund management is scarce.

"Off-shore" institutionalisation, with the seat of business in one of the European donor countries, eliminates or reduces these risks. In Austria, the Netherlands or Germany, for example, appropriate foundation laws and tax structures are in place to varying degrees. A single off-shore institution with a regional focus has additional benefits: it could facilitate the optimal deployment and re-flow of funds, achieve potential economies of scale and synergies in fund management, and stimulate competition among recipients. It might also stimulate regional policy dialogue and promote the development of a regional financial market.

A single off-shore institution could consist of three bodies: a board, an advisory council and a secretariat. The board would make internal decisions and represent the foundation in its affairs with third parties. The advisory council would be a consultative body, providing advice on the foundation's policies and operations. The management would be based on a traditional fund management model. The fund manager, under contract to the foundation, would implement programmes that would target the refinancing of suitable partner banks, the investment of liquid funds, the maintenance of accounts and the monitoring of projects and funds. A foundation secretariat would support the fund manager and be responsible for market surveys, bank risk assessment and contacts with the local partners. Staffed by local professionals, the secretariat could progressively assume more responsibilities from the fund manager.

Looking Ahead

Institutionalised European Funds could play a significant role in the financial markets in Southeast Europe. On the financial services front, they could help to introduce innovative banking products and to extend financial services to the poorer sections of society. On the political front, by preserving funds to be used indefinitely for further development purposes in the region, they would send a strong signal in favour of regional collaboration. This would contribute to re-building the countries of Southeast Europe, foster intraregional cooperation and promote integration with Western Europe.

CHAPTER 5

Strengthening Financial Sectors in Transition Countries: IFC's Contribution

Syed Aftab Ahmed

Manager, Global Micro and Small Business Finance Group, IFC, Washington, USA

The 1990s were defining years for the International Finance Corporation (IFC), a member of the World Bank Group. During this period, IFC realised its enormous potential for delivering development impact by explicitly linking its investment strategy to reducing poverty in its developing and transition member countries. The latter, consisting of Eastern Europe and the former Soviet Union, posed challenges that the Corporation had not faced previously. In essence, the challenge was to help these transition countries: a) develop the legal and regulatory framework of their financial sectors, b) transfer state ownership of assets into the hands of the general population, and c) develop the private sector financial institutional infrastructure.

Implementing Structural Change in Finance

Creating and strengthening the legal and regulatory frameworks of the local financial sector – an enormous and complex task – was made more challenging by the fact that these states controlled all means of production and owned all financial assets. State ownership covered everything, from industrial complexes to agricultural land and the housing stock. This situation was unique: if nobody owned anything of value to exchange, what would financial institutions intermediate? It was therefore necessary to help governments find practical, but swift methods of transferring state-owned financial assets into the hands of the population.

Transferring ownership of financial assets was an enormous task. The process had to be transparent, equitable and, given the political imperative, relatively fast. However, for the transfer to occur successfully, the supporting legal and regulatory frameworks and institutional infrastructure needed to be in place. Thus the legal framework for the financial sector had to be established at the same time as the state-owned assets were transferred.

In this context, IFC had a powerful development impact. With strong support from bilateral donors (US$ 87 million between 1990 and 2000), IFC offered an integrated package of consultancy, technical assistance and advisory services to transition country governments – and complemented those efforts by catalysing investment in the development of financial institutions. By helping in the design and implementation of the voucher system and the management of auctions of small businesses, by helping in the review of the laws and regulations and in the creation of modern stock exchanges and securities and banking regulatory authorities, IFC played a key role in the first wave of privatisation and building institutional infrastructure in transition countries.

In my opinion, the political will of the governments and consequently the methodologies chosen for the transfer of state assets determined the quantum, quality and benefits of the first wave privatisation for these economies. The decisions made in this first phase continue to be reflected in the uneven pace of second wave privatisation and relative economic development of the transition economies.

Significant strengthening of the private financial institutional infrastructure was required to create a lasting transition from a centrally-controlled to a market-based economy. IFC played an important catalytic role in mobilising private investment to strengthen the full range of privately-owned financial institutions such as commercial banks, investment banks, leasing and insurance companies, brokerage houses and other financial institutions. IFC investment in transition countries, US$ 881 million from 1990 through 2002, is a testament to its commitment to its developmental goals.

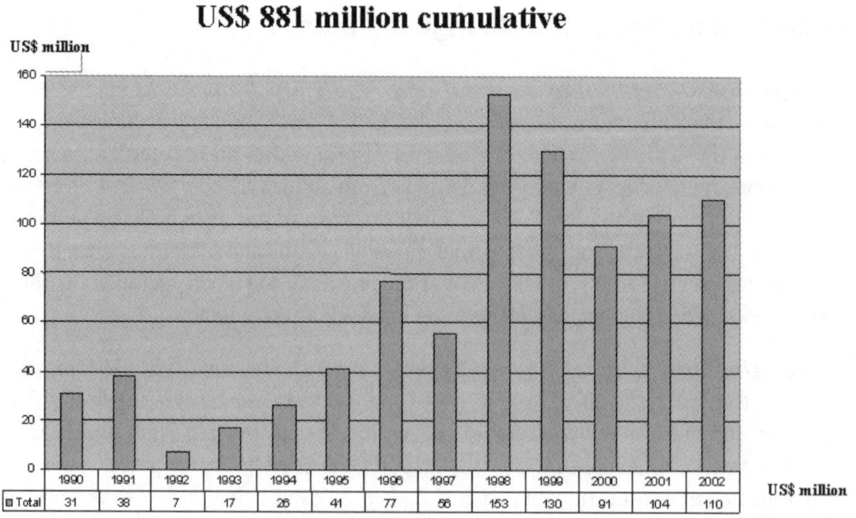

US$ 881 million cumulative

	1990	1991	1992	1993	1994	1995	1996	1997	1998	1999	2000	2001	2002
Total	31	38	7	17	26	41	77	56	153	130	91	104	110

Figure 1. IFC Investments in Transition Economies

Creating Employment with a New Model

The privatisation and rationalisation of the industrial base created significant efficiency and output gains in transition countries. But, large investments in the industrial sector created only a limited number of new jobs compared to the alarmingly high number of dislocated workers, a pool that swelled with each successive privatisation and the modernisation of existing production facilities. The bulk of employment would have to be created in the micro and small business (MSE) sector, particularly by enhancing its access to commercial finance, which would achieve the World Bank Group's goal of reducing poverty and unemployment.

Earlier initiatives met with only limited success in strengthening private sector lending through existing commercial banks by downscaling or through small and medium-sized enterprise (SME) credit lines. In most transition economies commercial banks were not and are not adequately offering loans of less than US$250,000. A new model for delivering credit and other financial services to MSEs was needed. There was a clear case for a specialised form of financial institution to demonstrate that on-lending to MSEs and the provision of other financial services to the "lower end of the market" could be successful and profitable.

The essential features of the model developed for this purpose by IFC are:

- Creation of specialised MSE-focused financial institutions, preferably commercial banks

- Time-bound technical assistance (TA) for an initial two years

- equity risk sharing with the TA provider as the manager responsible for project implementation

- gradual diversification from microfinance to include small business loans

- a strong shareholder group and corporate governance

This model of a target-group oriented commercial microfinance bank was launched with the creation of the Micro Enterprise Bank (MEB) in Bosnia and Herzegovina in 1997. In terms of its development impact, I rate this innovation as one of the most exciting in development finance in recent years.

Replication of the MEB Model

The success of the MEB model made it a key plank in IFC's strategy for strengthening MSE finance in Eastern Europe. The network of banks that are jointly owned by IFC, KfW, EBRD, FMO, IMI and Commerzbank will be familiar to many readers and are elaborated in other chapters of this book.

Table 1. MEB Model Banks ranked by Portfolio Size (September 2002)

	Total loan portfolio in million EUR	Number of outstanding loans	Average outstanding loan amount
Microfinance Bank of Georgia	32.9	28,970	1,136
Micro Enterprise Bank, Bosnia	28.4	6,538	4,337
Micro Enterprise Bank, Kosovo	19.5	3,737	5,210
Miro Bank, Romania	8.2	1,870	5,551
Microenterprise Credit, Moldova	3.6	737	4,882
FEFAD Bank, Albania	24.9	4,979	4,995
Microfinance Bank, Yugoslavia	24.6	3,251	6,819
Microfinance Bank, Ucraine	20.7	4,490	4,605
ProCredit Bank, Bulgaria	20.6	3,811	5,411
Total	**183.3**	**58,383**	**3,139**

While IFC conceived the idea and worked hard for its implementation, success has been in large part due to the very high level of cooperation between the international financial institutions involved. Results to date are very encouraging. As of September 2002, the combined outstanding loan portfolio of the nine institutions stood at 58,000 loans with a volume of over €180 million. These banks support the livelihood of some 300,000 people.

The operations of these banks clearly play a significant role in the financial sector of their respective countries despite the fact that most were founded recently. For example, the MEB model was replicated in Albania in 1999 with the receipt of a bank charter by FEFAD Bank in Albania. FEFAD was originally a foundation established with German financial assistance devoted to microfinance. At the close of 2002, FEFAD had a deposit base of €52 million, an outstanding loan portfolio of €25 million and 5,000 business loans. It is the fifth largest lender to the private sector in Albania, accounting for 8% of total loan volume. FEFAD is at the forefront of innovation in lending; it has recently introduced a popular housing loan product, and in a move to upgrade customer services it introduced ATMs in 2003. It finances a significant proportion of its loan portfolio from local deposits and has achieved sustainable levels of profitability. Commerzbank recently bought a 20% stake in FEFAD Bank, paying a premium over book value, probably the first large bank to make an arm's length investment in microfinance. FEFAD's other shareholders are KfW (25%), IFC (20%), EBRD (20%) and IMI (15%).

Expanding Services and Outreach

The core strategy of the MEB model is initially to offer micro loan products and then to introduce small business loan products as the institution stabilises and establishes its credibility in the market, building on the core microfinance business to offer larger loans and a broader range of services. For example, at Micro Enterprise Bank in Bosnia, recent growth in portfolio volume is increasingly attributable to small business loans larger than € 10,000, although the number of loans disbursed will always be dominated by micro loans of less than € 10,000. MEB is developing from a micro-only bank to a "micro and small business bank" providing a broad range of products for both types of customers.

This trend is paralleled across the network of transition country microfinance banks and is to be welcomed because it strengthens the commercial sustainability of the institutions, provides a wider scope of services to the target group, sets a good example for other local banks and strengthens the financial sector as a whole. The competencies developed at MEB banks in client orientation, rigorous analysis and high levels of efficiency make them well placed to serve small and medium-sized enterprises in addition to micro businesses.

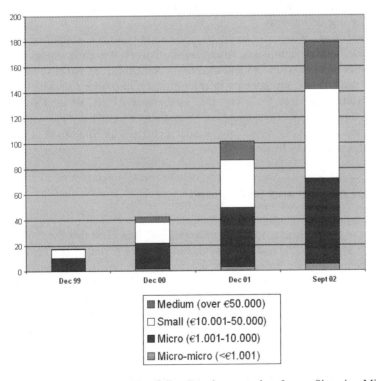

Figure 2. Business Loan Portfolio Development by Loan Size in Microfinance Institutions in which IFC participates in Eastern Europe and Georgia

Elements of Success

The key ingredients for success of these microfinance banks have been:

- a clear governance structure with a group of like-minded investors who share the twin goals of financial sustainability and development impact;

- technical assistance in the first years to support expatriate experts and the training of local personnel;

- international refinancing to support the growth of the institutions until they develop their own deposit base; and,

- strong management support.

I would like to dwell briefly on the last of these points. I believe that an essential reason for the success of the MEBs is that the management services provider – IPC – participates in the ownership of these banks through its investment company IMI. This is a model that IFC fought hard for. There were many who claimed that linking management services with ownership meant conflict of interest, whereas we believed it aligned interests.

It is a model that we are now trying to replicate in other IFC-supported micro and SME (small and medium-sized enterprise) initiatives. It is encouraging to see how many microfinance operators and consulting companies are establishing their own equity vehicles for investments in microfinance institutions to which they provide consulting services for a fee. IFC established AFRICAP in 2001 with Calmeadow, and ACCION Investments in Microfinance (AIM) in 2003 with AC-CION International. IFC is developing similar entities with Shorebank, FINCA International, Opportunity International and others.

Priorities, Lessons and Reflections

Looking to the future, where do IFC's priorities lie? It is clear that the move towards private sector lending and the institutionalisation of financial intermediation in the European transition economies is proceeding too slowly. Key barriers remain to effective private micro and small business lending in traditional commercial banks. These include cultural barriers, low technical skill levels and concerns about weak collateral and enforcement systems. Rather than lending, it is simply easier and less risky for these banks to earn income on fee-based activities and treasury bills. Assistance from international financial institutions (IFIs) such as IFC will therefore remain important over the next few years in order to achieve further improvements in transition economies' financial sectors.

IFC will continue to strengthen the existing network of microfinance banks in Eastern Europe because such focused business banks have an important impact and play a pathfinder role. As an owner of these institutions, IFC will support initiatives to accelerate and secure financial independence, strengthen small business lending, and build on the synergies between the networks of these European banks.

One lesson is that if the IFC contribution is to be leveraged and genuinely catalytic, then there is great value in cooperating with scale players that can carry skills and strategies across borders. To this end, IFC is supportive of initiatives such as IMI and the creation of a holding company for the Eastern European microfinance banks. Such consolidated efforts appear to be the best way to secure these institutions' target group orientation over the long term, whilst at the same time enhancing their financial viability and ultimately offering IFC and other multilateral and bilateral investors the opportunity to exit from their equity participation when their development role in these banks is complete.

The third element of IFC's financial sector strengthening strategy is to link MEBs to the local commercial banking debt market for local currency refinancing. The outstanding loan portfolio of most of these Eastern European microfinance banks is growing by over € 1 million per month. This means that in 2003 alone, over € 100 million in new money will be required. IFC is exploring a range of risk sharing mechanisms which will facilitate wholesale lending by local commercial banks to microfinance banks for on-lending to micro and small businesses. One such IFC initiative, the MSE/LCB Linkage Programme, would initially support risk-shared lending by local commercial banks and IFC, with the IFC's share of the risk gradually phasing out as local banks become comfortable lending directly to MEBs. The MSE/LCB Linkage Program would complete the circle of MSE institutional support – Create/Transition, Sustain, Link – around which IFC's MSE strategy revolves.

But, I pause to ponder. Obviously, the task for IFC in transition countries was enormous and the resources at our disposal were limited. The challenges ahead remain great, but nevertheless much has been achieved in a short period of time. Looking back, it is very clear that all this could not have been possible without the amazing cooperative spirit and dedicated joint efforts of many multilateral, bilateral and private sector institutions and the invaluable contributions of many people. Some of the finest people in the world of development finance dedicated themselves to the task and made changes that have benefited so many. EBRD, KfW, FMO, the DOEN Foundation, Commerzbank and IPC shared their vision with IFC and stood their ground against enormous odds to bring about change, and made all this a reality.

CHAPTER 6

EBRD's Micro and Small Enterprise Lending Programmes: Downscaling Commercial Banks and Starting Greenfield Banks

Elizabeth Wallace

Director of the Group for Small Business, EBRD, London, United Kingdom

The investment activities of the European Bank for Reconstruction and Development (EBRD) are centred on private enterprises and reach from the Adriatic and Baltic to the Pacific. These operations include micro and small enterprise (MSE) programmes in 24 early and intermediate transition countries. MSE projects take a number of forms in response to local market conditions, especially the state of the financial sector and differing institutional objectives and priorities based on local market conditions in each country receiving assistance. Since the beginning of these activities in 1994 through the end of 2002, almost 250,000 MSE loans were issued. More than 40% of these loans were issued in Russia. More than one-third were made in Southeast Europe through the Caucasus (Figure 1). About one-fifth of these

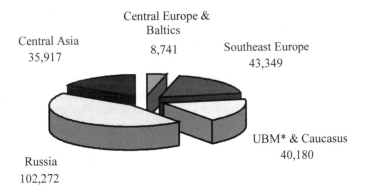

Central Europe & Baltics
8,741

Central Asia
35,917

Southeast Europe
43,349

UBM* & Caucasus
40,180

Russia
102,272

Total: 231,000 sub-loans

* UBM: Ukraine, Belarus, Moldova

Figure 1. Number of MSE Loans Issued 1994-2002

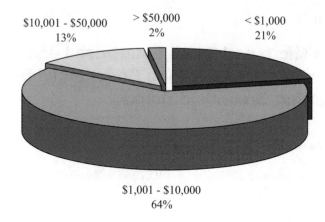

Figure 2. Loan Size Frequency Distribution by Number of Outstanding Loans – MSE Projects

loans were for amounts of up to $1,000, and about two-thirds were for amounts between $1,001 and $10,000 (Figure 2).

The primary objective of these activities is to ensure that the target group of micro and small entrepreneurs will have access to financial services on a permanent basis. Two strategies are applied and two instruments are used to secure this objective. The *strategies* consist of creating new microfinance institutions (MFIs – which increasingly also serve small and a few medium-sized businesses), and downscaling existing commercial and other banks (i.e., partner banks) so that they will engage micro and MSE clients, most of whom cannot offer the traditional types of collateral preferred by commercial banks.

The *instruments* are financial and managerial. The major financial activity is making debt and equity investments in MFIs and lending to partner banks. The managerial contribution is linked to this financial support and consists of technical assistance for institution building in the MFIs and also in partner banks. The major target group in each case is microenterprises, because of the severe gap in the market and the large numbers that can be reached. Emphasis is placed on first-time borrowers who have had little or no access to formal finance. Stimulating the MSE sector is also important because it creates employment, it contributes to demonopolising the industrial structure and helps create a middle class.

Partner Banks

The first EBRD programme designed to reach micro and small firms was the Russia Small Business Fund (RSBF), launched in 1994 with G-7 and EU support to provide commercial finance for working capital and the acquisition of fixed assets. By the end of 2002, more than 4,000 loans were being disbursed monthly through partner banks and KMB-Bank, a specialised micro and small business lending bank in which EBRD is a part-owner. More than 100,000 loans were outstanding and the portfolio at risk was less than one percent. (Portfolio at risk includes the entire outstanding balance of loans on which one or more instalments are at least 30 days overdue, expressed as a percentage of the total portfolio.)

Technical cooperation for downscaling micro credit was provided by IPC, and small lending activity within the RSBF was implemented by Shorebank (a well-known community development bank based in Chicago) and by the Bank of Ireland. Partner banks were selected through financial due diligence and an assessment of potential commitment to the MSE sector. They accepted the entire credit risk of microlending and an increasing share of the risk of small business lending. Micro enterprises were defined as owner-operated firms having up to 20 workers. The initial maximum loan size was $20,000, although the average was about one-third this limit. Later, the maximum was decreased to $10,000, which is the accepted 'industry standard' for this part of the world.

How Big Is Small?

When RSBF was being designed, it became clear that commercial bankers were very reluctant to make loans of less than $100,000, which led to the definition of a small loan as anything between the $20,000 micro loan limit and $100,000. Small firms in production and service sectors having up to 50 workers (later increased to 100) were offered longer-term loans of from $20,000 to, in a few cases, $125,000. By global microfinance norms these loan amounts are very large, but in a relative sense and in the Russian context they are not. Many young firms existed that, with properly structured loans, would have debt capacities of $20,000 or more. (Debt capacity is defined as the amount of debt that a borrower could service on a sustainable basis.) Hence, RSBF was created pragmatically to fill a very large hole in the financial system, demonstrating what would be possible, and through funding for commercial banks willing to sign on.

Crisis and Resilience

Given the fragility of the Russian banking sector prior to the 1998 financial crisis, portfolios created by EBRD funding were conditionally pledged to EBRD as security. The downscaling portfolio consisted of 6,500 loans that approached $100 million on the eve of the August 1998 crisis, when more than 500 loan officers had been trained and 13 Russian banks were participating.

The strategy of lending to the micro and small target group was wonderfully demonstrated during the crisis of 1998, in which EBRD's MSE portfolio held up quite well while most partner banks and many other commercial banks collapsed. The crisis quickly reduced the number of partner banks from 13 to four. Loans at risk amounted to about $35 million, but by the end of 2001, EBRD's unrecovered losses were only $7 million from six failed banks. RSBF losses from the crisis were proportionately lower than those of other EBRD investments in Russia.

What is the explanation for relatively good performance of micro and small enterprises in times of crisis and also for the high quality of MSE portfolios supported by EBRD throughout the region? Stability can be explained by the fact that daily life goes on during most financial collapses. People still buy everyday items. Also, MSE activities are usually flexible and hence not so vulnerable to market conditions as larger, more complex businesses. Owners, who also operate these businesses, and their family members or other workers can act more quickly to cut cost and move into new product areas.

High quality portfolios also result from appropriate lending technologies, defined as the manner in which relationships with borrowers are organised. One of the great achievements of microfinance is the development and refinement of lending technologies that are like chameleons, a harmless creature that blends well into any cultural or legitimate business environment. For example, the basic IPC micro lending technology is based on current rather than projected cash flow, and on the finances of the economic unit, which is the household including the enterprise, rather than the enterprise separate from the household. Collateral consists of whatever is convenient and workable: therefore a well-run business will not be excluded because it has no 'bankable' assets that can be pledged.

Supported by other donors interested in promoting intense institution-building efforts, the RSBF downscaling model has been replicated by EBRD in Armenia, Belarus, Georgia, Kazakstan, Kyrgyz Republic, Ukraine and Uzbekistan. More than 300 branches of partner banks have "graduated," that is, they conduct target group lending business without continued outside support. More than € 1.3 billion has been disbursed and arrears on an at-risk basis are less than one percent of the combined portfolio. The next step for these institutions is to diversify further their funding sources and to discontinue technical assistance. Questions remain, however, about whether the programmes are sufficiently robust in various partner banks to continue in the same manner, given the opportunity costs perceived by these banks, without the involvement of the international financial institutions (IFIs) that have funded this effort to get it underway. Large expansion of outreach remains the challenge. How can "lending factories" be created throughout Russia and the region?

Microfinance Banks

In addition to its downscaling activities, EBRD has participated with other donors and partners to establish microfinance banks. The reasons for establishing microfinance institutions (MFIs) differ by country, as follows from EBRD's perspective: banks were founded in Albania, Azerbaijan and Yugoslavia in response to dysfunctional banking systems, and time was of the essence in Yugoslavia. MFIs were set up in Bosnia and Herzegovina and in Kosovo to assist recovery following war – Kosovo had no functioning banks when peace was restored. Following disappointing attempts to locate satisfactory local partner banks, MFIs were set up in Bulgaria, Moldova, Romania, Ukraine, and also in Georgia, where another motive was to counteract financial instability. KMB-Bank in Russia was formed by the EBRD's RSBF in response to the financial crisis of 1998. It was also clear in many of these countries that a transparent and efficient bank focused on micro and small enterprise would be needed to lead the way so that others could follow.

While the ownership composition and stakes in these banks vary from case to case, the most active partners collaborating with EBRD are other international financial institutions (IFIs): the International Finance Corporation (IFC), the German KfW Group and FMO from the Netherlands. Other investors in many of the banks are Internationale Micro Investitionen (IMI) and Commerzbank. Further financing for IMI is provided by Stichting DOEN of the Netherlands, BIO from Belgium, and private investors including IPC. Local banks in some countries were initially solicited as investment partners in accordance with the policies or preferences of some participating IFIs, but this requirement has been relaxed in response to experience.

The MFIs owned by these consortia are comparatively efficient and effective, especially where other banks are not interested in MSE. More than 125,000 loans amounting to €1.2 billion have been made in these countries, and again, arrears are less than one percent. Loan sizes range typically from €50 to €200,000 and vary greatly from bank to bank.

Table 1. Loan Size Distributions by MFI

Outstanding Portfolio Composition by Loan Size when Issued, end-2002

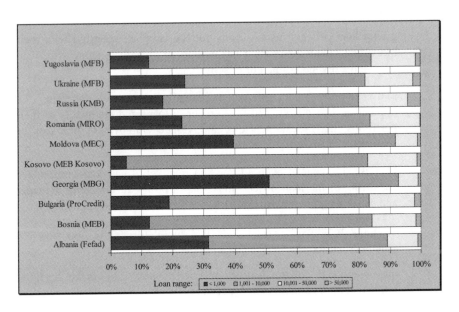

Institution Building

What factors contribute to the overall success of these banks? With respect to partner banks, regional or local conditions are important, but much less important than having receptive partner institutions. Banks with nation-wide branch networks seem slightly more interested in the target group than do small, local banks, but of course there are important exceptions. Cooperation among IFIs through joint participation in a programme is clearly more productive than having different and possibly competing operations within a single partner institution. Finally, the quality of consultants can make or break the programme.

Structural Issues and Costs

Institution building in partner banks requires patience. Everything seems to take longer than anticipated, which occurs because banks have not previously had any interest in acquiring MSE clients and because institution building requires the creation of new internal structures and procedures that will reduce the relatively high costs of making small loans.

- low costs can be achieved with flat rather than hierarchical organisational structures, which may run counter to the local banking orthodoxy.

- responsibility for working with micro clients may be entrusted to people without previous experience in the bank (i.e. not spoiled by bad practices) which can create friction within the ranks, especially when great progress is achieved.

- giving loan officers responsibility for the entire relationship with their individual clients (excluding accounting and handling money) may go against the division of labour in some banks.

- motivating these loan officers individually by bonuses based on the number of their clients, and the number of loans and the quality of their portfolios, may create tensions and violate employment practices or sentiments of solidarity in some countries and institutions.

- likewise, frequent or even ad hoc and relatively small loan committees consisting of the loan officer presenting a proposal, the credit manager and MSE department head, may seem too risky to traditional bankers.

- economy requires a certain pace that in micro-lending may threaten sedentary habits.

- unconventional collateral used in microfinance may make bankers, internal auditors and regulators nervous.

Working through banks is often risky: financial instability, lack of commitment and varying views of integrity can threaten downscaling programmes and block institution building. Institution building's requirement of sustainable outreach to the target group is not simply a question of training loan officers or a mechanical matter of covering costs. It is also a matter of opportunity costs: banks that are interested in serving the target group, or finding out what it takes to serve that group, have to evaluate these costs and returns against those of other, conventional lines of banking business. Simply put, institution building requires commitment by management and by owners.

The MFIs provide some lessons. They are usually more efficient than mainstream commercial banks that downscale to serve the target group. The MFIs exhibit a greater sense of teamwork internally and they understand what efficiency requires and that they have to be aggressive in order to survive. MFIs can become profitable within a reasonable period of time, but only if start-up costs are covered by technical assistance. Otherwise, and with very few exceptions, they would not attract investors because of the length of time that would be required to earn a competitive return on capital.

Technical Cooperation Costs

Technical cooperation (TC) is essential for regional expansion through new branches. Experience has shown it requires less assistance to set up an MFI than it does to work with commercial banks as partners. There are relatively little data available in the literature about TC costs on a per loan or per euro basis, but EBRD applies this rough test of cost effectiveness and efficiency. Results for MFIs and partner banks (PBs) are given in Figures 3 and 4. These show that cumulative costs per loan disbursed decline as productivity gains kick in. By the end of 2002, this approximated €250 in MFIs and about €700 in PBs. Per euro loaned, the cumulative cost was about 8 cents for partner banks and about 4 cents for MFIs at the end of 2002. The average marginal cost is 1.5 cents, which is indicative of banks that are graduating from TC and of greater efficiency in those banks still receiving TC and/or new partners.

The experience of KMB-Bank was dramatic, as indicated in Figures 5 and 6. The annual cost of technical cooperation per loan disbursed in the first two months of operation was about $2,500, while in 2002 this cost was about $150 on a cumulative basis, and about $75 per loan issued in 2002. The annual TC cost per dollar of cumulative loans issued was about 16 cents in 1999 and about 2 cents in 2002, while the corresponding annual costs in 1999 and 2002 were about 19 cents and 1 cent. These data and their trends indicate that technical cooperation costs are material when institution building efforts are devoted to constructing sustainable institutions, but that these costs decline relatively rapidly as scale economies are realised through increases in loan volume and more efficient lending operations.

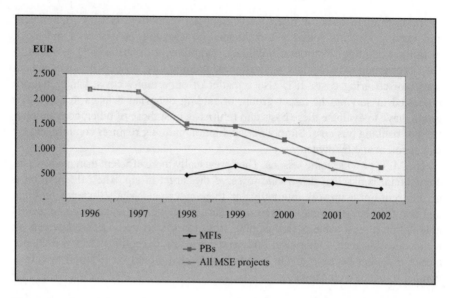

Figure 3. Cumulative Technical Cooperation Cost per Loan Disbursed

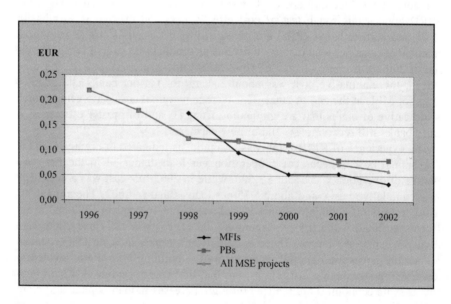

Figure 4. Cumulative Technical Cooperation Cost per Euro Disbursed

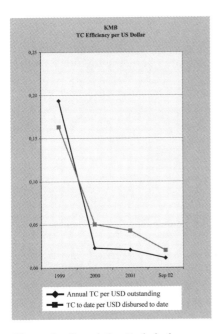

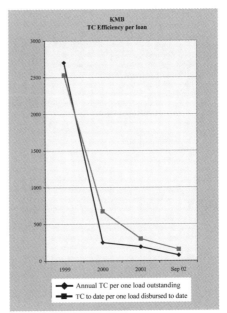

Figure 5. Cumulative Technical
Cooperation Cost per Loan
Disbursed by KMB-Bank

Figure 6. Cumulative Technical
Cooperation Cost per Dollar
Disbursed by KMB-Bank

Exit

Exit is easily described in downscaling. The programme establishes SME units in partner banks. Trainees are usually new recruits with a bachelors degree or similar qualification, whose salaries are paid by RSBF for approximately six months, at which time they join the partner bank as staff members at a higher base salary than they received as trainees. When the unit is functioning effectively, the MSE advisors move on to other branches. Exiting from the entire PB occurs when the PB has gained sufficient capacity to expand on its own without external assistance – at this point continuation generally depends on availability of sufficient liquidity to continue to grow the portfolio and opportunity costs.

Exit from MFIs in which EBRD has a stake is complex if the owners waver in their view of the long-term mission of these banks. A potential threat to the MFIs can occur when there is a change in their shareholding structure. An example would be purchase by a commercial bank that viewed the MFI acquisition as a means of entering a new national market, motivated by the attraction of corporate lending or other activities far removed from micro and small enterprises. The greatest challenge will result when IFIs exit. This requires not so much simply finding a way out for the highest price, but rather to whom participations could be sold so that the commitment to the target group is maintained. Given the mandate of these banks and the donor funding that has gone into them, this is imperative.

CHAPTER 7

Surviving the Crisis: Microfinance in Bolivia, 1999-2002

Elisabeth Rhyne

Vice President, ACCION International, Washington DC, USA

This paper examines the performance of Bolivian microfinance from 1999 to mid-2002, which was undergoing its first major crisis after emerging as a significant force in Bolivia in the early 1990s. The paper evaluates the performance of the microfinance industry during the crisis.

The case of Bolivia is important. Microfinance has advanced faster and farther in Bolivia than in many other countries, and therefore it anticipates developments that may emerge soon elsewhere. Among these are the rise of commercial microfinance institutions, competition among institutions, and experience with regulation and supervision of microfinance.

Bolivia exemplifies the financial systems approach to microfinance. A commercial vision has guided development. Microfinance has largely graduated from donor dependence and has become a full-fledged part of the financial system. The boundaries of the financial system have widened to include a major portion of the low-income population, especially the self-employed and informal entrepreneurs. The performance of Bolivian microfinance during its recent serious testing period can shed light on the long-term viability of the commercial approach to microfinance.[1]

Microfinance in 1998: The Crest

It is useful to begin on the eve of the crisis, with a quick review of the status of Bolivian microfinance at the end of 1998, after approximately a decade of devel-

---

[1] This paper is part of an ongoing documentation of Bolivian microfinance that I have been carrying out starting with the publication of *Mainstreaming Microfinance: How Lending to the Poor Began, Grew and Came of Age in Bolivia* and continuing with a case study in *The Commercialization of Microfinance: Balancing Business and Development* published by Kumarian Press, Bloomfield, Connecticut in 2001 and 2002, respectively. With this paper, events in Bolivia are updated to the middle of 2002.

opment. That year represents the peak of optimism about microfinance. A large number of institutions were providing microfinance, with a total portfolio of US$180 million and outreach approaching 400,000 loans. Providers included a commercial bank, several finance companies, many NGOs, and a number of credit cooperatives. Some providers made individual loans, some used solidarity groups, and others used village banking methods. Growth seemed a foregone conclusion: the industry grew significantly every year of the decade, more than tripling in portfolio size from 1994 to 1998.

Most noteworthy were the four leading microfinance institutions (MFIs): BancoSol, Caja Los Andes, FIE and Prodem, which had all emerged from NGO origins to become licensed financial institutions (Prodem's transformation was still in process). The performance of these MFIs in terms of growth (aggregate portfolio up 90% in two years), asset quality (portfolio at risk more than 1 day averaging 5.1%), and profitability (average return on assets of 28%) impressed Bolivia's financial leaders and international microfinance experts alike. The trend toward commercial microfinance appeared unstoppable. The Superintendency of Banks had created a special regulatory category, private financial funds (FFPs), to accommodate microfinance institutions, and there was a queue of new entrants, both NGO and private, seeking to become FFPs. NGOs increasingly targeted the edges of the industry – serving the poorest clients and moving farther into rural areas. On the other side, some private, commercially-oriented investors had begun to become involved as shareholders in MFIs.

Table 1. Status of Leading Microfinance Institutions, end 1998

	BancoSol	Caja Los Andes	FIE	Prodem*
Portfolio (US$ millions)	74.1	28.6	14.1	16.7
Growth since 1996	56%	140%	81%	104%
Active Borrowers	82,000	32,000	21,000	42,000
Growth since 1996	14%	33%	50%	56%
Portfolio at Risk Rate (over 1 day)	4.5%	5.7%	4.5%	5.6%
Return on Equity	29%	27%	32%	22%

* Prodem portfolio and clients as of June 1999.

Growth of traditional MFIs and entry of new commercial players created a competitive environment with benefits to consumers including falling interest rates, increased efficiency, faster loan approval, and increased range in product offerings.

The significance of microfinance for Bolivia's economic development was not well documented. Nevertheless, evidence at the aggregate level suggested that the client base was flourishing, as shown by the increased use of electricity and new equipment, by the growth of demand for loans in the upper size ranges of microfinance, and by rising numbers among the upper segment of the informal sector (manufacturing microenterprises with several wage employees) especially in comparison to the segment of the informal sector seen as a choice of last resort (one-person vendors, particularly those lacking a fixed location). Client impact studies of individual entrepreneurs indicated that a high percentage benefited in measurable ways from the new credit services.

With all this good news, participants and outsiders alike saw microfinance in Bolivia as a success story.

The Crisis

In 1998, the internal causes of the subsequent crisis were already in operation. In early 1999, a major external shock occurred from the financial crisis that began in Brazil and spread throughout the region. We can briefly summarise the causes of the ensuing microfinance crisis, starting with the elements external to microfinance:

- Bolivia's interdependence meant that regional problems sparked an extended recession in Bolivia. When Brazil devalued, thousands of Bolivian exporters to Brazil suddenly became uncompetitive. When Argentina began experiencing problems, millions of dollars of remittances from Bolivians working in Argentina suddenly dried up. Bolivia's economy stagnated or shrank in each of the next four years.

- Economic problems led to political instability, with street protests and a government facing increasing pressure to make populist concessions.

- A customs reform implemented in 1999 eliminated much of the informal cross-border trade that had been a crucial source of revenues and/or merchandise for thousands of microfinance clients, including importers, exporters and vendors.

Many microfinance clients suddenly found that demand for their products and services had shrunk and some failed to keep up their loan repayments.

The economic crisis provoked serious difficulties within microfinance because of factors internal to the microfinance industry:

- By far the most important factor was the rapid rise and subsequent collapse of consumer lending, which competed directly with microfinance and brought a set of operating principles into the marketplace that proved incompatible with microfinance.

- At the same time, competition among traditional microfinance providers was increasing as prime urban microfinance markets became saturated.

The lending growth that propelled MFIs and consumer lenders created a bidding war, with competitors vying for clients by offering larger loans, faster service, and lower interest rates. This momentum inflated the total amount of debt in the informal sector. Once the economy stalled, it quickly became evident that thousands of clients held more debt than their reduced level of economic activities would allow them to service. Overindebtedness was rampant. A proportion of clients had loans outstanding from multiple lenders.

Among microfinance institutions, overindebtedness and the economic slow-down resulted in rising delinquency, an abrupt halt to growth, and falling profits due in large part to increased loan loss provisions. Competition for the remaining good clients intensified. Lenders faced a stiff challenge: become more efficient, lower prices, develop attractive new products and *at the same time* cope with the highest rates of delinquency yet experienced and a dearth of fresh clients.

Among microfinance clients, the vast majority struggled to repay while learning hard lessons about risk-taking. However, a very small, vocal minority, spurred on by "professional" organisers, took to the streets. Debtor associations formed and engaged in high-profile protests against consumer lenders and microlenders. These protests featured hunger strikes, throwing garbage at head offices, tearful testimony by indigenous clients, and demands for debt forgiveness. In July 2001, protesters strapped dynamite around their bodies and took over the offices of the Superintendency of Banks, holding employees hostage. This and every other protest event was successfully resolved, but the protest movement continues to plague the microfinance industry.

The crisis began in early 1999. In its early and most intense stage it focused on the fall of the consumer lenders and the microfinance institutions' large population of overindebted clients. This stage ended as the consumer lenders disappeared (while still trying to collect debts). The crisis then moved into a second stage during which each microfinance institution sought a new formula for stable, profitable operations. Unfortunately, no economic upturn occurred and political tensions remained high. Nevertheless, there is some evidence that the situation began to level off in 2002.

How Have Bolivian Microfinance Institutions Performed during the Crisis?

The remainder of this paper examines how MFIs performed during the difficult period 1999 to mid-2002, first comparing microfinance institutions to other parts of the financial system, and then looking at differences among MFIs.

Microfinance in the Overall Financial System

In comparison to the other parts of the Bolivian financial system, MFIs, particularly the five regulated institutions (BancoSol, Caja Los Andes, FIE, Prodem, and EcoFuturo) performed well. As Tables 2 and 3 show, all parts of the financial

Table 2. Portfolio Growth by Segment of the Financial System (US$ million)

	1998		1999		2000		June 2001	
	Portfolio	Growth	Portfolio	Growth	Portfolio	Growth	Portfolio	Growth
Banks	4024	26%	3787	–6%	3175	–16%	2769	–26%
Mutuals	283	11%	286	1%	280	–2%	264	–12%
Cooperatives	186	9%	171	–8%	186	8%	179	–7%
MFIs (Regulated)	132	19%	153	15%	165	8%	159	–7%
MFIs (NGOs)	52	37%	57	11%	58	1%	53	–16%

Source: Gonzalez-Vega and Rodriguez-Meza, Table 2. Mutuals are similar to savings and loans or building societies.

Table 3. Portfolio at Risk by Segment of the Financial System (over 1 day)

	1998	1999	2000	June 2001
Banks	4.8%	7.0%	11.6%	16.6%
Mutuals	10.2%	10.5%	10.4%	14.4%
Cooperatives	10.8%	17.0%	17.2%	18.4%
MFIs (Regulated)	3.8%	7.2%	7.9%	11.9%
MFIs (NGOs)	3.8%	7.0%	12.1%	20.8%

Source: Author's calculations, based on data from Gonzalez-Vega and Rodriguez-Meza, Tables 2 and 3.

system suffered increasingly poor performance during the period. Microfinance, however, was the only sector whose portfolio did not shrink. In comparison, the commercial banks reduced their active portfolios by about one third.

Delinquency rose throughout the period, but the regulated microfinance institutions managed to contain delinquency more successfully than the mainstream financial institutions. Differences in loan portfolio performance are a major cause of the different levels of profitability achieved by the banks and MFIs. Four of the five regulated MFIs showed profits by late 2002, and FIE and Caja Los Andes were among the most profitable financial institutions in Bolivia. By contrast, several commercial banks remained in the loss column.

Preliminary hypotheses can be offered regarding some of the reasons for the differences in relative performance of microfinance institutions and banks:

- the informal sector may be able to adapt itself more quickly to economic stress than the corporate sector served by commercial banks.

- the commercial banks may have moved out of small enterprise lending, while the microfinance institutions took up some of their customers.

- poor commercial bank performance includes the shedding of poorly-performing consumer loan portfolios by several banks.

- MFIs, as newcomers to the financial system, were being regulated conservatively, and therefore were well-provisioned and less highly leveraged than the banks. Their solvency and profitability was better protected.

An important consequence of the integration of microfinance institutions into the mainstream financial system became evident during the crisis. Pressures to ameliorate the stress on the financial sector became extreme during the crisis, and the government included relief measures in its recovery programs. These included amnesties to allow banks to reschedule debt without penalty, deferral of provisioning requirements and other ways to soften regulatory treatment to allow banks to survive. A Ministry of Financial Institutions was created. This may increase political influence over the Superintendency of Banks, which had effectively distanced bank supervision from political interference. Measures such as these may undermine the high levels of financial discipline and transparency in the microfinance industry. It is difficult to maintain a strict provisioning policy and transparent financial statements when other institutions are being invited to soften theirs.

Performance of Microfinance Institutions

The relative performance of key Bolivian MFIs during the crisis illustrates the proposition that long term comparative advantages strongly influence performance. The ability of each institution to survive and prosper can be attributed to the specific history and endowments of each.

Table 4. Regulated Microfinance Institutions, 1998-2002: Loan Portfolio (US$ million)

	1998	1999	2000	2001	2002 (June)
BancoSol	74.1	82.3	77.8	81.1	79.3
Caja Los Andes	28.6	35.9	46.8	52.6	55.8
FIE	14.1	18.5	22.5	27.5	30.2
Prodem	24.2	21.8	23.6	33.6	39.9
TOTAL	141.0	158.5	170.7	194.8	205.2

The best performing institutions, Caja Los Andes and FIE, grew and maintained their profitability. Their success is attributed primarily to their lending methodology and market niche, as well as to stable ownership and management. Both have always made individual loans and have deep expertise in the processes of making such loans. Once markets began to be saturated, with clients gaining access to a variety of providers, many clients moved from group to individual lenders. Caja Los Andes and FIE have also benefited from continuity in management, allowing them to focus intently on survival in a highly competitive and depressed market. Nevertheless, both institutions experienced severe stress and worked intensively to reduce costs and improve service.

Table 5. Regulated Microfinance Institutions, 1998-2002: Number of Active Loans (000)

	1998	1999	2000	2001	2002 (June)
BancoSol	82	73	61	54	51
Caja Los Andes	32	37	43	43	44
FIE	21	24	23	n/a	24
Prodem	47	40	26	23	22
TOTAL	182	174	153	120	150

Table 6. Regulated Microfinance Institutions, 1998-2002: Portfolio at Risk (over 1 day)

	1998	1999	2000	2001	2002 (June)
BancoSol	4.5%	7.0%	12.3%	14.7%	13.4%
Caja Los Andes	.7%	6.5%	7.7%	8.4%	6.8%
FIE	1.5%	6.2%	7.9%	8.2%	6.8%
Prodem	5.6%	7.0%	4.8%	6.3%	4.9%

BancoSol and Prodem performed adequately, maintaining approximately a break-even level of operations. This is attributed partly to the fact that they entered the period as primarily solidarity group lenders, and therefore lost clients to individual lenders before they could implement individual lending programmes of their own. Moreover, in a recession group lending may actually be more risky than individual lending. When one group member encounters difficulties, her colleagues, already on the edge, may be unable to step in and the group as a whole may default. At BancoSol, delinquency was highest in the solidarity group portfolio. A great deal of staff reorientation and training, as well as system adaptation, is required to move from being a group lender to an individual lender. These changes take time and are difficult in the highly pressured, competitive environment the institutions faced. In addition, BancoSol was involved in changes of ownership and management which perhaps diverted high level attention away from the crisis. Prodem, primarily a rural lender, faced the additional uncertainties of the vulnerability of the rural economy to shocks such as low commodity prices. BancoSol was able to sustain itself in part because of its strong financial and market position going into the crisis. These two key attributes gave it the breathing space to adjust to changing conditions.

Two new MFIs, EcoFuturo and Fassil, performed very poorly. Fassil, a mixed consumer and microenterprise lender, was hit very hard by the consumer lending collapse. It never established a clear market identity as a microenterprise lender. It was relatively thinly capitalised and lacked access to resources outside the country. EcoFuturo, a new institution created by four microfinance NGOs, was attempting to establish its market presence and internal organisational development during this difficult time. Whatever the particulars of these two institutions, the survival of the newer, less established institutions was jeopardised because they lacked market presence and internal organisational and financial strength. The regulated microfinance industry was consolidating around the four established MFIs – BancoSol, Caja Los Andes, FIE, and Prodem.[2]

NGOs' performance varied. Pro Mujer and Crecer have been noteworthy, growing steadily while maintaining strong portfolio quality. Both are village banking programmes for women. Crecer works in remote rural areas, Pro Mujer in urban areas. Their success may be attributable to two principal factors. First, they aim at a less hotly contested portion of the microfinance market, segmenting the market by gender and poverty level, and in the case of Crecer also by location. The village banking methodology may have some built in stabilisers during times of economic stress: the larger group size offers greater diversification than occurs among small solidarity groups, and the internal account system can operate as an emergency loan fund.

Lessons from Recent Bolivian Experience

Increased Use of Credit Bureaus

It is often said that the credit bureau operated by the Superintendency of Banks was not sufficiently inclusive and up-to-date to prevent the crisis of overindebtedness. It is true that the credit bureau was still in the early stages of operation, and did not include non-regulated MFIs. However, until the crisis hit, many lenders,

---

[2] Although Prodem was only licensed as an FFP in 2000, its transformation from NGO to FFP did not involve significant change in operations or management, and therefore it can be regarded among the group of established MFIs.

especially the consumer lenders, were willing to lend to borrowers who already had outstanding debt at other institutions. Not until borrowing from multiple institutions led to increasing default did institutions (and the Superintendency) begin to crack down.

It is clear that the development of a top-notch credit bureau is among the priorities for Bolivia (and particularly a bureau that includes non-regulated MFIs), but it is also clear that credit bureaus cannot prevent crises. Lenders must believe that they will benefit from using them. The dynamics of competition mean that risky practices such as making relatively large loans or lending to the good borrowers of other institutions will attract clients. To prevent this, some countries have safe lending rules requiring that lenders obtain and follow the findings of credit bureau reports. The situation in Bolivia leads one reluctantly to conclude that such rules may become necessary whenever overlending appears.

Increased Knowledge by the Superintendency

When the crisis began, the Superintendency was still relatively unfamiliar with microfinance and unprepared for the entry of consumer lending, and it acted too late to prevent its collapse. The consumer lenders and the Superintendency failed to recognise that the techniques of the consumer lenders could not be applied to the clients of microenterprise lenders: it failed to appreciate the differences between lending to the salaried and to the informal sector. Over the years, the regulatory authorities gained greater understanding of microfinance, and developed more detailed and appropriate supervisory tools. This took several years, even at a Superintendency that was one of the more competent in the region and that responded positively to the emerging microfinance movement.

Widening Range of Clients Served and Products Offered

Nearly all the MFIs attempted to attract clients and find growth markets in the wake of difficult market conditions. Several added new products in an attempt to retain existing microenterprise clients and attract similar clients away from other institutions. These include housing loans, lines of credit and payment services. The institutions also sought new types of clients. One of the clearest trends is the move up-market to small business lending, where competition is perceived as not so strong, particularly if commercial banks retreat from this market.

With donor assistance, NGOs focused on poorer clients and savings became a priority. With respect to the rural clients of the regulated MFIs, arguably the least well served group, the trend was generally negative. Some rural branches were closed, and Prodem, the one regulated lender with a rural base, opened urban branches to diversify its dependence on the rural economy. Overall, while a great deal of innovation occurred, the regulated MFIs attempted to innovate in what they perceived as safer ways, leaving the NGOs to take the risk of pushing the farther frontiers.

Industry Consolidation

As a result of the crisis, new entry into the Bolivian microfinance market decreased. The perception of saturation in microenterprise lending and high risk in consumer lending will keep commercial players from entering the market for some time. There have been merger talks as formal institutions consider whether they can survive over the long term. However, no mergers have actually been concluded, as the difficulties have outweighed the perceived advantages. Exit from the sector is taking place through the closure of consumer lenders that experimented with microenterprise finance, and one or two of the weaker microfinance institutions may be forced to close.

In 1998, it seemed inevitable that successful NGOs would try to obtain licences as FFPs. In 2002, the queue has disappeared, as NGOs recognise that the FFPs face tough market conditions, whereas their markets are somewhat better protected because they are not yet commercial, and that their frontier-pushing mission may keep them as NGOs. Some leaders of FFPs believe that long-run survival requires becoming a bank, and some are making preparations to apply for a banking licence.

Learning to Live with the Debt Protestors

The debt protestors will be a fixture on the microfinance scene for some time. They have the ability to damage the microfinance industry and/or specific institutions far beyond the validity of their claims: only a small fraction of the agitators are actually borrowers. Despite their questionable claims and tactics, they have altered the public image of MFIs, garnering significant sympathy among various audiences. Microfinance institutions will have to counter the threat. First, they must become more adept at responding to specific protest events, including negotiating with the protesters. Second, they must proactively move to capture the moral high ground by articulating and advocating more clearly that good lending practice is beneficial to borrowers. This could include measures such as codes of conduct or consumer education campaigns.

Decreases in Interest Rates and Administrative Costs

Throughout the 1990s, the increasing competence of MFIs led to falling administrative costs, which decreased interest rates. This trend continued throughout the crisis, as consumers began to be acutely aware of comparative pricing. For the first time there was evidence that some customers would switch institutions on the basis of price. For example, in 1994, a time of very low competition, BancoSol's portfolio yield (interest income divided by average portfolio size) was 50%. By 1998, the yield had fallen to 33% and by 2001 to 24%. At Caja Los Andes, yield fell from 40% in 1995 to 25% by 2001, and yields at Prodem and FIE in 2001 were even lower (22%). Not only did yields fall, they also narrowed as institutions priced their services on a competitive basis rather than on the basis of their own internal costs. These reductions in income required improvements in administrative efficiency. Ratios of administrative costs to portfolio ranged from 12% at FIE to 19% at largely rural Prodem in 2001. In 1995, these rates had been in the mid to upper 20s. MFIs were able to achieve these improvements for three reasons: 1) as their growth slowed, expenditures on new infrastructure and staff dropped; 2) loan sizes and loan maturities continued their upward trend; and 3) most institutions had intensive cost-cutting campaigns.

Table 7. Portfolio Yield and Administrative Efficiency at Leading Bolivian MFIs

	1994	1995	1996	1998	1999	2001
Banco Sol						
Yield	50%	33%	47%	33%	29%	24%
Admin/Portfolio	21%	22%	20%	17%	16%	14%
Los Andes						
Yield		40%	35%	31%	27%	25%
Admin/Portfolio		27%	20%	13%	13%	13%
Prodem						
Yield						22%
Admin/Portfolio						19%
FIE						
Yield						22%
Admin/Portfolio						12%

Note: 1997 and 2000 omitted

More Competent Institutions

Participants in the microfinance industry generally express their belief that difficulty results in stronger institutions. For example, Pedro Arriola of Caja Los Andes claims that institutions have strengthened their credit evaluation processes and increased staff training. If not stronger, the MFIs of 2002 are certainly wiser than in 1998. In 1998 there was a sense of triumph among microfinance institutions, a victor's sense of having achieved an unprecedented goal. By 2002, the sense among the same institutions was one of gritty determination and survival. Institutions understand their vulnerabilities more completely and have developed better means of protecting themselves against the volatility of the financial, economic and political landscapes.

Lessons for Other Markets

The Balkans are far from Bolivia, but both have active microfinance markets and are not immune from instability. What advice could be offered, based on Bolivia's experience?

First, lenders' capital ratios should reflect the risk of the lending business. This applies to consumer lenders, which were the source of many problems in Bolivia, as well as to micro and SME lenders that intend to survive crises. Second, credit bureaus can be useful in monitoring indebtedness and thereby curbing overindebtedness through the sharing of information among lenders. Whether these should be operated by regulators, private actors, or by lenders acting in concert remains an open question, but it is clear that these bureaus must function very well if they are to be of use. Third, group lending exhibited weaknesses in Bolivia that are now understood as being structural defects when group and individual lenders compete head to head. Finally, good relationships with clients are essential so that problems can be more easily resolved, and in a manner that is less likely to become politicised. Lenders may wish to take the lead in defining pro-consumer lending practices for the community at large. Promulgation of good lending practice may help to head off the pernicious tendency to over-lending in competitive markets.

References

The following sources were particularly helpful in preparing this update:

ASOFIN, CIPAME and Finrural, *Microfinanzas: Boletín Financiero.* No. 9, La Paz, December 2001.

Claudio González-Vega and Jorge Rodríguez-Meza, "La Situación Macroeconómica y el Sector de Las Microfinanzas en Bolivia", SEFIR-DAI Project, USAID/ Bolivia, undated.

Pedro Arriola Bonjour, "Crisis y Competencia: La Prueba de Fuego para las Microfinanzas Bolivianas", La Paz, unpublished, 2002.

CHAPTER 8:

Institutional Development and Commercialisation – Optimal Exit for Equity Financiers

Volker Neuschütz

Vice President of the Europe, Middle East and Central Asia Department, DEG, Cologne, Germany

The Role of the Financial Sector in Developing Countries and Southeast Europe

A financial system provides services that are vital for a modern economy. A stable currency facilitates trade and thereby the specialisation of production. Financial assets with attractive yield, liquidity and risk characteristics encourage savings in financial form. Institutional investors contribute to a more efficient use of resources by evaluating alternative investment options and monitoring borrowers' business activities. The availability of a broad range of financial tools offers economic entities the opportunity of bundling, analysing and shifting risks. Trade, the rational use of resources, saving and the acceptance of risks are the cornerstones of a growing economy.

In the past and especially before the fall of the Iron Curtain, governments in Eastern Europe utilised comprehensive policies to control and direct credit. The risk of inappropriate intervention has considerably increased in a global environment characterised by rapid changes of relative prices, extreme currency fluctuations, complex economic structures and the continuous development of financial markets. Resource allocation could be improved and the financial system consequently made more stable if the number and size of special credit programmes and interest subsidies were scaled back more rapidly following reconstruction and economic reorientation. It is better to rely on credit availability rather than to grant long-term interest subsidies that interfere with the functioning of financial markets. Special programmes should be devoted only to activities that may be inadequately covered even in a developed financial sector. But even such interventions cannot guarantee the desired development of the financial sector. A weak legal system, weak accounting systems as well as inadequate management processes are a poor basis for modern finance.

Commercial banks are the dominant institutions in developing and transition countries. The operational efficiency of these banks can be increased by improving their management systems, marketing, sales, risk management and processes. The entry of foreign banks into these countries may stimulate competition and encourage the introduction of "best practice" standards.

Most developing countries have an informal financial sector serving small clients – households, smallholders and small enterprises. Pawnbrokers provide considerable credit to those with acceptable pledges, while moneylenders do so for the remaining clientele. Government programmes that "encourage" domestic commercial banks to issue loans to small borrowers are often a burden for these banks and yield only low profits. Nor is this customer segment particularly attractive for foreign competitors. The institutions of the formal sector find the credit risk of this group difficult to estimate and assume it is costly. However, informal lending has serious drawbacks. Loans are small, the service offered is narrow, the markets are fragmented and the interest rates often exorbitant. Such conditions inhibit the growth of small and medium-sized enterprises, which is required from the macroeconomic and developmental points of view. Some countries have recognised this and created programmes to achieve closer cooperation between the formal and the informal markets. The most successful programmes for small clients make use of systems which have been developed over years; these stimulate investment and lending and enable credit providers to charge cost-covering fees.

The biggest difference between rich and poor countries is the efficiency with which they use their resources. The contribution of financial systems to economic growth is specifically based on their capacity to increase this efficiency. Smoothly working financial systems lower the cost of intermediation from investors to borrowers, leading to an increase in interest rates paid to investors and a decrease in the costs involved for borrowers. The possibility for borrowers and lenders to compare interest rates offered in different markets improves the allocation of financial resources.

The Tasks of Development Cooperation Institutions

International development cooperation finance institutions have the following aims concerning financial sector development: a) strengthened financial sectors at both the institutional and sectoral levels, and b) improved access for the private sector – especially small and medium enterprises (SMEs) – to loans, equity and other finance products that are offered insufficiently or not at all by commercial banks. This is called the "complementary strategy".

The pursuit of these two aims ensures that financial institutions render as substantial a contribution as possible to the development and transformation processes in the financial sectors in which they operate. On an institutional level this objective is pursued by supporting existing financial institutions, by privatising and restructuring state-owned institutions and by the formation of private financial institutions. In addition to the banking sector, special priority is given to the development of the capital market and to launching a private sector insurance industry.

Sectoral level aims include improving the financial framework (e.g. introduction of market based participants, free market access, enhanced competition), strengthening mechanisms for monitoring and control as well as expanding the range of products and services offered. In addition to financing projects and investment programmes, consultancy services on a sectoral level are also offered. The promotion of small and medium-sized companies is considered the primary task of financial institutions.

The following principles of funding apply in general:

- finance projects should have a positive effect on a country's development or transition processes.

- projects in the financial sector should be carried out in strict compliance with regulations and best practice standards.

- terms and conditions of funding should be oriented to market conditions; implemented gradually and/or phased out over time.

- projects should work with, not against private activities.

- the instruments applied are:

  o Equity participations in banks and other financial institutions,

  o Direct loans to banks and strengthening of financial institutions,

  o Credit lines and guarantees to support the supply of credit to the private small and medium-sized enterprise (SME) sector.

The allocation of technical assistance to financial institutions and sub-borrowers often plays a vital role in the operations of financial institutions. This applies particularly to private equity funds, apex facilities, credit lines and equity participation in banks. In this context, a clearly defined time limit should be applied to support activities.

The Role of Equity Financing, Especially in the Financial Sector

Many of the enterprises operating in DEG's (Deutsche Investitions- und Entwicklungsgesellschaft mbH) target countries require long-term capital beyond their own resources in order to exploit their growth potential. The development of efficient, small and medium-sized companies is particularly retarded by poorly developed capital markets and financial systems. The lack of equity and long-term loans is frequently the decisive bottleneck for economic development in developing and transition countries.

The growth of financial institutions is considerably influenced by the capital resources available to them. Although developing and transition countries in general
exhibit high market potential, their capital resources are limited by the regulatory
and economic requirements facing financial institutions. The self-financing of
financial institutions is frequently insufficient to guarantee the growth of capital
required to meet increasing customer credit demand. If self-financing can no
longer be achieved by means of capital increases, many institutions are left only
with the possibility of joining a financially stronger partner or trying to increase
income by merging with a partner who has equal financial clout. Many countries
have "overbanked markets", which make acquisitions and mergers generally welcome. However, as the takeover process often places a heavy financial burden
upon them, the acquiring institutions also frequently need to stabilise their financial structures through equity increases.

Regulatory and legal requirements are placed on capital primarily to protect
borrowers. The capital ratio requirement and restrictions on ownership are intended to ensure supplementary financing capacity for growth and for liquidity
and are the decisive parameters influencing refinancing capacity and its associated
costs. The resulting interest margin has a strong impact on self-financing capacity.

Volatile markets and unstable political situations in countries in which DEG invests allow only limited predictability of liquidity and credit risks. The provision
of capital to a financial institution is therefore a crucial buffer against the crises
that threaten profits.

Structuring the balance sheet to provide adequate shareholder value is one of
the greatest operational challenges for financial institutions. If the equity base is
too low, there is a latent threat to the company as a whole in times of crisis, while
excessive capital resources result in low or negative value added. The introduction
of new financial tools such as "mezzanine finance" is intended to overcome these
conflicts.

Different Sources of Equity Financing, Especially for the Finance Sector

Given the economic importance of a stable financial system and that financial
institutions require adequate capitalisation, the question arises as to how these
conditions can be ensured.

Unlike industrialised nations, most developing and transition countries do not
have a comprehensive capital market that would allow local financial institutions
to raise equity. The only sources are usually big investors, whether individuals,
conglomerates, private investment companies or foreign competitors. But often
these investors have only a limited capacity to mobilise sufficient funds. They are
either inadequately capitalised, have severe conflicts of interests or utilise only a
small portion of the available and economically useful market potential.

This is why additional equity resources have been provided with governmental support to encourage the development of the banking sector in developing and transition countries. Some of the funds provided by technical and financial cooperation are made available by implementing organisations – usually under bilateral agreements between governments. A considerable share of government aid also reaches the market via non-governmental organisations (NGOs). The major part of this aid consists of very long-term soft loans and subsidies, with special requirements imposed on their utilisation. The repayment terms of technical and financial cooperation funds in effect give them the character of equity finance.

In their role as development agencies, international financial institutions have both a developmental and a banking function. Their business purpose and financing methods may be totally or partially focused on productive investments in developing and transition countries. Development agencies from the industrialised countries should contribute to private entrepreneurial equity – i.e. genuine venture capital – directed to productive investments. They also fulfil this mandate through equity financing of credit institutions. International financial institutions (IFIs) promote and support private enterprise in developing and transition countries by mobilising savings and contributing to capital generation. Progress in these fields will improve the investment climate, thereby also improving the prospects for attracting private investors from industrialised countries.

The Tasks and Aims of Equity Financiers

The basic task facing every equity financier is to create the foundations for capital that will enable an enterprise to generate real economic value with yields commensurate with the risks incurred. The correlation between yield and risk is important on the one hand for preventing exploitation, and on the other for balancing the assumed risks and potential profit expectations in order to reduce moral hazard.

The aims and tasks of the investor also include the direct and indirect monitoring and control of management to ensure that it fulfils the objectives of creating jobs, securing economic prosperity, increasing shareholder value, and gaining prestige and influence.

To achieve their strategic goals, IFIs engage in a broad range of activities in addition to financing projects in the financial sector:

- identifying projects: determining requirements and niches for projects in the financial sector, plus identification of regulatory obstacles, mobilisation of technical support, and appraisal of tax and regulatory issues.

- searching out potential investors, especially strategic investors: sponsoring the initial feasibility studies used for market evaluation and as a basis for project appraisal.

- structuring project finance: defining the investment strategy, management structure and corporate governance; definition of legal form, exposure guidelines (prudential guidelines), assistance in obtaining official authorisations (in the role of "honest broker").

- mobilising funds: promoting self-financed investment to encourage financing by third parties, preferably private investors, and underwriting.

- providing consultancy and monitoring inputs: obtaining a seat on the supervisory board and participating regularly in its activities for the purpose of monitoring investment, and for providing advice and initiating training measures.

The General Importance of Exit and Potential Risks for Investors

Ever since its foundation, DEG has provided equity finance involving very different types and degrees of risk. At first, this included only German joint ventures, but was later extended to international and to local partners. While exit plans were previously of secondary importance, exit strategy is now an integral part of the negotiations at the beginning of cooperation. This process is similar at other IFIs.

In the early years, DEG's portfolio at times consisted of up to 50% in equity investments, which led to some severe yield-related problems and losses through the early 1990s. Devaluation losses caused by economic crises in individual countries were often larger than increases in the companies' net asset value. Profits achieved in local currency were destroyed by devaluation. This situation and equity finance agreements that failed to take exit into consideration made participations difficult to sell. Commitments for up to 20 years were not unusual. Another major problem was the conflict of interest between DEG as the investor on one hand and the German partner company on the other. While DEG earned no dividend income during the projects' early years due to start-up losses, later developments led to situations in which the protection of the partner's market interests was often considered more important than making profits commensurate with investment risks. The result was a sluggish equity portfolio that tied up funds and required high consultancy expenditure.

DEG's equity policy was redefined during its reorganisation in the late 1980s. A policy of revolving the equity portfolio was adopted so that sales of investments could provide funds for new commitments. Participation is generally not undertaken without a clearly defined exit strategy. Profit and upside potential as well as foreign exchange income to offset devaluation losses must be convincingly outlined to justify participations. A company's profitability can be influenced by the partners' intervention, requiring arm's length agreements to limit downside risk.

Investment appraisals are necessary in order to avoid implicit operational risks related to insolvency, currency and markets. Additionally, it has become indispensable at the point of entry to align the strategy of the target company toward an exit, and to use membership on the board to facilitate achievement of the company's strategic targets. In this respect, it is necessary to identify potential financial or strategic investors at the very start of the investment without neglecting the developmental mandate. The target company can, for instance, be structured by the IFIs in a way that makes it attractive to a strategic investor, e.g., by closing production gaps at a later date (using leasing, for example) or to expand into regional markets. If an exit is intended to be made through a liquid capital market, the company must be fit to go public. In some cases, DEG has successfully sold its participations in banks on the stock exchange.

Convergence of Economic Rationalism and Developmental Priorities

DEG's new investment policy was a result of experience, but also of the ever-scarcer availability of financial aid in a changing environment. While public donors faced a growing shortage of funds, the willingness of private investors to invest in transition countries and selected developing countries began to grow. IFIs had to allocate their scarcer funds even more selectively and revolve them more frequently in order to increase their multiplier effect.

The IFIs' current equity policy is to devise an exit strategy as soon as they become involved as an equity financier. Projects have to be economically successful to attract an investor to buy out the IFI interest. Only in this way is it possible for projects (and thereby their developmental aims) to continue to prosper in the long run.

If it is impossible to find a strategic investor, financial institutions and particularly development banks (which are mainly owned by western IFIs) can grow only if the owners inject further funding. This is the case in many African development banks. The intended business purpose of the local development banks was to provide equity and long-term loans according to market conditions. But this objective has not been realised because of their weaknesses: sponsors without entrepreneurial responsibility, limited access to local refinancing, shareholders with limited resources, one-sided and risky financial products, limited profitability subordinated to other objectives, lack of proximity to customers and partly subsidised refinancing. Development banks which failed to address these issues have largely ceased to fulfil their functions. However, some local commercial banks have increasingly played a role since the markets were liberalised in the early 1990s.

IFIs' efforts to transform these local development finance companies have so far shown little success and they continue to depend on their owners for refinancing. Their integration into the local market has at best been only partially successful owing to the local commercial banks' reluctance to deal with such institutions. In such cases, exit by IFIs appears to be extremely unlikely with possible liquidation looming in some cases.

Elements of a Successful Exit Strategy for a Promotional Investor

There are two elements of a successful exit strategy: first, to achieve an internal rate of return (IRR) reflecting the risk upon exit, and second, to reach the development goal agreed at the outset of the investment. Essential factors related to the successful attainment of an adequate IRR are, in particular, a "best execution" at the start of the investment, strategic alignment and control in working towards the exit, as well as the timing and "best execution" upon exit. The question therefore is the degree to which IFIs are positioned between the poles of these two elements. Institutional development and commercialisation are not mutually exclusive terms, but rather define the first and the final stages.

After six to eight years, when the economic independence of the company appears to be safe, a strategic investor who will not abandon the original business purpose should be brought into the project. It is advisable to engage an investment bank for this purpose. The equity financier (IFI) should be able to attain adequate yields in the form of a risk premium, which is of course necessary to maintain and increase the financial power of the IFI. Put and call options used as exit vehicles should not be executed prematurely, since project delays frequently occur in difficult partner countries, thus retarding the realisation of profits. This is certainly a complex decision-making process: the experience of a Swedish private equity fund has shown that exit can also be unnecessarily delayed through the independent, individual interests within an IFI. These include consistently false signs of improvement in the profit prospects or the reluctance to relinquish prestigious board appointments. In calculating an acceptable level of profitability of an investment, the IFI also has to take into account that the recovery of the acquisition cost is but a nominal consideration at the end of the investment phase. There might actually be substantial asset erosion in real terms, particularly over long repayment periods. This is why intermediate dividend payouts are of particular importance.

A buyer that subsequently changes the character of the project should be obliged to repay all or some portion of the donor money contributed to the project. This compensation for donors might make exit more difficult. The buyer/strategic investor should have to report to the donor for a certain period of monitoring. It is therefore important to thoroughly explore right from the start whether a common set of values and objectives exists. Projects in which an exit is not possible have in a way missed the target because they cannot survive in their particular market. They can survive only with the continuous injection of new external funds or the provision of finance by the owners, in either case relying on donors or IFIs as trustees. They do not assist market-economy development and at the same time inhibit new commitment and thus reduce further developmental benefits.

The time schedule for an involvement can vary considerably depending on the developmental status of the country. For transparency, it is helpful for all partners involved to define clearly the target exit time frame at the outset of the project, integrating this element into strategic decisions. Attention to the following aspects throughout the 6 to 8-year period of IFI participation is paramount for a successful exit strategy:

- the company has to be an attractive size in order to interest strategic investors.

- the project should have "additionalities" such as market acceptance and access to target groups that would otherwise be inaccessible to the partners.

- the financier should be commercially oriented and have reliable management; good corporate governance is indispensable.

- economic transparency provided by information systems and proper accounting are equally indispensable.

- the financier should cultivate and maintain relations with partners at home and abroad to offer a broad range of options in choosing a strategic investor.

Examples of Successful and Timely Exits by IFIs

In Latin America and more recently in the Baltic states, it has proved possible to transfer development finance companies relatively swiftly to private owners. This has been facilitated by the comprehensive and rapid supply of credit from private banks. The available credit know-how (analysis, structuring of agreements, etc.) has enabled the commercial banking sector to serve its clientele effectively. The commercial banks established in those years are today's strategic partners for banks in the CIS countries.

RZB – Bosnia-Herzegovina

Raiffeisen Banka Bosnia-Herzegovina, formerly Marketbanka, is a private bank established in 1992. International financial institutions such as Soros Economic Development Funds and the European Bank for Reconstruction and Development (EBRD) invested in this bank in 1997 and DEG joined in 1999. In 2000, Raiffeisen Zentralbank Österreich AG took control as majority shareholder from the IFIs. The bank has expanded and now has 12 offices throughout the country and a staff of approximately 380. The bank's contribution to capital market development is noteworthy. It provides new finance products such as customer and sales and housing financing, start-up financings, and the mobilisation of local savings.

SKB Banka AD – Slovenia

The Slovenian commercial bank SKB grew out of the state-owned Ljubljanska Banka and was transferred to a very large extent into private ownership. The bank went public on the Lubljana Stock Exchange in 1997 and issued GDRs (German depository receipts) traded on the Munich, Frankfurt, Berlin and London stock exchanges.

EBRD and DEG acquired shares in 1995, helping to stabilise the financial structure and to improve corporate governance in preparation for takeover by a foreign partner. The IFIs and other shareholders used an international investment bank to search for and select a suitable strategic partner, using a bid procedure which is customary in international banking. At the conclusion of the successful tender in May 2001, the share capital was almost completely transferred to the French Société Générale.

The entry of this large international commercial bank brought the overall organisation, processes and product range up to international standards, making an important contribution towards the further development of the Slovenian financial sector. Engaging an international investment bank and using a bid and selection procedure set an example in Slovenia that led to finding suitable foreign strategic partners for other local banks.

Examples of Planned Exits by IFIs

Crnogorska Komerciljana Banka AD in Montenegro has received substantial support from KfW in the form of long-term credit programmes and technical assistance. FMO and DEG are major shareholders. The intended exit strategy is to include a strategic foreign investor as majority shareholder as soon as possible in order to introduce state-of-the-art banking know-how.

Euromarket Banka AD in Montenegro was founded in late 2000 by the Soros Economic Development Fund, DEG and RZB Bosnia. Over the medium term, the bank considers a takeover by a foreign investor as an exit possibility that would have positive consequences for the bank and the Montenegrin financial sector.

In the spring of 2002, a consortium consisting of the Soros Group, EBRD, DEG and a private shareholder took over the majority of the mainly state-owned Belgrade-based Eksim Bank through a capital increase. The exit strategy is intended to enhance the bank's profitability, systems and corporate governance in order to attract an international investor that will purchase the majority of its share capital.

Summary

The banks described above are examples of IFI exit strategies that are generally agreed with a strategic partner at the start of the investment. However, strategic investors in financial institutions are not as a rule attracted to countries with poorly developed macro-economies and finance sectors. IFIs and other private financiers face the medium-term task of assuming a bridge function in terms of providing equity commitments and expert know-how that will make the local financial institutions attractive for a takeover by strategic investors. It is necessary from the beginning to work towards achieving the sustainability of the local bank in order to ensure that the developmental mandate is fulfilled.

Outlook

This essay explores issues relating to the timely exit of equity investors in financial institutions in developing and transition countries. Efforts to promote this developmental activity face several difficult challenges. For example, developing and transition countries are often discussed as if they were all more or less identical despite the fact that policies and experience differ from country to country. The human and political dimensions of financial sector promotion have often been treated superficially relative to the attention devoted to the development of the manufacturing sector, where the problems can be defined in terms of factories and machines. While financial performance requirements can be rewritten overnight with the help of regulations, genuine changes are not brought about in this way. The acquisition of the necessary banking skills takes time. The training of new employees, the implementation of new institutions and the task of motivating staff have proved to be great challenges for development. We will continue trying to promote the expansion of efficient financial systems that are capable of raising and distributing funds on a voluntary basis.

In addition to the implementation and stabilisation of financial institutions, future priorities in the sector should focus on intermediaries that promote small and medium-sized enterprises. The countries of Eastern Europe that are not yet EU accession candidates are expected to be the principal focus of our activities. However, we will continue to direct our efforts towards the less developed countries in Africa, Asia and Latin America. Private investors play a major role, because sustainable development cannot be attained in the absence of professional private-sector initiative.

PART III:

Pioneering Banks and Bankers in Southeast Europe

Introduction to Part III

Three experts experienced in banking in Southeast Europe outline how their organisations entered the SEE market, each in a different way. Their pioneering activities reveal a variety of commercial strategies and incentives, focusing on different banking functions and market segments.

RZB's Strategic Entry into SEE Banking

The Raiffeisen Banking Group (RZB), Austria's largest privately-owned financial institution, established 10 banks and acquired four others in Eastern Europe and Russia between 1987 and 2001. Alexander Witte compares the options of either opening a greenfield bank or of acquiring an existing bank in a transition market. The greenfield bank starts with a clean slate, often replicates an existing model and is therefore less costly to set up; it can usually achieve rapid growth and gain market share quickly, especially where local banks are not dynamic. Acquisition provides instant market share, a familiar local brand name, a loan portfolio and a deposit base. The question is whether an acquisition is worth the price. Integrating the acquired bank into the existing corporate structure is often painful and time-consuming, in many cases large numbers of staff have to be let go, and skeletons may be found in the closet.

Raiffeisenbanka Jugoslavija, a greenfield entry, started operating in June 2001. IFC holds a 10% equity stake, and EBRD provided €10 million in subordinated debt. These investors also have stakes in large enterprises in Serbia, making these firms more attractive to commercial lenders such as Raiffeisenbanka Jugoslavija. Another benefit provided by IFC and EBRD is their assistance in helping governments to modernise regulations and infrastructure in ways that lower the costs of doing business. By the end of 2002, Raiffeisenbanka Jugoslavija's loan portfolio exceeded €40 million, of which approximately €2 million consisted of retail lending. The bank had managed to attract deposits of about €150 million, partly due to citizens' mistrust of locally owned banks. It is active in the money market, broke even in its first year, and provides 15-year mortgage loans.

Microenterprise Banks as Private Sector Vehicles for Commercial Development

A number of microenterprise banks (MEBs) have been established in Southeast Europe: FEFAD Bank in Albania, MEB Bosnia, ProCredit Bank in Bulgaria, Microenterprise Credit in Moldova, Miro Bank in Romania, MEB Kosovo, and the Microfinance Bank in Yugoslavia. Two others, the Microfinance Bank of Georgia and Microfinance Bank in the Ukraine, operate in their respective Eastern European markets.

Claus-Peter Zeitinger founded Internationale Projekt Consult (IPC) more than 20 years ago. The firm has advised and managed many microfinance institutions (MFIs). It became an enthusiastic investor in and co-founder of new MFIs as a result of participation in an initiative launched by IFC in BiH in 1996 in which the technical assistance provider was also required to become an equity partner, as described by Ahmed's paper in Part II above. In 1998, and based on this experience, IPC founded IMI (Internationale Micro Investitionen AG), an investment company specialising in microfinance that provides capital to MFIs in which IPC has an interest. Current shareholders in IMI include KfW, BIO, Commerzbank, DOEN Foundation, FMO, IPC and others. IMI constitutes an indirect link between microfinance and capital markets, offering potential for the development of direct links.

Zeitinger lists three defining characteristics of MEBs: supervision by a bank regulator, emphasis on lending to micro and small enterprises, and thirst for local deposits as a basis for loan portfolio growth. By the end of 2002, IMI's equity capital totaled € 26.5 million and it had participations in 17 institutions. These institutions generally require start-up subsidies for a period of two or three years. Zeitinger notes that although these banks, like NGOs, are in some respects unconventional, their commercial banking skills enable them to provide clients with loans of between € 1,000 and € 50,000 on a profitable basis. The great bulk of these client loans are for amounts of less than € 10,000. The MEBs are financially sound and their results highly satisfactory (see www.imi-ag.com), often superior to those of local commercial banks in SEE.

The rapid growth achieved by these banks is made possible by three factors: a simple yet thorough approach to credit analysis, loan officers motivated by incentives, and acceptance of unconventional collateral. MEBs in several markets have been exceedingly successful in deposit taking, but growth has been so rapid in the region generally that more funding, especially equity capital, is urgently sought.

The MEBs are designed to offer a full range of banking services useful to the target group. Full-service banking is worthwhile and profitable for institutions that can provide such services efficiently. Jan Baechle describes the characteristics of microfinance banks in which Commerzbank has invested, following initial experience acquired in MEB Kosovo. Baechle outlines the general characteristics of these banks: a relatively uniform shareholder structure centred on IMI's involvement, initial capital of € 5 – € 10 million, total assets of € 100 million within two or three years of operation, a return on investment of 15% after tax, loan sizes of up to € 250,000 with maturities not exceeding three years repayable monthly, portfolio arrears rates of 3% or less, a staff of up to 200 trained by IPC, a wide branch network, a range of retail banking services, national and international payments capacity including import and export financing and settlements, and good management information systems in line with IAS. Commerzbank serves as the correspondent bank for each of the MEBs in which it has invested.

Commerzbank may be the first multinational commercial bank to make arm's length investments in microfinance, apart from some cases outside SEE in which local banks are part-owners of microfinance institutions to which they provide local currency funding and related services. Between 2000 and 2002, Commerzbank invested in MEBs in Albania, Bosnia and Herzegovina, Bulgaria, Georgia, Kosovo, Romania, Serbia and Montenegro. It supplies specialists in transactions and systems and also trains local staff in these areas. Commerzbank's participation has demonstrated beyond doubt the developmental importance of payments services for micro, small and medium-sized businesses, and for many other account holders who receive or send funds locally or across national borders. The level of demand in Southeast Europe surprised even Commerzbank. The result is better integration of businesses and financial sectors throughout the region due to the reduction in transaction costs associated with foreign and domestic trade.

One of Commerzbank's strategic objectives is to capitalise on its state-of-the-art payments mechanisms by creating platforms in these new banks without the costs of establishing full branches under its own banner. At the same time, it is gaining valuable country-specific know-how and contacts. Due to the successes achieved to date, Commerzbank has no plans to exit the markets it has helped create. It does not rule out increasing its regional presence through these banks, especially where strategic goals are being achieved by the MEBs ahead of schedule.

CHAPTER 9:

Market Entry in Southeast Europe – Raiffeisenbank Belgrade

Alexander Witte

Head of Risk Management, Raiffeisenbank a.d., Belgrade, Yugoslavia

RZB Group

Raiffeisen Zentralbank Österreich AG (RZB) is the central institution of the Austrian Raiffeisen group. RZB has for many years recognised the vast potential of the emerging Central and Eastern European (CEE) markets on its doorstep. In 1987, before the fall of the Berlin Wall, RZB started to penetrate these markets by co-founding a joint venture bank in Hungary in collaboration with a German commercial bank and the International Finance Corporation (IFC). The opening of the CEE markets in 1989/1990 gave RZB's growth strategy a major boost: in many cases it was the first Western commercial bank to enter these markets, as in Poland, Slovakia and Bulgaria. Today, RZB has subsidiaries in 14 countries in the region (see Box 1) with 600 branches employing more than 12,000 people. The total assets of RZB's CEE network reached €45 billion in 2001, and the CEE subsidiaries contributed more than 50% to the group's total earnings.

Why Yugoslavia?[1]

As the people of Yugoslavia took to the streets in 2000 to bring about the peaceful changes that would set the country on its way towards democracy and a market economy, RZB's board commissioned a feasibility study for a subsidiary bank in Yugoslavia. RZB's reasons for such a quick move into this new emerging market were several:

---

[1] Author's note: This article was written prior to the assassination of the Serbian Prime Minister Zoran Djindjic on 12 March 2003. I have since reviewed this article in the light of this tragic event and the developments following it, and I feel no need to change my optimistic assessment of Serbia's economic future and Raiffeisenbank's prospects in the Serbian financial market.

Box 1: Development of RZB's CEE Network

Year of Entry	Bank	Country	Head Office
1987	Raiffeisenbank Rt.	Hungary	Budapest
1991	Raiffeisenbank Polska S.A.	Poland	Warsaw
1991	Tatrabanka a.s.	Slovakia	Bratislava
1993	Raiffeisenbank a.s.	Czech Republic	Prague
1994	Raiffeisenbank (Bulgaria) A.D.	Bulgaria	Sofia
1994	Raiffeisenbank Austria d.d.	Croatia	Zagreb
1997	CJSC Raiffeisenbank Austria	Russia	Moscow
1998	Raiffeisenbank Ukraine	Ukraine	Kiev
1998	Raiffeisenbank Romania S.A.	Romania	Bucharest
2000	Raiffeisenbank Bosna & Herzegovina d.d.*	Bosnia and Herzegovina	Sarajevo
2001	Raiffeisenbank HPB*	Bosnia and Herzegovina	Mostar
2001	Banka Agricola S.A.*	Romania	Bucharest
2001	Krekova Banka*	Slovenia	Maribor
2001	Raiffeisenbank a.d.	Serbia and Montenegro	Belgrade

* acquisition

- with a population of 10.5 million, Yugoslavia presented one of the few remaining untapped markets in Central and Eastern Europe;

- with only one Western bank operating in the country at the time, the first wholly-owned subsidiary of a Western bank would enjoy a decisive first mover advantage;

- RZB had confidence in Yugoslavia's prospects for rapid transition: as one of the last to embark on the transition process, Yugoslavia (and the multinational donors active in the country) would be able to draw on the experience gathered in other CEE countries;

- the Raiffeisen brand was already well known in Yugoslavia. Many Yugoslav nationals working in Austria in the 80s and early 90s placed their savings in local Raiffeisen banks;

- experience in Croatia, Bosnia and Herzegovina and in other successor countries of ex-Yugoslavia in which RZB had been operating for several years, indicated that this was a favourable opportunity. Synergies could be generated as the traditional trading links between the ex-Yugoslav republics were restored.

Federal Republic of Yugoslavia[2]

Yugoslavia is the largest successor state of the late Socialist Federal Republic of Yugoslavia. It comprises the former Yugoslav republics of Serbia and Montenegro, and includes Kosovo, an autonomous province within Serbia.

Apart from plunging the country into four successive wars, the Milosevic regime delayed the transition to a market economy by some ten years. Attempts to privatise state enterprises resulted in either an inefficient transfer of ownership to employees or in giving away the "crown jewels" to cronies of the regime. The country's banking system also suffered: four of the largest banks were declared bankrupt in January 2002.

After the democratic changes, Serbia's new government under Zoran Djindjic embarked on an ambitious reform programme with emphasis on rapid privatisation and attracting foreign investment. The initial results are encouraging: foreign debt has been largely rescheduled and in part forgiven, a number of large enterprises (notably cement plants) have been sold to major foreign investors, inflation is now stable and average per capita income (€ 140 in 2002) is gradually rising. Nevertheless, much remains to be done and success will ultimately depend on foreign direct investment (FDI), support from multinational donors and the population's realisation that improvements in the living standard will not come overnight.

On the basis of its feasibility study, RZB decided to limit the subsidiary's area of operations to Serbia proper and to manage operations in Kosovo via a separate unit. RZB later acquired the USAID-sponsored American Bank of Kosovo. Montenegro, the smaller partner republic with a population of 600,000, is pursuing an independent economic policy, with the euro as the official domestic currency and an independent central bank. A separate licence would be required to set up an outlet in Montenegro.

Banking Sector

At the close of 2002, 47 banks were operating in Yugoslavia, which leaves ample space for consolidation. Several Western banks (mainly German and Greek) entered the market after RZB, but the degree of foreign ownership still remains very low at 8% of aggregate capital. Despite the comparative stability of the dinar,

---

[2] The Federal Republic of Yugoslavia ceased to exist in February 2003, having been replaced by a loose confederation of Serbia and Montenegro.

practically all transactions between Yugoslav economic entities are either indexed to the euro or performed directly (and illegally) in foreign currency.

With numerous banking scandals in the early 90s and the collapse of the four largest banks in early 2002, one would expect public confidence in the banking system to be severely shaken. Although the constant growth in retail savings deposits shows that the remaining banks do enjoy a certain degree of confidence, it is estimated that only 25% of total savings is held in banks, with the remainder, around €4 billion, still stashed under mattresses.

Without a functioning capital market, long-term finance is hardly available in Yugoslavia and interest rates remain high, making badly needed investments in new equipment extremely difficult.

Acquisition vs. Greenfield Investment

It has long been RZB's strategy to enter new markets with a 100% greenfield investment. The reasons for such an approach are that:

- it avoids having to take over a troubled loan portfolio and superfluous staff;

- no restructuring costs are incurred;

- organisational "blueprints" already proven in other markets may be used;

- initial investment can be kept low to minimise risk.

This strategy proved its worth in the early stages of CEE market penetration, when RZB was in many cases the first entrant into a new market and competition from international and domestic banks was low. However, with the growing sophistication of local competition and accelerating economic development, the need for "instant market share" has become increasingly pressing, and RZB has decided to acquire existing banks in several new markets.

Quick Set-up, Rapid Development

A greenfield approach was chosen in Yugoslavia because local competition was comparatively weak and international competitors had only a limited presence. This concept has been proved right.

After obtaining a banking license in March 2001, Raiffeisenbank a.d. started operations in July 2001 – the fastest set-up within RZB's CEE Network. Raiffeisenbank's initial capital amounted to €10 million and has since increased to €35 million, including a €10 million subordinated loan provided by EBRD. RZB, as the parent company, holds 90% of the shares, 10% being held by the International Finance Corporation (IFC), with which RZB has enjoyed good working relations since entering CEE markets in the late 80s. The window of opportunity seized by RZB has since closed: in August 2001, the National Bank of Yugoslavia stopped issuing licenses for foreign bank subsidiaries, forcing new entrants to acquire existing Yugoslav banks. One of the reasons for this change in strategy is to shift some of the burden of restructuring the banking system to foreign entrants.

At the end of 2002, Raiffeisenbank employed 350 people in 10 branches throughout Yugoslavia. Only four employees were expatriates. Most local employees have 3-4 years experience and were hired from domestic banks. Most required very little training during the conversion to Western banking practices. The former Yugoslavia was open to the West, and knowledge of foreign languages is widely spread; many people are highly proficient in English and often in German. The skills and the enthusiastic attitude of the young local staff were among the major reasons for Raiffeisen's rapid expansion and growth in the Yugoslav market.

At the close of 2001, the bank's corporate loan portfolio amounted to a mere €2.75 million, but a major success was achieved in retail banking: at end-2001, foreign currency deposits exceeded €100 million, making Raiffeisenbank the second largest in terms of deposits, with a market share of 20%, close behind a domestic bank with a 10-year track record in this market.

By the end of 2002, Raiffeisenbank's corporate loan portfolio had reached €50 million, with an additional €5 million in retail loans. This rapid growth was achieved by adopting a focused strategy based on a clear definition of the bank's target client group and a proactive approach to clients, clearly a novelty in the local financial market. The fact that Raiffeisenbank posted a profit in the first full year of operation underscores its favourable development.

The bank has actively supported the privatisation process by advising international companies interested in investing in Yugoslavia, offering payment and foreign exchange services and providing working capital finance to newly-privatised companies. Though loans of up to one year still account for 80% of the portfolio, long-term finance (typically for tenors of three to five years, depending on the asset financed and projected cash flow) is increasingly offered to selected clients. Loan collateral usually comprises a combination of mortgages, pledges on inventories and assignments of export receivables. Loans to subsidiaries of foreign corporations are typically secured by a guarantee or a letter of comfort issued by the foreign parent company. The main challenges in corporate credit are the notoriously unreliable financial statements, legal uncertainty concerning collateral and slow and cumbersome court procedures.

Retail and SME

Despite success in attracting retail deposits, much remains to be done in retail lending. Low per-capita income dampens the demand for retail loans, which have been slow to gather pace. Another reason for the comparatively low demand for personal loans is a specifically Yugoslav phenomenon: while incomes may be low at present, a major part of the population still has access to savings from "better times". Major purchases are made in cash rather than by taking an expensive bank loan. Prohibitively high insurance charges make car loans unattractive.

Mortgage finance is a potentially attractive market due to Yugoslavs' traditional preference for home ownership. However, progress in this area is constrained by the lack of long-term funds and legal uncertainty – more than 80% of property is still not registered. According to Raiffeisenbank, mortgage loans still have excellent potential once the government's land registration efforts are successfully concluded and a mortgage insurance agency is in place.

For several reasons, SME finance will constitute an important element in Raiffeisenbank's future corporate strategy. With the expected market entry of major Western competitors, such as Citigroup and ING, margins for large corporate business are likely to erode. However, experience in other CEE countries has shown that healthy margins can be earned in the SME segment at comparatively low risk. Besides, the fast-growing SME market has been largely neglected by most domestic banks and foreign entrants.

Outlook

Raiffeisenbank's vision is to become one of Yugoslavia's three major banks. To achieve this goal, the bank's future strategy will focus on the SME and retail segments while maintaining a strong position in the corporate market. With the transfer of the domestic payment system from the Central Bank Clearing Office (ZOP) to commercial banks, the last "protected sector" has been opened to competition. Raiffeisenbank, with a client base of 36,000, is well positioned to acquire a significant share of this new market.

Well aware of the risks inherent in deficient legislation and jurisprudence, Raiffeisenbank will nevertheless start a residential mortgage programme with tenors of up to 15 years, which are yet to be matched by other foreign-owned banks. This strategy is based on RZB's favourable experience with mortgage lending in other CEE markets and Raiffeisenbank's confidence in the rapid recovery of the Yugoslav economy. The bank will also selectively explore opportunities in commercial property development projects involving international property developers who have a proven record in the region, and with reliable general contractors and attractive anchor tenants.

In a move to meet the pent-up demand for investment finance, Raiffeisenbank will establish a leasing subsidiary in cooperation with Raiffeisen Leasing International, RZB's CEE leasing arm. This company will give local clients access to modern Western equipment, and also offer car leasing to retail customers.

Branch development will continue at a fast pace to keep up with Raiffeisenbank's corporate clients' demands, while also targeting areas with attractive retail business opportunities. Branching will be complemented by Raiffeisenbank's recently launched an e-Banking product that has been well received by the bank's corporate clients and will soon be offered to retail customers.

Completing its second year of operations in 2003, Raiffeisenbank looks well set to achieve its vision of becoming one of the leading banks in Yugoslavia.

CHAPTER 10:

Sustainable Microfinance Banks – Problems and Perspectives

Claus-Peter Zeitinger

Managing Director, IPC GmbH, Frankfurt, Germany

In 1998 we founded Internationale Micro Investitionen AG (IMI), the first private institution established to invest in commercially-oriented microfinance banks (MFBs) worldwide. By MFBs we mean institutions which

- are subject to supervision by a banking supervisory authority and required to adhere to banking legislation;

- have a clear focus on lending to micro and small enterprises; and

- attract local deposits, which helps the MFB become less reliant on international credit lines.

IMI's founders consisted exclusively of private investors: IPC GmbH, IPC-Invest GbR and two foundations: DOEN and ProCrédito. Later they were joined by IFIs (international financial institutions): DEG (KfW Group), IFC (World Bank Group), the Dutch FMO, the Belgian BIO and more recently by KfW. As of June 2003, IMI's equity capital stood at €35.1 million, provided by the following shareholders: IFC (19%), IPC GmbH and IPC Invest GbR (33%), DOEN (19%), FMO (9%), ProCrédito (2%), KfW/DEG (9%) and BIO (9%).

As of June 2003, IMI's capital was invested in ten institutions in Eastern Europe[1], five in Latin America and the Caribbean and three in Africa and the Philippines.

Although these financial institutions are still very young – all but two founded since 1998 – their initial start-up losses have been low: 12 of the 18 institutions are already earning a profit. This is possible only because many organisations supported the establishment and development of the new MFBs, providing TA (technical assistance) funds for institution building and training.

---

[1] The 10 institutions in Eastern Europe include nine banks and one finance company (Micro Enterprise Credit, Moldova).

Features of MFBs

In addition to the opportunities which present themselves to this new type of bank, there are also limitations and problems. These factors, both positive and negative, can be illustrated by looking at the nine institutions in Eastern Europe in which IMI has a share or which the management consultancy IPC has supported during their start-up phases. These MFBs typify the network as greenfield commercial banks that provide credit and other banking services to the target group. The average loan size is higher in Eastern European banks than in Latin America or Africa, but the basic features are highly similar.

Ownership

All are majority-owned by IMI shareholders: four organisations hold over 66% of total equity capital.

Table 1. Shareholder Structure of the Eastern European Microfinance Banks (million)

	Bosnia & Herzegowina (€)	Albania (€)	Georgia (US$)	Kosovo (€)	Ukraine (US$)	Serbia (€)	Bulgaria (€)	Romania (US$)	Macedonia (€)	
KfW/DEG	0.6	1.9	2.0	1.66	3.0	2.0	2.4	2.8	1.25	17.61
IMI	4.6	1.1	3.9	1.66	3.0	2.0	2.4	1.6	1.55	21.81
IFC	–	1.5	1.6	1.66	3.0	2.0	2.4	2.6	0.95	15.71
FMO	–		–	1.66		2.0		0.9		4.56
EBRD	1.8	1.5	1.0	1.66	3.0	2.0	2.4	2.8	1.25	17.41
Commerzbank	1.0	1.5	0.1	1.66		2.0	2.4	2.8		11.46
IPC			1.4							1.40
others			0.1		3.0					3.10
total	8.0	7.5	10.1	10.0	15.0	12.0	12.0	13.5	5.0	93.06

Lending Operations

MFB's lending operations focus primarily on microenterprises taking loans of less than € 10,000. As of mid 2003, 93.3% of all loans outstanding at eight banks (excluding the bank in Macedonia, which started operating in July 2003) were to enterprises taking loans of less than € 10,000. A further 5.9% of all outstanding loans went to enterprises borrowing between € 10,000 and € 50,000. We define this group as small loan customers. The remainder, i.e. 0.8% of all outstanding loans, went to enterprises taking loans of more than € 50,000, i.e. medium loan customers.

As of mid 2003, the eight banks then in operation had almost 96,000 loans outstanding. This roughly reflects the number of enterprises or entrepreneurs who

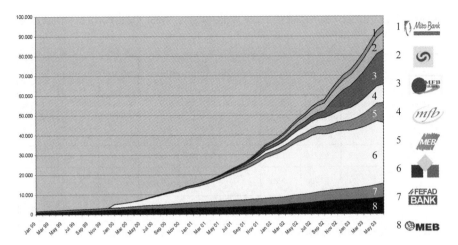

Figure 1. Eastern European Banks' Number of Outstanding Loans, January 1999–June 2003

received a loan. In most cases, they could not have obtained a similar loan from a traditional commercial bank. To illustrate the level of productivity being achieved, about 12,000 loans are disbursed every month by about 700 loan officers employed in these banks.

MFBs issue loans after meticulous and labour-intensive analysis, but without applying the rigid requirements normally set by traditional banks, such as certified accounts, a business plan and excessive collateral. Precisely because of this information-based and not primarily asset-based lending, the MFBs' portfolio quality is very high – considerably higher than at most other banks – as the arrears rates for a recent three-year period illustrates. The arrears of eight Eastern European banks expressed as portfolio at risk (more than 30 days overdue) and measured at month-end from January 2001 to June 2003 averaged less than 1%. Six banks had average arrears rates of less than 1%. Four banks had no instances in which their arrears rates exceeded 1.5%. ("Portfolio at risk" consists of the entire outstanding balance of loans on which one or more instalments is overdue, and is commonly expressed as a percentage of the gross loan portfolio.) Write-off rates also indicate robust portfolio quality.

Development Outreach

MFB loans are intended to integrate small enterprises into the economic system and thus into the new societies emerging in their respective countries. It is precisely this small-enterprise sector which creates new jobs when downsizing and plant closures decrease employment elsewhere in the economy. Thus, we should focus on the number of loan contracts concluded, which roughly reflects the number of customers we have reached. Overall portfolio volume is a secondary concern.

Table 2. Eastern European Banks' Total Write-offs vs Total Loan Portfolio, December 2001–June 2003

	2001			2002			June 2003		
	Total Loan Write-Offs in Year (€ '000s)	Total Out-standing Loan Portfolio at Year End (€ '000s)	As %	Total Loan Write-Offs in Year (€ '000s)	Total Out-standing Loan Portfolio at Year End (€ '000s)	As %	Total Loan Write-Offs in Year (€ '000s)	Total Out-standing Loan Portfolio at Year End (€ '000s)	As %
MEB, Bosnia	57	19,310	0.3%	82	31,967	0.3%	95	38,345	0.2%
FEFAD Bank, Albania	89	17,700	0.5%	74	28,406	0.3%	0	38,789	0.0%
Microfinance Bank, Georgia	178	31,180	0.7%	1,482	33,097	4.5%	163	34,007	0.5%
MEB, Kosovo	0	10,590	–	20	22,600	0.1%	45	48,172	0.1%
Miro Bank, Romania	0	4,820	–	91	10,104	0.9%	42	12,386	0.3%
Microfinance Bank, Ukraine	0	10,033	–	0	24,815	0.0%	0	33,817	0.0%
Microfinance Bank, Yugoslavia	0	8,800	–	0	32,222	0.0%	31	52,939	0.1%
ProCredit Bank, Bulgaria	0	5,330	–	9	27,921	0.0%	1	45,567	0.0%
Total	324	107,763	0.3%	1,758	211,132	0.8%	378	304,091	0.1%

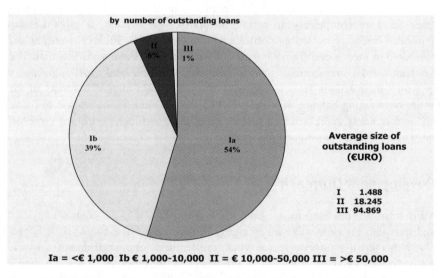

Figure 2. Breakdown of the Combined Portfolio of the Eastern European Banks by Loan Size (June 2003)

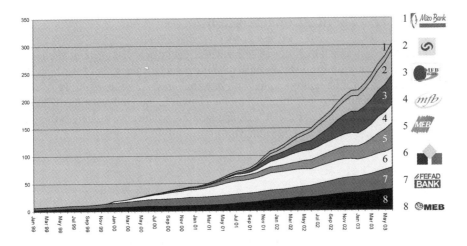

Figure 3. Eastern European Banks' Volume of Outstanding Loans, January 1999 – June 2003

At the end of 1999, when the first four MFBs had been in existence for about a year, they had a total of just 5,000 loan clients. In the course of 2000, new MFBs were added, and the total number of customers reached about 14,000 by the end of that year. By the end of 2001, this figure had more than doubled to 30,000, and by the end of 2002 it was almost 62,000. It is realistic to assume that the MFBs will have 100,000 borrowers by the end of 2003.

Portfolio growth by volume has been at least as impressive, if not more so. This is due to the considerable increase in the number of new customers and to the expanding volume of business with repeat borrowers. From a modest € 20 million in 1999, the total portfolio climbed to € 40 million in 2000 and to € 110 million in 2001. By mid-2003, the eight banks achieved a combined portfolio volume of € 300 million. With their existing infrastructure and excellent human capital, the banks' combined portfolio will reach € 1 billion between 2005 and 2006.

The Necessity of Innovation and Expansion

The growth in the MFBs' international money transfer business over the last three years illustrates their development as universal banks and their widening business and income base. To remain competitive and dynamic, these banks require the capacity to offer larger loans for medium-sized enterprises, and to manage these customers' accounts, which includes executing domestic and international payment transactions on their behalf. Products and services such as letters of credit, e-banking, consumer lending, credit cards and ATMs have a key role in enabling the MFBs to build successful business relationships with these types of customers.

Funding and Service Considerations

One major constraint which could prevent the banks from exploiting their full potential, however, is the liability side of their balance sheets, i.e. financing the banks' growth through equity capital and external funds. The availability of outside capital depends first and foremost on the growth in the volume of local deposits and on the willingness of the IFIs to accept a higher level of risk by providing more capital.

Deposit Growth

The total deposits held by the network of Eastern European microfinance banks exceeds their total outstanding loan portfolio. However, the bulk of the deposits is accounted for by only two countries, Kosovo and Albania. For regulatory reasons, these funds cannot be used to finance related institutions in other countries.

In order to achieve controlled and steady growth in deposits from local customers, the MFBs must increasingly act as full service banks and offer all of the products customers demand. However, this means that the banks must attract deposits from medium-sized enterprises and private households. They can do this by offering appropriately designed banking products on both the liability side and the asset side. This process has begun at most of the MFBs, and it is enhancing their level of professionalism and raising the level of technology they employ.

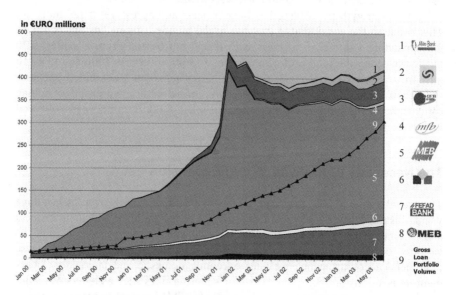

Figure 4.   Eastern European Banks' Deposit Volume Development vs Gross Loan Portfolio, January 2000 – June 2003

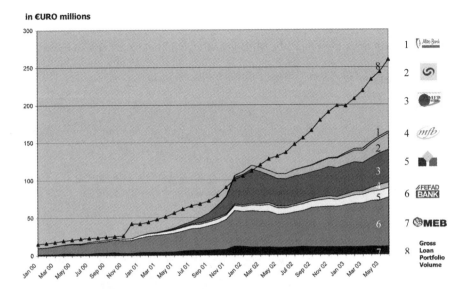

Figure 5. Deposit Volume Development vs Gross Loan Portfolio, January 2000 – June 2003, Eastern European Banks excluding MEB Kosovo

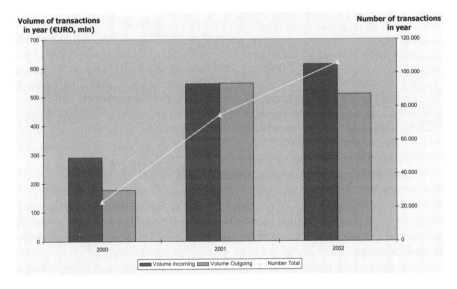

Figure 6. Eastern European Banks' International Money Transfer Business, 2000, 2001 and 2002

The Essential Role of IFIs

Without credit lines from the IFIs, MFB growth would not have been so robust.

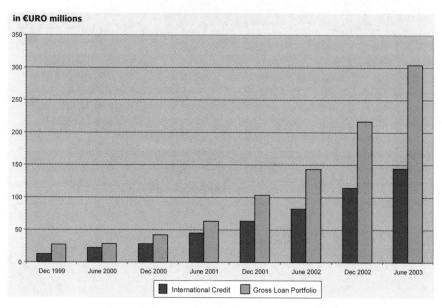

Figure 7. Eastern European Banks' International Credit Lines vs Gross Loan Portfolio,
December 1999–June 2003

An important role has been played in particular by the EBRD and KfW, which together provided some 68% of the nine MFBs' international onlending funds at the end of June 2003. Most other IFIs seem to find it comparatively difficult to make credit lines available at the right time or on an appropriate scale. At the end of 2002, it was still virtually impossible to obtain onlending funds from commercial banks. Either they regard the MFBs as too small, or their internal risk classifications tell them that the country risks associated with the MFBs are too high.

Without further external lines of credit, the MFBs will not be able to sustain their present rate of portfolio growth. This is because there is a limit to the degree to which deposit growth can be accelerated, even if the MFBs offer substantially increased interest rates. Deposit growth is determined by the reputation a bank is able to build, and also by the extent to which it expands its branch network. Both of these take time.

The growth of the banks makes it necessary to increase their equity capital on a continuous basis. To date, all of the MFBs' profits have been reinvested in the capital of the banks belonging to the network. Notwithstanding the MFBs' attractive growth prospects, it will probably take another five years before net cash flows come back to the owners. In early 2003, the group of eight MFBs had combined equity totalling roughly € 75 million, and the positive trend is expected to continue.

Extraordinary Success and Consolidation

The picture presented so far of the MFBs in Eastern Europe is one of success in development policy terms, more success than we ever dreamed of at the outset. Precisely because the formal markets neglect the financing of small enterprises, these new banks are encountering tremendous demand. The further the banks' already impressive branch networks expand, the stronger this demand becomes.

And this demand is not only for small enterprise loans, but for all kinds of banking services. Therefore, we are forced to consider whether this success – and the understandable desire to perpetuate it and build upon it – obliges us to contemplate a more appropriate and efficient structure for the MFBs in Eastern Europe. That is why IMI, as the strategic investor, proposed to the other shareholders of the Eastern European MFBs and the other MFBs worldwide the creation of a single framework for all of these banks. The reasons for this have already been made clear above:

- the growing need for equity,

- the continuing appetite for onlending funds from external sources,

- the necessity of using deposits mobilised by the more successful deposit-takers to provide loanable funds to the other MFBs, thus balancing out liquidity mismatches,

- the potential to achieve a substantial reduction in the at present comparatively high administrative costs and corporate governance expenses associated with running a loose network of legally independent banks, and

- the considerable potential for synergies among the MFBs.

The single framework now being discussed entails the establishment of a commercial bank to be registered in Frankfurt which, apart from conducting limited banking business in Germany, would primarily function as a holding company for the MFBs worldwide. They would become subsidiaries of the newly created international bank. This would generate numerous advantages over their current status as independent MFBs:

- key treasury operations could be managed centrally, and thus more efficiently and economically.

- some of the deposits from "liquidity surplus countries" could be reinvested in "liquidity deficit countries".

- the German bank holding company, with its diversified portfolio of investments, could obtain funds on much better terms than the individual institutions.

- the costs associated with the management and corporate governance of the individual institutions could be significantly reduced.

- further savings could be achieved by centralising training and software development and by enabling the efficient promotion and spread of best practices in products, procedures and marketing, and not least,

- a public listing of this new business entity would attract new shareholders and provide the participating IFIs with an exit strategy.

In addition to the obvious potential for increased efficiency that a holding structure of this kind would imply, there are a number of development-related arguments in favour of this proposal:

- to achieve the goal of reaching hundreds of thousands of customers it is necessary to have a solid structure from which to launch our activities.

- to mobilise loanable funds, mainly in the form of local deposits rather than international credit lines, it is important to have a competitive international bank with a strong brand and a favourable image.

- to go beyond our core business with micro customers and serve the still underdeveloped SME market, as a technically sophisticated, professionally competent bank offering a wide range of products is essential.

That bank would play a key role in most of the financial markets of developing and transition countries in which it operates, and it would make a decisive impact in improving the supply of financial services, especially for small businesses.

CHAPTER 11:

Equity Participation in Microfinance Banks in Southeast Europe and Georgia – A Strategic Option for a Large Private German Bank?

Jan Baechle

Former Senior Vice President and Head of the Central and East Europe Department, Commerzbank AG, Frankfurt, Germany

What Are Microfinance Banks?

Microfinance banks are institutions that concentrate mainly on issuing small and very small commercial loans to small businesses and private persons in developing countries and transition economies. This group of institutions is large in number and comprises banks with widely different attributes.

In Southeast Europe and Georgia, Commerzbank has invested in microfinance banks which have the following common characteristics:

- uniform shareholder structure: at their inception, the microfinance banks' shareholder structures are very similar, with share capital provided in approximately equal amounts by five institutions: the European Bank for Reconstruction and Development (EBRD), the International Finance Corporation (IFC, part of the World Bank Group), Kreditanstalt für Wiederaufbau and Deutsche Investitions- und Entwicklungsgesellschaft mbH (KfW Group), Internationale Micro Investitionen and Internationale Projekt Consult (IMI AG and IPC GmbH) and Commerzbank AG. In some cases, two Dutch entities, the development corporation FMO and the DOEN Foundation, also participate.

- similar basic financial and operating structure in terms of a) balance sheet: a target of approximately €100 million in total assets within two to three years of the commencement of operations; b) share capital: depending on national regulations, initial share capital amounts to between €5 and €10 million; c) number of staff: up to 200, trained and instructed by IPC GmbH, a specialised consulting company in Frankfurt; d) loan portfolio arrears rate: the total outstanding balances of loans more than 30 days in arrears is less than 3%; e) return on equity: the target is approximately 15% after tax; f) wide branch network: aggressive branching where feasible; g) maximum loan size: € 250,000 or less. Amounts exceeding the upper limit require approval by the supervisory board; h) term of loans: up to 3 years, repayable in monthly instalments; i) other banking services: domestic and international payment transactions, import and export financing and settlements. Simple private customer products such as current account management, savings accounts and term money accounts, credit cards; j) business and accounting practices: in accordance with international standards using the most up-to-date EDP equipment in compliance with IAS.

In Which Microfinance Banks Has Commerzbank Participated?

Commerzbank participates in the equity capital of FEFAD Bank, Tirana, Albania; ProCredit Bank, Sofia, Bulgaria; Microenterprise Bank, Sarajevo, Bosnia and Herzegovina; MIRO Bank, Bucharest, Romania; Microfinance Bank, Belgrade, Serbia and Montenegro; Microenterprise Bank Kosovo, Prishtina, Kosovo; Microfinance Bank of Georgia, Tbilisi, Georgia. In all these countries, Germany is among the leading foreign trade and investment partners.

Commerzbank's Business Motives

- a regional concept for Southeast Europe and Georgia: structural reforms have reached an advanced stage in many transition countries, such as Hungary, Poland, the Czech Republic, Slovakia and Slovenia, while the reforms in Bulgaria, Romania and the successor states of Yugoslavia began later and have progressed more slowly. Until recently, direct foreign investment in industry and trade in these latter countries was also correspondingly lower, which meant that there was no customer base that would justify banks' setting up their own branch networks – a practice successfully adopted by Commerzbank in industrialised countries. Participation in microfinance banks thus offered an alternative to the go-it-alone approach.

- risk limitation: Commerzbank's total investment in the microfinance banks in these seven countries amounts to approximately € 10 million. This limits and spreads risk, which seems appropriate in these high-risk countries.

- concentration on the bank's strengths: as a trading bank with a great tradition which handles about 17% of German trade with Central and East Europe, Commerzbank can have a positive impact on the micro-finance banks by contributing its expertise in international trade and international payment transactions. In these microfinance banks, Commerzbank assumes responsibility for precisely this task. While the other shareholders concentrate mainly on their development mission, international payment transactions and foreign trade are at the forefront of Commerzbank's efforts.

- serving Commerzbank's small and medium-sized clients in challenging locations: through its network of microfinance banks in Southeast Europe, Commerzbank serves its small and medium-sized clients, particularly in Germany, in two respects. First, it offers payment transaction services and an opportunity to expand international business activities, albeit with limited credit facilities; second, it assists sales financing. This is also valuable for large German companies operating in the seven countries.

- cooperation with the other shareholders: close and trusting cooperation with the world's largest development institutions, which are all active in the Balkan countries and Georgia, sometimes leads to unexpected but interesting business opportunities that would not otherwise be possible. We cooperate closely, for instance, with EBRD's trade facility programmes and with Kreditanstalt für Wiederaufbau's loan guarantees for countries such as Bosnia and Herzegovina. KfW's guarantee enables us to make longer-term loans available, which we would be unable to do at our own risk. In the longer term, it is quite conceivable that we shall carry out joint capital market operations in conjunction with funding from the microfinance banks. This would be facilitated by the first-class ratings of the supranational and national development institutions among the microfinance banks' shareholders, helping counter the impact of the country risks inherent in the microfinance banks.

Experience from Two Years of Practice

The first joint founding of a microfinance bank in which Commerzbank participated took place in January 2000 in Kosovo. The most recent participation was in September 2002 in Bosnia and Herzegovina.

How can we sum up the experience gained up to the end of 2002? All microfinance banks in which we have equity investments are operating successfully. On the basis of their conservatively prepared business plans, positive results are becoming evident earlier than anticipated. To a large extent this is due to the efficiency of IPC, which provides the management. Indirectly via its investment affiliate, IMI AG, and directly as a shareholder, IPC participates in the success or failure of these institutions. IPC plays a role which extends far beyond its traditional consulting business in development finance.

The contribution of the national and international development institutions mainly consists of three elements, all of which work successfully:

- they share the risk and participate in business success through their equity interest.

- through their technical assistance funds they make non-repayable subsidies available for the start-up phase of 1 to 2 years. These are used to purchase systems hardware and software, upgrade premises, train local staff, and remunerate expatriate management.

- under their development assistance mandate, they provide long-term loans at market rates which are not yet available in the interbank market. In so doing, they secure funding for the microfinance banks over the long term, allowing them, in turn, to provide loans with maturities of up to 3 years.

Commerzbank's role is also clearly defined: in addition to handling foreign trade and international payment transactions, Commerzbank provides expert staff for temporary or longer-term assignments at the microfinance banks or with IPC. It also offers specialised training for staff from the countries in question, usually at its own expense.

To date, payment transactions and foreign trade services have generated significant earnings for Commerzbank in Kosovo, where the political and economic circumstances place special demands on business activities. We see growth potential in this field for all other microfinance banks, too.

As a shareholder in the microfinance banks, Commerzbank is entitled to a seat on their supervisory boards. Experienced managers are assigned to represent Commerzbank at the supervisory board meetings. These meetings take place four or five times a year and are characterised by their constructive atmosphere and the spirit of trust which prevails – notwithstanding the fact that this constellation of corporate stakeholders is completely new. We regard this as the basis for success. Commerzbank acts as a clearing house for the entire network of microfinance banks and implements active cash management.

Outlook

Even though the reforms in the Balkan countries and Georgia began later and proceeded more slowly than in the other transition countries, there can be no doubt whatsoever that these countries too have "joined the train to Europe". Through our participation in the microfinance banks, we are helping drive this transformation. In a challenging regional setting, we are gathering country know-how which we could otherwise acquire only at very much higher cost.

The shareholders in the microfinance banks agree in principle that ownership structures in these banks should remain unchanged for the first four or five years after their foundation. Only after this period has elapsed, do they intend to consider changes in ownership, for instance because the development mission has been largely accomplished. From Commerzbank's present point of view, it would be worthwhile to continue cooperation for an indefinite period, especially as the microfinance banks are experiencing dynamic growth and require regular injections of capital. These capital increases can be more easily shouldered by several institutions rather than one on its own.

Although the current credit policy primarily targets small and medium-sized clients, many of these will grow by harnessing the dynamic forces of their economies, which will increase their demand for larger loans. Evidence of this is already apparent. In meeting the challenges posed by the increasing commercialisation of development finance in general, Commerzbank – as a bank with a traditional corporate-client focus – can make a meaningful contribution.

Is participation in microfinance banks in the Balkan countries and Georgia a viable strategic option for Commerzbank? On the whole, the question can be clearly answered in the affirmative, both in the current setting and for the longer term. The crucial factor remains the shareholders' commitment and willingness to continue supporting these interesting joint activities, which have got off to such a good start. Initially, the joint founding of microfinance banks was a risk for all shareholders, the more so for Commerzbank as a major private bank. All parties concerned can now be sure that they have developed a concept which is viable on a long-term basis for the promotion of economic development in one of Europe's most challenging regions.

PART IV:

Research and Impact Analysis for Accountability and Management

Introduction to Part IV

KfW's efforts to improve financial sectors in Southeast Europe have been supplemented by impact analyses that include market research. Research has been conducted at the financial sector level, at the level of institutions using KfW-managed funds, and at the level of the entrepreneurs and firms receiving loans and access to other financial services. Relationships among these levels have also been explored. Impact analysis has many controversial aspects based on attribution problems (that is, accurately linking cause and effect) and other limitations of social science research and survey tools. However, KfW supports impact analysis in an effort to improve its analytical techniques and their interpretation, and as an essential element in accountability in the use of public funds. Impact analysis broadly defined includes elements of market research, which is not controversial and especially useful for operational purposes and for refinements in project design.

This Part begins with a statement explaining how rural finance research changed perspectives on activities at the small end of financial markets, where the poor transact. These insights provided a basis for microfinance and stimulated institution building. Evaluation of the impact of interventions in finance has developed more recently, using social science research technique. Applications have focused primarily on microfinance, which is subsidised and often intended to go beyond commercial activity to include poverty alleviation, advancement of women's access to finance, and other social and even environmental objectives.

The Contribution of Research

Recent attempts to identify the impact of financial sector projects and credit lines have roots in research begun in universities during the popularity in rural finance in the 1970s and 1980s. The issues identified at that time provided a basis for more comprehensive approaches and exploration of more complex relationships. Throughout, the question has been how to make finance more productive for the intended beneficiaries of development projects and for society in general.

Franz Heidhues of the University of Hohenheim describes six crucial contributions by the research community over the last 30 years that have illuminated government and market failure and led to innovations in public policy and alternative models of the role of finance in development. First, low interest rates of credit projects in the past produced adverse consequences because they created the wrong incentives. Low repayment rates resulted. Second, in the informal sector, group formation and social cohesion resolve information problems and keep costs low through honourary (volunteer) management. Borrowers can generally use loan funds as they please, according to their private priorities. Third, savings are an important component of a sustainable rural financial system: rural savings are highly valued and their volume is substantial.

Fourth, the relevance of rural finance is proportionate to outreach. Greater outreach occurs only when institutions increase their efficiency and improve the quality of their services. Subsidies for institution building are justified in those cases in which microfinance is a public good. Fifth, microfinance is a means of poverty alleviation, especially when it is directed toward women. Loans and other services enable poor households to increase their income, diversify their activities, and to deal with risks more effectively. Sixth, markets for credit and savings are also markets for insurance. Creation of larger networks offer scope for dealing with local covariate risk. Consumption smoothing through saving and borrowing permits households to get through lean periods and regain their normal standard of living without sacrificing their material assets. In this way, access to rural finance can prevent transitory insecurity from causing chronic poverty.

Professor Heidhues offers prescriptions for innovations in the regulatory framework, in the structural and operational reform of financial institutions, and for the provision of high quality services to small entrepreneurs.

Methodological Issues in Impact Analysis

Elizabeth Dunn of the University of Missouri provides a comprehensive view and definitive statement of the issues involved in determining the impact of projects in which donors make funds available to micro, small and medium-sized businesses and build financial institutions that serve this target group. She indicates that consensus about impact analysis best practice is emerging among donor agencies and researchers in a field having a relatively short but controversial history. She outlines how impact analysis has developed, and offers detailed guidelines and practical procedures for structuring surveys, conducting fieldwork and interpreting results. Professor Dunn briefly summarises the two studies that follow her contribution in Part IV and indicates where they are located within the context she describes.

Enterprise-Level Impact of KfW-Managed Projects in Southeast Europe

Abenaa Addai and Kristine Nienborg of LFS Financial Systems conducted analyses of the European Funds administered by KfW in Bosnia and Herzegovina, Kosovo, Montenegro and Romania. These funds provided money to retail financial intermediaries such a microbanks and commercial banks to fund housing loans and business loans, as described in earlier papers. Their research focus includes clients who use these funds and the banks through which these funds are channeled. The authors note that, "Impact assessments explore whether objectives are being met and whether underlying assumptions are realistic," and that their research task "combined feed-back for KfW on the attainment of programme objectives with a market research study for the partner banks." Market research examined partner banks' existing and new products offered, their delivery systems and their responsiveness to demand.

Addai and Nienborg identified the three most important objectives of these programmes: private enterprise development, job creation, and improved access to financial services. Their survey included a sample of about 60 borrowers in each country, a control group of non-borrowers (except in BiH) and case studies. They conclude that KfW's efforts reached its target group of enterprises having fewer than 50 employees. In Romania and BiH most borrowers reported improved business results, while in Kosovo and Montenegro this did not occur because of events exogenous to the projects. Employment increased in sampled enterprises in all four countries, although this effect was relatively weak. Possibilities for obtaining alternative sources of credit varied greatly, with borrowers in Kosovo having the fewest prospects and hence the greatest degree of dependence on the project, while borrowers in Romania had the greatest range of choice. Put in another way, the Kosovo project had the greatest relative impact because few alternatives existed. Research indicated that household income and savings had a similar pattern: a highly positive impact in Romania, with much less positive results in Montenegro and Kosovo.

Addai and Nienborg concluded that access to credit had a positive overall impact on business development and household income, although in Montenegro it appears that loans obtained for business objectives was used primarily for household purposes. The degree of impact varied by length of programme operation and by country context. They note that methodological issues inherent in impact analysis temper the interpretation of results. In addition, caution is required regarding the findings for the Kosovo and Montenegro programmes because of their short history: different impacts occur in different time frames. At the same time, the authors recommend more tightly defined objectives in project design.

Impact on the Financial Sector

Sylvia Wisniwski of Bankakademie International and Klaus Maurer, a consultant, examine the impact of KfW-managed projects on financial institutions and the financial sectors of Albania, BiH, Kosovo and Romania. Impact analysis at the levels of institutions and sectors are relatively new and few, and hence no general agreement has emerged regarding practices in this type of impact analysis. This pioneering study should help to generate informed discussion about the research issues that remain outstanding.

These projects examined by Wisniwski and Maurer include refinancing lines and technical assistance (TA) to greenfield banks and in downscaling projects that encourage commercial banks to make tiny loans. The authors found that impact depended on framework conditions of the financial sector, the scope and length of programme intervention, and the behaviour of other government and donor activities and of commercial entities.

Wisniwski and Maurer ascribe two objectives to private commercial banks: strengthening their market positions, customer base and sales, and increasing their profitability. They confirm that banks in BiH using KfW-managed funds have offered longer maturities for products such as housing loans, refined their approaches to SME lending, expanded portfolio diversification, introduced more services, strengthened their client orientation, and gained credibility through their links with international supporters. Loans supported by KfW-managed funding were also more profitable than those funded by the banks' own resources.

The effect of greenfield banks is innovative in all cases. New products create new opportunities, and other banks copy good practices. However, as these new banks move up-market in response to declining margins on very small loans, they are less willing to share their practices with competitors. Greenfield banks have influenced regulatory practices and provide services on a commercial basis to microcredit NGOs. Peripheral institutions such as deposit insurers, credit information services, property registries and bank associations (also known as bank trade associations) have been formed around these innovations.

An important observation is that KfW-managed interventions are usually modest relative to the size of the financial sectors they studied. However, KfW's policy of "picking winners" permits it to realise considerable leverage, qualitatively and quantitatively.

In summary, the results identified by the two series of impact studies are positive. KfW management and funding are constructive interventions throughout the region. Impact differs across the region due to local circumstances arising from different economic conditions, market structures and states of governance.

Reviews of best practice also offer challenges for project designers, policy analysts and implementing organisations, as suggested by Dunn. KfW and other donors together with MFIs should use impact studies as a management tool, and to support further efforts to refine impact analysis at the institutional or meso level, as well as at the sector or macro level.

CHAPTER 12:

The Contribution of Science and Research to the Development of Microfinance

Franz Heidhues

Professor for Development Theory and Policy, Department of Agricultural Economics and Social Sciences in the Tropics and Subtropics, University of Hohenheim, Stuttgart, Germany

Introduction

The way the financial sector functions, particularly the credit side, has on occasion been illustrated by a quotation from the Bible: "I say to you, to everyone that has, more will be given; but from the one that does not have, even what he has will be taken away" (Luke 19:26).

Microfinance, with its new approaches, is the result of a process that challenges such views of financial sector performance. In the following I highlight what I consider to be the most important steps in transforming the narrow focus on credit into a comprehensive financial sector approach that integrates small farmers and enterprises and poor households into its activities.

After outlining the traditional approach to development credit, I shall discuss six essential contributions that the research community has made and which have initiated important changes in thinking on financial sector approaches and practice. I would like to emphasise that this change process was the result of an extremely productive cooperation between research and development practice. The experiences of development institutions stimulated researchers to look for remedies, and in development institutions and the banking sector their research findings have fallen on fertile ground. The paper concludes by looking ahead and delineating the work yet to be done.

The Traditional Approach to Small Enterprise Credit: Concept and Issues

The traditional approach to small enterprise credit was based on a development model that posited two factors as the binding constraints to development: the savings gap and the foreign exchange gap. In this two-gap model, the savings gap had to be overcome by means of domestic resource mobilisation, and the foreign exchange gap through external resource mobilisation. Domestic savings mobilisation, however, would be a futile exercise in rural areas, where incomes are low. Thus, building credit institutions that could finance small enterprises' investments and innovations required outside funding, primarily from government sources and bilateral and multilateral donors. The approach to small enterprise credit that emanated from this two-gap model was simple and its logic persuasive: the government created, supported and funded development banks that provided credit to small enterprises for "productive activities", that is, business investments and activities that promoted production.

This approach turned out to be deficient in a number of ways, and it failed more often than it succeeded. Dale Adams and his colleagues at Ohio State University (Adams and Graham 1981; Adams and Vogel 1986; Adams and Von Pischke 1992) and J.D. Von Pischke (Von Pischke et al, 1983) spearheaded research that brought the failures and lacunae of this approach into the open. They highlighted the negative impact of low interest rate policies: resources were misallocated in favour of capital intensive technologies and processes that inhibited growth and tended to bias resource allocation against employment creation; low interest rates discouraged savings mobilisation and created excess demand for funds which the market could not allocate. Thus, substitute rationing mechanisms, i.e. non-interest factors including economic and political power, determined who obtained these scarce funds. Often, recipients were not the poor and small farmers and businesses that the approach claimed to favour.

Low interest rate policies had a negative impact on institution-building because low interest rates squeezed institutions for funds, making it impossible for them to build up their own capital and cover costs. In such circumstances, lenders tended to direct their loans to larger borrowers who were able to offer valuable collateral and imposed low administrative and risk costs. To summarise, this research showed that access to external funding and subsidised interest rate policies on retail loans led to institutions that provided credit to only a few, mostly larger clients, rather than to small enterprises and the poor. Ultimately, this tended to weaken these institutions and worked against growth and employment creation.

Important work at Hohenheim pointed to a link between the low repayment rates achieved by these agricultural credit institutions and distorted agricultural price policies. Taxing agriculture through agricultural price policies, under which farmers were paid far below the world market price for their crops, induced farmers to consider credit from governmental institutions as a mechanism for reimbursing them for the low prices that the government paid for their crops. Thus, they did not feel obliged to repay loans to government credit institutions. Low repayment rates pushed banks into dependency on ministries and government officials who tended to interfere in the credit allocation processes, often for their own political or personal benefit. Under the combined effect of these factors, many institutions collapsed.

Performance of the Informal Financial Sector

In contrast to the dismal performance of the formal credit institutions, there was a thriving and expanding informal sector in many countries. The research community asked how the informal sector was able to lend sustainably to poor people without government support. It looked at many informal sector institutions and analysed their strengths and limitations. Their strength was due to the fact that they worked in small groups characterised by a high degree of social integration and interpersonal contact. Through group formation and social cohesion, they managed to overcome two major constraints facing traditional agricultural credit institutions:

- they solved the information asymmetry problem at low cost through the close-to-perfect information that group members had about each other;

- they often operated with honorary (volunteer) management, keeping the costs of operation and management low.

By not demanding physical assets as collateral (which formal institutions require to lower their risk costs and to overcome the information disadvantage they have vis-à-vis their borrowers), they were particularly accessible to small enterprises, women, the landless and the poor (Schrieder and Cuevas 1992). In addition, they did not supervise members' use of credit, letting borrowers select their own priorities, thus reducing administrative costs. They were also extremely flexible, unbureaucratic and quick to respond.

As well as revealing their many advantages, research also highlighted their limitations. With few exceptions these groups focused on relatively small, short-term loans; they were locally based and had no mechanism for intermediating between different groups at regional or national levels. Fragmentation was a key feature of these groups, and financial market intermediation was limited or absent.

The conclusion was that the informal finance sector demonstrated many valuable features and provided lessons for the formal sector. However, it was unable to fulfil the functions of a financial system in a growing economy; the important task of building an effective and functioning formal finance sector remained.

The Importance of Savings

Governments often proved to be an unreliable source of funding for small enterprise credit institutions because governments regularly fail to balance their budgets and run deficits. This fact and the informal sector's general reliance on its own funds led researchers to emphasise savings as a most important component of a sustainable rural finance system. The Ohio State University group described savings as the "forgotten half of rural finance" (Vogel 1984).

While the informal sector demonstrated that there were savings in rural and urban areas, researchers looked more closely at the amount that could be mobilised, the stability of savings mobilisation, the motives for savings and the factors that determined savings mobilisation. Research revealed that there were substantial amounts of savings to be mobilised, even in rural areas, and that in these areas there was a pronounced and urgent need for appropriate savings instruments. Numerous studies found that the demand for proper savings instruments was often larger than the demand for credit. Appropriate savings instruments required low transaction costs. Savings institutions had to be close at hand within villages, and both safe and reliable. Savers wanted to be able to withdraw at any time. Savings institutions serving these clients would have to accept and pay out small amounts of cash.

Another issue linked to the priority of savings mobilisation was the question of whether to start building microfinance institutions with savings or with credit. Whether the "savings first" approach is the more successful, or whether starting with credit and concomitantly building up the savings side is more appropriate, depends on local circumstances. Grameen Bank successfully followed the savings first approach, but other successful institutions have built up savings together with or subsequent to their initial credit activities. Undisputed is that savings mobilisation and improved savings instruments are an integral part of microfinance and a most important feature of sustainable institution building.

Outreach to the Poor

If microfinance is to make a meaningful impact on small enterprises, financial institutions have to serve a large and growing number of poor people. To achieve this goal, they must offer high quality financial services adapted to small clients. At the same time, their efforts need to be directed at increasing efficiency and financial soundness in order to ensure their own viability and thus sustainability (Erhardt 2002).

Can microfinance institutions be shaped such that they are both accessible to the poor and financially viable without subsidies? This question still figures prominently in current discussions on microfinance. On the one hand, Grameen Bank has shown that it can serve the poor. It also claims to provide credit to them on a sustainable basis and to operate without government subsidies. Others argue that the costs of lending to the poor are high because transactions are small; the poor can provide little collateral and they are limited in their ability to bear the full credit costs. IFPRI and other researchers show that rural financial institutions can be made accessible as long as the borrowing poor are able to exploit effectively their main production factor – labour. To meet this condition, borrowers have to be in good health and not otherwise impaired in the use of their labour. This research emphasises that the disabled, the young and the old require other means, such as social security systems.

IFPRI researchers also conclude that when offering microfinance services to the poor involves the provision of public goods, government support for building pro-poor finance institutions is warranted. Furthermore, they make the case for subsidising institution start-ups, capital and initial training. With such initial support, microfinance institutions for the poor can be made to operate sustainably and at the same time cover costs.

The Impact of Microfinance on Poverty

There is increasing evidence that microfinance has helped poor families improve their livelihoods. Poverty has many dimensions and is reflected in such issues as food insecurity, malnutrition, illiteracy, ill health and lack of entitlements (Chung et al. 1997). The effect of microfinance on poverty is thus often analysed by looking at the impact on basic-needs indicators, such as food insecurity and malnutrition, and more generally on household income.

The picture that emerges is diverse. In a comprehensive study of 13 microfinance institutions and their impact on the poor in Asia, Africa and South America, Hulme and Mosley (1996a and 1996b) show that the benefit of microfinance is not scale-neutral, i.e., they found that the upper and middle income poor tended to benefit more than low income clients. Mosley and Hulme (1998) confirmed a greater preference on the part of poorer households for consumption loans, but also their greater vulnerability to income shocks and their more limited range of investment opportunities.

In their multi-country study (1998), Zeller and Sharma found that access to credit positively influenced the absolute amount of household income and that households with improved access to credit were better able to adopt innovations. Thus, those with better access to credit were found to have higher adoption rates for high-yield crop varieties. This in turn produced a positive effect on natural resource management as smaller areas of fragile land came under cultivation (Rashid, Sharma and Zeller 2002). These findings were confirmed by Mourji's study (2000) which found that almost two-thirds of the clients of microcredit institutions had increased their income over the preceding 12 months while only 39% of non-clients were able to do so. A key factor was that credit supported the expansion of clients' enterprises and a greater diversification of income-generating activities. Furthermore, the study conducted on a village bank credit programme for women in Côte d'Ivoire revealed a higher degree of income diversification among those women participating in the programme (Schäfer 2002).

In the analysis of microfinance impacts, poverty and gender relations are important. Women, who represent 75% of the world's poor, are frequently the focus of microfinance activities. Women are more likely than men to spend additional income on their children's nutrition, health and education (World Bank 2002), making them a prime target group for poverty oriented microfinance programmes. Improving women's access to credit is likely to have a greater effect on poverty alleviation than credit made available to men (Sharma 2001). Pitt and Khandker examined the impact of credit on welfare indicators in a study of 87 villages in Bangladesh. They found that lending to women increased non-land assets substantially more than lending to men. However, before drawing policy conclusions, more research is needed to determine whether loans to women were actually used by the women themselves, or whether their access to loans simply made it easier for men to obtain finance through intra-household transfers.

Microfinance as Insurance

Just as the Ohio School coined the term the "forgotten half of rural finance" in their efforts to promote savings mobilisation (Vogel 1984), IFPRI's research led Zeller to emphasise insurance in rural financial market development, labelling insurance as the "forgotten third of rural finance" (Zeller et al. 1996). IFPRI's research, closely linked with food security and vulnerability research, found that rural households in fragile environments are particularly exposed to a number of risks that threaten their food security and survival. They found that the informal sector provided rural households with an important mechanism for insuring against certain risks.

Informal groups were found to be able to cover individual risks but unable to cope with covariate risks affecting whole regions. Rural finance institutions could be an efficient and effective instrument for covering both individual and (limited) covariate risks. Thus, microfinance institutions can certainly assist people to bridge transitory stress, such as food insecurity, over short periods. Having access to credit allows them to maintain their productive assets, for example animals, tools and other production materials, which, in the absence of access to finance they might have to sell in order to survive. Households that do not have to sell their productive assets (because they are more able to endure periods of stress by means of access to microfinance institutions) recovered after the stress periods more quickly and were able to resume production activities faster than other households. Access to microfinance in stress periods can thus prevent transitory food insecurity from turning into chronic poverty and food insecurity.

Microfinance as Part of the Financial System

The goal of building sustainable, self-reliant finance institutions as the base for a sound financial sector strategy is widely supported by researchers and development practitioners alike. It is seen as a prerequisite for reaching the poor on a long-term basis (Erhardt 2002). However, building a sustainable microfinance sector also requires creating a conducive financial and economic environment for microfinance institutions. These requirements became particularly apparent in transition countries, where microfinance development is hampered by market distortions, rampant inflation, the continued channelling of government funds through the banks in order to keep loss-making enterprises afloat, and the lack of a reliable and enforceable regulatory framework without effective bank supervision (Heidhues et al. 1998).

Microfinance in Transformation Processes

The successful reform of financial systems and the successful building of microfinance institutions in transformation countries in Central and Eastern European countries (CEECs) has been a particularly difficult challenge of fundamental importance to the economic transition of these regions (Heidhues and Schrieder 2000). Moreover, their increasing integration into the world economy makes the efficient functioning of a domestic financial systems even more crucial (EBRD, 1996; Davis and Hare, 1997; Heidhues 1995).

The most important functions of a financial system in a market economy are to maintain an efficient medium of exchange, mobilise and allocate resources, pool risk, exercise financial discipline over enterprises, and to provide a policy framework and instruments to ensure economic stability. The financial intermediaries that the CEECs inherited from the central planning era were not suited to these tasks. In many CEECs, the development of the financial system suffered and continues to suffer for a number of reasons:

- banks still finance loss-making state-owned enterprises, most notably in agriculture;

- banks continue to carry large bad-loan portfolios and do not effectively control corporate governance and policy;

- regulatory systems are ineffective and bank supervision poor. There is a shortage of skills and experience in evaluating risks, creditworthiness and investment profitability.

Moreover, financial markets in transition economies, particularly in rural areas, lack many features that are taken for granted in developed market economies. Poorly developed communications and transport infrastructure makes the use of financial services costly for potential clients. For the rural sector, insufficient land and lease markets, distorted relative prices in input and output markets and the lack of extension for private farmers reduce the ability and willingness of potential investors and creditors alike to engage in financial transactions.

The building of an efficient and effective financial market requires a multifaceted approach. First, an essential requirement is financial discipline and monetary stability. This cannot be achieved if the government requires the central bank to finance loss-making state enterprises. Such government interference with the central bank undermines efforts to strengthen the financial system. Second, to improve access to the financial market for small private enterprises, financial innovations are required at four levels (Heidhues 1998):

- at the financial system level, creating a reliable, fair and enforceable regulatory framework with an effective supervisory structure;

- at the organisational level, restructuring banking institutions to better serve the small client market, or strengthening existing finance institutions such as credit cooperatives;

- within financial intermediaries, streamlining loan applications, approvals and supervision processes; and integrating participatory client involvement; and

- offering new, high-quality services geared to the small-enterprise clientele.

These are innovations that require a major long-term effort in terms of education and training, gathering experience, changing laws, and restructuring institutions and organisations. This requires time, patience and persistence; a shock approach will not succeed.

Conclusions

Looking ahead with a view to meeting the challenges this sector will face in the future, it is important to take into account that:

- microfinance can be a suitable and effective tool in fighting poverty, particularly if it integrates women into the clientele;

- in many countries, particularly transition countries, structural weaknesses continue to hamper financial sector development. Development in this sector needs to be complemented by structural policies that address these problems. Microfinance is not a panacea for structural weaknesses;

- building and maintaining efficiency in the microfinance sector requires competition. Competitive structures are the best guarantee for the dynamic development of the sector and its continuous adaptation to changing opportunities;

- microfinance services should be demand-driven. As opportunities change and expand in the course of development, so must the services provided by the microfinance sector. Thus, in a country that is recovering from war or natural disaster, top priority may be given to housing, reconstruction, and start-up financing. At later stages, loans for expansion and modernisation may take first place. The goal of reaching a growing number of borrowers can best be achieved through proper client orientation. There may also be a case for linking microfinance institutions with groups and social organisations in order to include the poorer clientele in their outreach;

- the sustainability of microfinance institutions depends vitally on their efficiency and competence. This calls for the recruitment of high quality staff, systematic and continuous staff training and incentive systems;

- finally, internal monitoring and evaluation have always been and will remain important instruments for the early detection and correction of problems. This is also an area with considerable scope for exploiting synergies with the field of research.

Microfinance has come a long way towards refuting the validity of the biblical quotation from Luke 19:26. By addressing these challenges, it will continue to move in the right direction.

References

Adams, Dale W; Graham, Douglas H. (1981): A Critique of Traditional Agricultural Credit Projects and Policies, in: Journal of Development Economics, Vol. 8, pp. 347-366.

Adams, Dale W; Pischke, J.D. Von (1992): Micro-enterprise Credit Programmes: Déjà vu, in: World Development, Vol. 20, No. 10, pp. 1463-1470.

Adams, Dale W; Vogel, Robert C. (1986): Rural Financial Markets in Low-Income Countries: Recent Controversies and Lessons, in: World Development, Vol. 14, No. 4, pp. 477-487.

Chung, K., Haddad, L., Ramakrishna, J., Riely, F. (1997): Identifying the Food Insecure: The application of mixed-method approaches in India. Occasional Paper. Washington, D.C., USA: International Food Policy Research Institute (IFPRI).

Davis, Junior R; Hare, P. (1997): Reforming the systems of rural finance provision in Romania: Some options for privatisation and change, in: Quarterly Journal of International Agriculture, Vol. 36(3), pp. 213-234.

EBRD (1996): Transition Report 1996: Infrastructure and savings. Brussels, Belgium: European Bank for Reconstruction and Development.

Erhardt, Wolfram (2002): Financial Markets for Small Enterprises in Urban and Rural Northern Thailand. Development Economics and Policy, Series edited by Franz Heidhues and Joachim von Braun, Vol. 28, Peter Lang Verlag.

Heidhues, Franz (1995): Rural financial markets – An important tool to fight poverty, in: Quarterly Journal of International Agriculture, Vol. 34(2), pp. 105-108.

Heidhues, Franz; Davis, Junior R.; Schrieder, Gertrud (1998): Agricultural transformation and implications for designing rural financial policies in Romania. European review of agricultural economics, Walter de Gruyter, Vol. 25/3.

Heidhues, Franz; Schrieder, Gertrud (eds) (2000): Romania – Rural Finance in Transition Economies. Development Economics and Policy, Series edited by Franz Heidhues and Joachim von Braun, Vol. 14, Peter Lang Verlag.

Hulme, D., Mosley, P. (1996a): Finance against poverty. Vol. 1 London, UK: Routledge.

Hulme, D., Mosley, P. (1996b): Finance against poverty. Country case studies. Vol. 2. London, UK: Routledge.

Mourji, F. (2000): Impact study of the Zakoura microcredit program. New York, NY, USA: United Nations Development Capital Fund (UNCDF), Micro-Start Program, Special Unit for Microfinance (SUM), www.uncdf.org/sum/reports/ impact/zakura.pdf (accessed October 2002).

Mosley, P., Hulme, D. (1998): Micro-enterprise finance: Is there a trade-off between growth and poverty alleviation. PRUS Working Paper No. 3. In Recent research on micro-finance: Implications for policy, Matin, I., Sinha, S., with P. Alexander (eds.): 1-12. Brighton, Sussex, UK: University of Sussex, Poverty Research Unit at Sussex (PRUS).

Rashid, S., Sharma, M., Zeller, M. (2002): Micro-lending for small farmers in Bangladesh: Does it affect farm households' land allocation? IFPRI Discussion Paper No. 45. Washington, D.C., USA: International Food Policy Research Institute (IFPRI).

Schäfer, B. (2002): Wirkungsanalyse von ländlichen Finanzprojekten. Eine Untersuchung des Projektes 'PADER-Nord (Programme d'appui au Développement Rural de la Région Nord), Côte d'Ivoire'. Endbericht an die Deutsche Gesellschaft für Technische Zusammenarbeit (GTZ) in Eschborn. Stuttgart, Universität Hohenheim, FB für landwirtschaftliche Entwicklungs- theorie und -politik in den Tropen und Subtropen (490a).

Sharma, M. (2001): Microfinance. In Empowering women to achieve food security, Quisumbing, A.R. and R.S. Meinzen-Dick (eds.): 19-20. Policy Brief No. 10. IFPRI Focus No. 6. Washington, D.C., USA: International Food Policy Research Institute (IFPRI).

Schrieder, Gertrud; Cuevas, Carlos E. (1992): Informal Financial Groups in Cameroon, Adams, Dale W; Fitchett, Delbert A. (eds), Informal Finance in Low-Income Countries, Boulder, Colorado, USA: Westview, pp. 43-55.

Vogel, Robert C. (1984): Savings Mobilization: The Forgotten Half of Rural Finance, in: Adams, Dale W; Graham, Douglas H. and Von Pischke, J.D. (eds): Undermining Rural Development with Cheap Credit, Boulder, Colorado, USA: Westview, pp. 248-265.

Von Pischke, J.D.; Adams, Dale; Gordon, Donald (1983): Rural Financial Markets in Developing Countries, Baltimore, USA: Johns Hopkins.

World Bank (2002): Integrating gender into the World Bank's work: A strategy for action. Washington, D.C., USA: World Bank.

Zeller, Manfred; Schrieder, Gertrud; von Braun, Joachim; Heidhues, Franz (1996): Review of Rural Finance for Food Security of the Poor: Concept and Implications for Research and Policy, International Food Policy Research Institute, Washington, D.C., USA.

Zeller, M., Sharma, M. (1998): Rural finance and poverty alleviation. Food Policy
    Statement No. 27. Washington, D.C., USA: International Food Policy
    Research Institute (IFPRI).

CHAPTER 13:

Best Practice Principles for Microfinance Impact Analysis

Research Assistant Professor of Agricultural Economics, University of Missouri, USA

Introduction

To promote financial sector development in Southeast Europe, KfW and its partners have implemented several projects to establish new microbanks and to downscale existing banks. These projects are designed to improve the performance of financial sectors in the region by establishing effective financial intermediation for micro and small enterprises. Effective financial intermediation can unleash the productive potential of the region's entrepreneurs with the ultimate objectives of expanding economic opportunities, promoting economic recovery, and improving economic welfare.

The performance of the financial sector in providing financial intermediation for micro and small enterprises can be evaluated in three critical dimensions: financial sustainability, outreach to the poor, and welfare impact. According to Zeller and Meyer (2003), this microfinance "triangle" corresponds to the three overarching policy dimensions of financial sector development. This chapter focuses on one leg of the triangle: analysis of the welfare impacts of microfinance. After reviewing some of the most important theoretical and empirical obstacles to impact analysis, a set of best practice principles for microfinance impact analysis are proposed. KfW studies are then reviewed within this framework.

KfW Impact Studies

KfW has commissioned several studies to analyse the impacts of its financial sector development efforts in Southeast Europe. The first set, summarised in another chapter of this book by Addai and Nienborg, used a similar approach to examine client-level impacts, including enterprise development and household welfare. These impact studies were conducted in Bosnia and Herzegovina,

Kosovo, Montenegro, and Romania. The impact analysis described in the chapter by Maurer and Wisniwski examines the impacts of financial sector development at two additional levels: at the meso level of partner banks and at the macro level of the financial sector.

These studies make an important contribution toward understanding the impacts of KfW's financial sector projects. The information they provide is useful for assessing programme impacts and for improving programme management.

Impact Controversies

Despite the growing interest in impact analysis within the microfinance industry, a great deal of controversy surrounds the topic. Disagreement tends to arise around three key questions:

- What kinds of impacts should be analysed?

- What methods should be used to measure and analyse these impacts?

- Is impact analysis even feasible and warranted for microfinance projects?

This chapter focuses on the first two questions, taking as a premise that impact analysis is feasible and warranted in certain situations.

The emergence of numerous distinct approaches to impact analysis reflects disagreement about what constitutes best practice in this field. There are two reasons that so many distinct approaches have emerged. The first is that there are different motivations behind impact analysis. The second is that there are several technical challenges associated with impact analysis in microfinance. The central argument of the present discussion is that no single impact analysis approach can resolve all of these motivational and technical challenges. However, it is possible to identify best practice principles that can be used to guide and strengthen microfinance impact analysis.

The next part of the chapter provides a brief introduction to the evolution of impact analysis and the current state of the art within microfinance. The third part examines the ideological tensions and theoretical challenges that set the stage for controversy in this field. The fourth part proposes a set of best practice principles to guide impact analysis for financial sector projects. The fifth part discusses the contributions of the KfW-sponsored impact studies, using the framework of the proposed best practice principles. The conclusion suggests logical next steps that KfW may want to pursue in analysing the impacts of its projects to promote financial sector development.

Impact Analysis in Microfinance

Impact analysis methods emerged and evolved largely in medical, environmental, and social science research. Medical research provides an easily understandable illustration of the basic objective of impact analysis. In medical research, the analysis attempts to measure the impacts of a specific medical treatment, such as a type of medicine or a surgical technique, on two groups of patients whose results are compared. These analyses normally follow an experimental design in which similar patients are randomly assigned to the treatment group or the control group. Random assignment helps to prevent the bias that could result if only the healthiest patients, or those most likely to respond, were assigned to the treatment group.

Early Scepticism

Early efforts at client-level impact analysis in microfinance were met with substantial scepticism, as being unnecessary, difficult, unreliable, and expensive. The facts that clients repaid their loans and took repeat loans were taken as *prima facie* evidence of positive impact. In addition, the technical challenges associated with impact analysis were considered too difficult to be effectively overcome. These technical challenges, including selection bias, fungibility, and attribution problems, are discussed later in this chapter. Because of the difficulty associated with addressing these challenges, there was not much confidence in the reliability of microfinance impact studies. Finally, part of the scepticism about the value of impact analysis was based on an implicit assessment of the relative costs and benefits. At a time when the primary challenge was to reduce costs and build sustainable financial institutions, it was hard to justify an impact study, particularly given the assumption that the results were not expected to be reliable.

Financial sustainability continues to be an important and challenging goal, and a well-designed impact analysis can promote sustainability by improving knowledge about the clients using microfinance services. The information generated in a client-level analysis can be used to understand how clients use financial services and to determine which product features are the most (or least) attractive and what types of new products and services would be useful.

Range of Efforts

Despite early scepticism, interest in the impacts of microfinance programmes has persisted. Among the first important studies were the research of Pitt and Khandker (1996) in Bangladesh and the multi-country studies described in Hulme and Mosley (1996). These studies helped to break down some of the early doubts about the legitimacy and feasibility of impact analysis.

The USAID-sponsored Assessing the Impact of Microenterprise Services (AIMS) Project was instrumental in developing a range of impact analysis methods for microfinance, and promoted impact analysis as a means of gaining knowledge about microfinance clients. Early products from the project included a survey of impact studies (Sebstad and Chen 1996) and a discussion of research methods (Gaile and Foster 1996). Before ending in 2002, the AIMS Project addressed many of the technical challenges related to impact analysis, while defining a range of impact analyses and developing impact methods for a variety of potential users.

Following the AIMS Project, there have been a number of important global efforts to develop better impact analysis methods. Some of the better-known global projects are listed in table 1.

Table 1. Global projects in microfinance impact analysis and client knowledge

Project Name	Emphasis Area(s) in Impact Analysis	Sponsor(s) and Website
AIMS Assessing the Impact of Microenterprise Services	Develop range of impact analysis methods from practitioner tools to advanced studies	USAID http://www.mip.org/
CGAP Consultative Group to Assist the Poor	Impact assessment working group; Poverty Analysis Tool (PAT); Impact Assessment Centre	29 member donors http://www.cgap.org/ http://www.microfinancegateway.org/impact
EDIAIS Enterprise Development Impact Assessment Information Service	Link impact analysis to sustained learning that empowers clients and improves programme management	DFID http://www.enterprise-impact.org.uk/
Imp-Act Improving the Impact of Microfinance on Poverty: Action Research Programme	Promote practitioner-focused processes to improve programme management while satisfying donors	Ford Foundation http://www.imp-act.org/
Microcredit Summit Campaign	Measure poverty and the impact of microcredit on the poorest families	RESULTS Educational Fund http://www.microcreditsummit.org/
Micro-Save Africa	Gather information on financial behaviour of the poor to use in market research and product design	Austria/CGAP/DFID/UNDP http://www.microsave-africa.com/

The Imp-Act Project, sponsored by the Ford Foundation, concentrates on generating information useful for microfinance providers (practitioners). The Consultative Group to Assist the Poor (CGAP) has made several contributions to microfinance impact analysis, including the development of a method for analysing the poverty levels of microfinance clients, while providing access to major impact analysis resources through the Internet. In addition, a number of international nongovernmental organisations have developed substantial impact analysis expertise in recent years. The growing interest within the microfinance industry for impact analysis and client-level information has also generated a divergence in methods and in their underlying philosophies.

Recent microfinance impact assessments in Southeast Europe have used a variety of approaches. The Microfinance Centre in Poland (MFC) has played an important role in developing impact analysis expertise in the region, offering training in the use of the AIMS-SEEP impact assessment tools for practitioner organisations. In addition, MFC heads a regional impact research consortium that is part of the Imp-Act Project.

Several impact analyses have been conducted recently in Bosnia and Herzegovina (BiH), in addition to the KfW-sponsored study. Two microfinance providers, ICMC and Mercy Corps, worked with MFC to apply the AIMS-SEEP impact assessment tools, while another microfinance provider (PRIZMA), used the poverty assessment tools developed by CGAP. A longitudinal study involving 3,500 microentrepreneurs from twelve microfinance organisations is currently underway in BiH to analyse the impacts of the World Bank-sponsored Local Initiatives Projects (LIP). Each of these projects has taken different analytical approaches.

Ideological, Theoretical and Empirical Challenges in Microfinance Impact Analysis

The diversity of methods being used in Southeast Europe and around the world are a legitimate response to several critical tensions and challenges. These arise from a number of factors, including a) ideological differences related to the overall purpose of impact analysis, b) theoretical challenges generally associated with social science impact analysis, c) other challenges unique to microfinance, and d) decisions related to the identification and measurement of impacts. No single impact analysis approach can address all of these tensions and challenges in a definitive way.

Ideological Differences

Stakeholders' Objectives

The three primary stakeholders in the microfinance industry—donors, providers, and users—have different motivations for impact analysis. Impact analysis has traditionally been associated with donors' needs for accountability in their use of funds, otherwise known as the "proving" role of impact analysis. Studies designed to "prove" the impacts of microfinance programmes focus on impacts related to the development goals of the donor. These studies are sometimes held to fairly high research standards and, consequently, tend to be more expensive to conduct.

Providers of microfinance services, while also interested in "proving" the positive impacts of their services, have more recently become interested in using impact analysis and related methods as managerial tools to improve their knowledge about clients and to develop better products and services. This use is sometimes referred to as the "improving" role of impact analysis. Providers' evolving objectives for impact analysis have opened up a broader agenda for collecting and analysing client-level information (see below).

Finally, microfinance clients may view impact analysis as an opportunity to participate, sometimes for the first time, in the discussion about how microfinance services should be offered. Some approaches rely on broadly participatory techniques to ensure that participants' perspectives are an integral part of the evaluation process. Impact analyses designed specifically to increase client participation will tend to differ from those having a primary objective of proving impacts or improving programme management.

Broader Agenda for Client Information

As the microfinance industry has grown and evolved, providers' attitudes toward clients have evolved as well. The early years were characterised by a product-centered approach, in which potential clients are offered a single, standardised product, usually working capital loans for use in enterprises. More recently, however, there has been increasing recognition that microfinance providers need to become more client-centered.

As microfinance providers evolve more toward a client-centered approach, they can benefit from the collection and use of client-level information in three specific areas (Dunn 2002a). First, basic information on client characteristics is useful for assessing the provider's progress in extending outreach to target populations. Some outreach-related information, such as client gender, can be routinely collected in the application process and maintained in the management information system. Other information, such as clients' poverty levels, may require special data collection efforts. Information about client characteristics can also be used for market segmentation analysis.

Second, providers need information about how clients use their products and services and how these fit into household financial management strategies. This information can be useful for product innovation, both to improve the features of existing products and to develop new products and services. Innovation can assist sustainability by improving the microfinance provider's ability to retain existing clients and to attract new clients.

Third, those microfinance providers with social objectives, or that receive support from organisations with social objectives, also need impact information to assess their progress. In addition to simply demonstrating that a microfinance programme has positive client-level impacts, impact information is required to evaluate the relative costs and benefits of alternative social investments. While impact analysis is warranted under these circumstances, there is no ideal way to collect the information.

Theoretical Challenges in Social Science Impact Analysis

Two important theoretical challenges that affect the design of microfinance impact analysis are the attribution problem and the selection bias problem, which are common across all types of impact analysis in the social sciences. To a large extent, these arise because of the nature of the impact problem and the fact that it is not usually feasible in the social sciences to use the experimental design commonly associated with medical impact analysis. Instead of randomly assigning individuals to receive or not receive microfinance services, the second best alternative is to use a non-experimental research design, as described below.

The Impact Problem

The basic challenge in impact analysis is to determine the effect of an intervention or treatment on an outcome variable. In the case of microfinance impact analysis, the intervention is the microfinance service and the outcome variables are the variables related to the programme's social objectives, such as household income, enterprise revenue, or enterprise employment.

Moffitt (1991) provides this description of the impact problem:

> "Suppose that we wish to evaluate the effect of a particular intervention (i.e., a treatment) on individual levels of some outcome variable. Let Y be the outcome variable and make the following definitions:
>
> $Y^{*}_{it} =$ level of outcome variable for individual i at time t if he or she has not received the treatment
>
> $Y^{**}_{it} =$ level of outcome variable for same individual i at same time t if he or she has received the treatment at some prior date.
>
> The difference between these two quantities is the effect of the treatment, denoted
>
> α:
>
> $$Y^{**}_{it} = Y^{*}_{it} + \alpha$$
>
> or
>
> $$\alpha = Y^{**}_{it} - Y^{*}_{it} .$$
>
> The aim of the evaluation is to obtain an estimate of the value of α, the treatment effect." (Moffitt 1991, 292-293)

Impact analysis seeks to measure the difference in outcome between an individual who received treatment and what the outcome *would have been* for the same individual, if he or she *had not received* the treatment. Obviously, the latter is an unobservable counterfactual event. The only practical alternative is to compare the outcomes for individuals who receive treatment with the outcomes for individuals who do not receive treatment. This is one of the fundamental problems in impact evaluation and the source of the associated selection bias problem.

Selection Bias

Selection bias exists if there are differences between those individuals who receive treatment and those who do not, and if these differences lead to incorrect measurement of the treatment effect. It can occur in microfinance impact analysis because people self-select (and are selected by credit committees) to become clients in a microfinance programme. The people who become clients may differ in important ways from those who do not become clients. Selection bias can also result from decisions made by the microfinance provider about where to place programmes and branch offices.

Selection bias can lead to overestimation of the true impact of a microfinance programme. This occurs if there are differences between the programme participants and non-participants that have a positive effect on the outcome variable. In this case, the measured difference in outcomes between the participants and the non-participants is partly due to pre-existing differences between the two groups that are unrelated to the programme.

Several situations in microfinance impact analysis could lead to selection bias. For example, selection bias might occur if clients have greater entrepreneurial talent than non-clients. This difference between the two groups could lead clients to have better business outcomes than non-clients, even in the absence of receiving microfinance services. In another example, clients' businesses may already be better positioned relative to the market, thus motivating them to seek microfinance services. In summary, selection bias can lead to an exaggerated measure of the impacts of microfinance services because it causes a divergence in outcomes that is not related to microfinance.

Non-experimental Research Design

The optimal method for eliminating selection bias is to use an experimental design, such as in medical impact analysis, in which qualified applicants are randomly assigned to receive or not receive microfinance services. However, most microfinance service providers have valid reasons for rejecting a random assignment procedure. Instead, it is usually necessary to follow a non-experimental research design in microfinance impact analysis, in which the outcomes for the client group are compared to outcomes for a constructed control group. The members of the control group do not receive microfinance services but are considered "similar" to the clients in critical ways that affect outcomes.

Rossi and Freeman (1989) describe several approaches for selecting control groups. The most commonly used method is to select individuals who share critical characteristics with the clients, then to control statistically for differences in other variables that are expected to affect outcomes (Rossi and Freeman 1989, 328ff.). For example, if males and females occur in different proportions in the client and control groups, and if gender is expected to affect the outcome variable, then gender differences between the client and control groups should be statistically controlled for in the analysis.

In this respect, the most useful type of data for reducing selection bias is panel data. Panel data, a specific type of longitudinal data, are created by interviewing the same respondents on the same variables, measured at more than one point in time. The advantage of panel data is that selection-bias related differences between the client and control group are reflected in the differences that already exist in the baseline period. Panel data can then be used to compare how outcomes change over time for the client and control groups. This helps to address the selection bias problem by accounting for the fixed effects of selection bias and for the exogenous effects on outcomes that are unrelated to programme participation (Dunn 2002b).

Attribution

Another important theoretical challenge in microfinance impact analysis is the problem of establishing a strong, plausible case for attributing the change in outcome to the programme services that were received. The attribution problem arises from two causes. First, while the statistical methods used to measure impacts can establish statistical correlation, they cannot be used to prove the existence of a cause-and-effect relationship. Second, controlled experiments in which all factors except the treatment (intervention) are held constant are difficult to conduct in the social sciences. The result is that it can never be proved incontrovertibly that the treatment led to the impact. Instead, the best that can be done is to establish a strong case in favour of attribution.

Even though the establishment of a statistical correlation between programme participation and improved outcomes can not "prove" that the programme led to the outcome, it is one important piece of evidence. Another component in constructing a plausible case for attribution is to build the research on an internally consistent conceptual model that links the intervention to the impact in a cause-and-effect relationship that is logical and credible. A third way to strengthen the case for attribution is to use qualitative research to identify and document the chain of events, ordered in time, that lead from the programme services to the impact.

Any of these approaches—statistical results indicating association between variables, a logically consistent conceptual model, or qualitative evidence linking the programme and the outcome—could be used alone to build at least a plausible case for attribution. By combining them, however, a mixed-method approach establishes a much stronger case for claiming that the observed difference in outcomes can be attributed to the microfinance services received by the client.

Analytical Challenges Unique to Microfinance

Unlike selection bias and attribution, there are some challenges that are relatively unique to microfinance impact analysis. Two are discussed in this section. The first is fungibility and the related issue of additionality. The second is the lack of available methods for assessing the wider impacts of microfinance.

Fungibility and Additionality

Money is fungible, which means that loan funds can be used in different ways. The fungibility of money makes it difficult to track the use of loan funds in order to link the actual credit received to changes in the enterprise. Loan funds may be used in the target enterprise, or some of the funds may be used in other enterprises or for purposes that are not business related. For example, loan funds may be used to purchase property, buy medicine, or finance children's education. Because of the fungibility of money, it can be very difficult to track how a household allocates the loan it receives.

Fungibility also relates to the problem of determining the additionality of the loan. Additionality occurs when the loan leads to some kind of investment in the business that would not have occurred (or would not have occurred at the same level) in the absence of the loan. If, in the absence of the loan, the same business investment would have been made by reallocating (fungible) money away from some other use within the household economic portfolio, then the loan has no additionality.

In the past, the fungibility of money was considered a major challenge to microfinance impact analysis. Clients may not spend the entire loan proceeds on the intended microenterprise, making it difficult to know how much of the loan funds were being used in the microenterprise. In addition, the household might mobilise other (non-programme) funds to support the enterprise. This would make it difficult to link specific changes in the enterprise to the financial services received, undermining the premise of impact assessment.

The issue of fungibility can be addressed by widening the unit of analysis. In addition to impacts on microenterprises, the analysis should be expanded to include the entire household economic portfolio within which the fungible capital might be used (Chen and Dunn 1996). In this way, it is not necessary to assume that all of the loan funds are spent on the intended enterprise nor, alternatively, to track how loan funds are actually spent.

Wider Impacts of Microfinance

While methods for measuring client-level impacts are evolving rapidly, much less is known about the wider impacts of microfinance. Nearly all current impact studies focus on the micro level of analysis, which includes households, enterprises, and individual clients. Methods for analysing impacts at the meso and macro levels have not yet been developed and applied, so there is little empirical information about the impacts of microfinance at these levels.

At the meso level, possible units of analysis include the community and the subsector. The measurement of community-level impacts is intuitively appealing but conceptually challenging. Many of the proposed community-level impact variables reflect political and social changes, such as improvements in social networks and local levels of political organisation, which can be difficult to measure.

While some methods have been developed for analysing market subsectors, an untested assumption is that economic impacts at this level are negative due to the crowding out of enterprises that do not receive financial services. On the other hand, it is also theoretically possible that microfinance has positive multiplier effects on the local economy. These multiplier effects could occur as clients' increased incomes and non-household members' increased wages circulate through local goods and employment markets to create welfare improvements for non-clients.

The third level of analysis is the macro level, which includes the financial sector and the macroeconomy. Where micro and small enterprises are a substantial part of the economy, the increased availability of microfinance may have general equilibrium impacts. Examples would include changes in prices and production levels in goods markets and changes in wages and employment levels in labour markets. In addition, there may be macro-level changes in financial markets affecting interest rates and the overall volume of financial intermediation.

In summary, there are three possible levels for analysing the impacts of microfinance. While there has been substantial progress in developing effective methods for impact analysis at the micro level, there has been less progress at the meso and macro levels. Until impacts at these levels have been empirically analysed, it will not be possible to gauge the full welfare implications of projects to develop the microfinance sector.

Impact Measurement and Indicators

Another set of challenges in microfinance impact analysis relates to the selection of the impacts to be measured and the development of appropriate indicators. This process involves a host of decisions, beginning with the selection of the specific impacts that will be measured and which represent the concepts to be measured in the study. Once the conceptual variables are selected, then appropriate empirical indicators must be developed to measure the concepts represented in the impact variables.

Common Micro-level Impact Variables

A number of factors will influence the selection of impact variables. These factors include the motivations for the study, the key questions to be answered from the results of the study, the time and resources available, and relevant findings from previous studies. It is also important that the selection of impact variables be grounded in a conceptual model that provides a plausible link between participation in the microfinance programme and the hypothesised impacts.

The household economic portfolio model is one example of a conceptual model that can be used to analyse the client-level impacts of microfinance programmes (Chen and Dunn 1996). In this model, the enterprise is embedded in the household economy. As one of the household's several economic activities, the enterprise shares a common resource base with other production, investment, and consumption activities. Microfinance services intermingle with the resource base, with possible implications for all of the household's resource allocation decisions. The household economic portfolio model can be used to generate impact hypotheses for three different units of analysis: the household, the enterprise, and the individual client.

The most frequently used micro-level impact variables at the household and enterprise levels are listed in box 1. While these are the most commonly used variables, there are many other household- and enterprise-level impact variables that have been analysed. For example, for client populations with low levels of income, some studies include behavioural variables related to risk management. At the level of the individual client, studies typically measure either changes in business skills or changes in psychosocial variables, such as those related to women's empowerment.

Box 1.   Common impact variables

Household	**Enterprise**
• Income	• Profits
• Assets	• Sales
• Housing	• Assets
• Food	• Employment
• Education	• Registration

Attributes of Good Indicators

Once the conceptual impact variables have been selected, the next challenge is to develop appropriate indicators to use in measuring these impacts. Good indicators have the attributes of simplicity, availability, reliability, and validity (Godsey 1996):

- A *simple* indicator is easy to implement, interpret, and communicate.

- An *available* indicator is compatible with the time and budget for the study.

- A *reliable* indicator is accurate, unbiased, and replicable.

- A *valid* indicator is closely related to the concept, unambiguous, and objective.

Normally, a number of possible indicators can be used to measure a single conceptual variable. The challenge is to select the indicator that provides the optimal balance between the four attributes described above.

Two Examples: Enterprise Profit and Household Income

Enterprise profit is a common enterprise-level impact variable. Many different indicators for enterprise profit have been used in empirical studies. Most of these indicators encompass one or more of the four components of profit: sales, labour costs, other operating costs, and depreciation of fixed assets.

Indicators for measuring profit can range from a complex, time-consuming accounting of all of the profit components to a single question asking the entrepreneur to provide an estimate for profit. An empirical study of four different profit indicators showed that each represented a different balance of simplicity, availability, reliability, and validity (Daniels 1999a, 1999b).

While household income is one of the most common impact variables, it can be difficult to measure. Two distinct approaches are used. The income-based approach measures income as the household receives it. The expenditure-based approach measures income indirectly by measuring household expenditures. For both the income-based and expenditure-based approaches, there are ranges of possible indicators: the simplest ones use one or two questions; the more complex ones are based on a large number of detailed questions.

Microfinance programmes that target low-income populations may be interested in assessing the poverty levels of client households. Poverty assessment is closely related to the measurement of household income and, consequently, can follow an income-based or expenditure-based approach. These monetary measures of poverty can then be compared to national poverty standards, such as the Living Standards Measurement Surveys (LSMS), or to international poverty standards, such as the $1/day and $2/day estimates. A third distinct approach for assessing poverty levels involves the creation of an index of physically observable variables, such as a housing index. Significant advances in assessing microfinance clients' poverty levels can be expected in the next several years, as donors are becoming increasingly interested in this issue.

Toward the Identification of Best Practice Principles

Interest within the microfinance industry for impact analysis is likely to persist, fuelled by pressures for accountability and improved programme management. At the same time, the tensions and challenges underlying impact analysis imply that no single approach will be optimal for all situations. Just because different approaches are needed to address different situations, this does not mean that all approaches to impact analysis are acceptable. Resources to conduct impact analysis are scarce: they should be used to produce reliable and credible results.

To ensure a good return on the resources used in impact analysis and to generate useful information for evaluating and improving programmes, the microfinance industry needs a set of best practice principles for impact analysis. Ten principles are proposed and briefly described below, offered as a starting point to initiate a dialogue leading to agreement on a set of best practice principles.

1. **Clarify the motivations for the study**: Before starting an impact analysis, it should be clear who are the stakeholders for the study and how study results will be used. The stakeholders' objectives and the key questions to be answered should play a critical role in selecting the appropriate levels of analysis and the specific types of impacts to be included. The motivations for the study should influence how potential methodological trade-offs are addressed.

2. **Develop the conceptual impact pathways**: In order to create a plausible case for attributing the observed impacts to the microfinance programme, the impact analysis should be based on a logically consistent conceptual (theoretical) model. The conceptual model should indicate the pathways by which participation in the microfinance programme might lead to the hypothesised impacts.

3. **Identify the counterfactual**: The counterfactual is what would have happened in the absence of the programme. The findings from an impact analysis should always be interpreted relative to a credible counterfactual. For studies based on an experimental or non-experimental research design, the control group provides the counterfactual. The control group for a non-experimental design should be constructed carefully. At the meso and macro levels of analysis, it may not be possible to construct a control group, but some credible counterfactual should still be identified.

4. **Choose impact variables and indicators carefully**: Impact variables should be closely linked to the objectives and conceptual model for the study. The number of impact variables should be limited to those that are directly related to the study objectives and that can be measured effectively given the resources available for the study. Possible indicators should be evaluated in terms of their simplicity, availability, reliability, and validity. Indicators that have been used in past studies should be reviewed, since these may be easily adapted to fit the current study.

5. **Accommodate fungibility**: The conceptual model, data collection techniques, and analytical methods should accommodate the fact that money is fungible within the enterprise and within the household economic portfolio. Assumptions about how funds are allocated should be avoided. It is usually difficult to elicit accurate survey information about how funds are used, particularly if respondents use funds for some purpose other than intended by the microfinance provider.

6. **Triangulate to improve validity**: Since there are no flawless impact analysis methods, a combination of methods that point to the same conclusion should be assembled to strengthen the validity of the impact findings. In particular, a mixed-method approach, which combines quantitative and qualitative methods, can be used to measure the size and direction of impacts and to provide detailed information about the processes by which they occur.

7. **Incorporate participants' perspectives**: In planning the impact analysis, attention should be paid to finding ways to include participants' own perspectives on impact. This will strengthen the interpretation of the findings and may lead to the discovery of unanticipated impacts. Participants' perspectives may be given centre stage through the use of participatory learning and action methods, or they may be incorporated in a more limited way through other qualitative techniques.

8. **Recognise and reduce bias**: The possibility of selection bias should be anticipated in all microfinance impact analyses. The goal of reducing selection bias should play an important role in selecting the counterfactual, the research design, and the analytical methods. While the level of bias should be reduced as much as possible, it should be recognised that all studies contain some degree of bias.

9. **Acknowledge the limitations of the approach**: Since all possible methodological weaknesses cannot be completely eliminated, the results of every study should be reported with an honest and explicit discussion of remaining limitations. This helps to place the findings in perspective, and it provides a more balanced basis for comparing impact findings across different studies.

10. **Utilise design and analysis experience**: It is important to draw on existing expertise in planning an impact analysis. While expertise may be developed internally or hired externally, some level of experience is needed to ensure adequate planning for data collection and analysis. If expertise is developed internally, then special attention should be placed on reducing the bias that might result if evaluators have a vested interest in demonstrating the positive impacts of their programme.

Contributions of the KfW-Sponsored Studies

Both impact studies presented in this book make significant contributions to the field of microfinance impact analysis. They cover three distinct levels of analysis. At the micro level, the chapter by Addai and Nienborg (2002) reports and compares findings from similar client-level impact studies in four countries of Southeast Europe. The chapter by Wisniwski and Maurer (2002) breaks new ground in attempting to analyse programme impacts at the levels of the financial institution and the financial sector.

Impacts on Clients

The micro-level study (Addai and Nienborg 2002) compiles results from client-level impact studies in Romania, Montenegro, Kosovo, and Bosnia and Herzegovina. A major contribution is that, by following similar methods in all four countries, cross-country impact comparisons can be made. Differences in the findings across the four countries suggest two conclusions. First, the differences highlight the importance and role of context in influencing programme impacts. Second, the differences indicate that the methods used are relatively unbiased and sensitive enough to detect a variety of programme outcomes.

The client-level studies have several design strengths, including incorporation of fungibility, triangulation of methods, and utilisation of design and analysis experience. Fungibility is addressed by measuring impacts not only on the enterprise, but on the household as a whole. This was particularly helpful in the case of Montenegro, where credit was not associated with improved enterprise performance. Instead, there were measurable impacts on household well-being during the study period.

Triangulation through the use of both survey and case study methods led to a deeper understanding of the impact processes and provided a consistent interpretation of the findings. Finally, the study relied on design and analysis experience in the selection of a well-tested survey instrument and in seeking external review of the conclusions from an internationally recognised expert. These and other design strengths are consistent with the best practice principles for impact analysis discussed in the previous section.

Impacts on Financial Institutions

For the meso-level study, Wisniwski and Maurer assume that positive impacts on the financial institution occur to the extent that the KfW programme helps the financial institution achieve its own objectives of improving its market position and increasing its profitability. These two impact indicators are compatible with acknowledged industry standards of improving outreach and financial self-sufficiency. In fact, the use of these criteria for finance programme evaluation has been proposed as an alternative to client-level evaluation (Rhyne 1994).

While outreach and profitability appear to be appropriate indicators for meso-level impact analysis, the challenge of using this approach to analyse the impacts of KfW's financial sector projects is the difficulty of identifying appropriate counterfactuals. For KfW projects that foster downscaling operations at existing banks, the authors compare the performance of the SME operation to the performance of the bank's other lending operations. For greenfield banks, the authors analyse the impact of these newly created banks on the financial sector as a whole.

Impacts on the Financial Sector

In the macro-level component of the impact analysis, Wisniwski and Maurer propose a number of qualitative indicators for the impact of KfW's financial sector projects on the financial sector. These indicators include enhanced leverage for the soundest financial institutions, creation of positive demonstration effects within former centrally planned financial sectors, and provision of a learning experience for bank supervisors and central bankers.

Clearly, this pioneering study has opened the door for continued analysis of macro-level impacts. Appropriate quantitative indicators are also needed at this level. In a situation such as in Kosovo, where the KfW programme provided almost 40 percent of total loans to the private sector in 2001, it might also be possible to estimate the impact of financial sector projects on macroeconomic variables, for example employment and GDP. This would represent a useful next step for future studies.

Conclusion

Taken together, the two studies measure the impacts of KfW's financial sector projects and suggest areas for improving programme management. This is clearly an advance over the earlier round of impact studies, which were conducted primarily to satisfy donors' requests for accountability. Any future impact analyses sponsored by KfW should increase the focus on generating and articulating results that can be used to improve programme management, both for KfW and for the partner banks. Additional work is also needed to continue the progress made in defining and refining impact indicators at the meso and macro levels.

This paper has described some of the tensions and challenges associated with microfinance impact analysis and the feasibility of conducting impact studies. Analysing the impacts of financial sector programmes such as undertaken by KfW is a legitimate response to a variety of constructive uses for this type of information. While no single impact analysis method is ideal for addressing every challenge, that does not imply that any and all methods are equally acceptable. To guide microfinance impact analysis, this paper proposes a set of best practice principles. With continued discussion and testing, it should be possible to refine this list and improve microfinance impact analysis.

References

Addai, Abenaa and Kristine Nienborg. 2002. *Enterprise Level Impacts of Financial Sector Projects in Southeast Europe*. Paper presented at the KfW symposium in Berlin.

Chen, Martha Alter and Elizabeth Dunn. 1996. *Household Economic Portfolios*. AIMS Project Report, USAID/G/EG/MD. Washington, D.C.: Management Systems International.

Daniels, Lisa. 1999a. *Alternatives for Measuring Profits and Net Worth of Microenterprises*. AIMS Project Report, USAID/G/EG/MD. Washington, D.C.: Management Systems International.

Daniels, Lisa. 1999b. *Measuring Profits and Net Worth of Microenterprises: A Field Test of Eight Proxies*. AIMS Project Report, USAID/G/EG/MD. Washington, D.C.: Management Systems International.

Dunn, Elizabeth. 2002a. It Pays to Know the Customer: Addressing the Information Needs of Client-Centered MFIs. *Journal of International Development* 14: 325-334.

Dunn, Elizabeth. 2002b. *Research Strategy for the AIMS Core Impact Assessments*. AIMS Project Report, USAID/G/EG/MD. Washington, D.C.: Management Systems International.

Gaile, Gary and Jennifer Foster. 1996. *Review of Methodological Approaches to the Study of the Impact of Microenterprise Credit Programmes*. AIMS Project Report, USAID/G/EG/MD. Washington, D.C.: Management Systems International.

Godsey, Larry. 1996. *Selecting Indicators of Sustainable Farming Systems*. Unpublished M.S. thesis. Columbia, MO: University of Missouri, Department of Agricultural Economics.

Hulme, David and Paul Mosley. 1996. *Finance Against Poverty*. Vols. 1&2. New York: Routledge.

Wisniwski, Sylvia and Klaus Maurer. 2002. *Impact of Financial Sector Projects in Southeast Europe – Effects on Financial Institutions and the Financial Sector*. Paper presented at the KfW symposium in Berlin.

Meyer, Richard L. 2002. *Track Record of Financial Institutions in Assisting the Poor in Asia*. ADB Institute Research Paper No. 49. Tokyo: Asian Development Bank Institute.

Moffitt, Robert. 1991. "Program Evaluation with Non-Experimental Data." *Evaluation Review* 15(3): 291-314.

Pitt, Mark and Shahidur Khandker. 1996. *Household and Intrahousehold Impact of the Grameen Bank and Similar Targeted Credit Programs in Bangladesh*. World Bank Discussion Paper 320. Washington, D.C.: World Bank.

Rhyne, Elisabeth. 1994. A New View of Finance Program Evaluation. Chapter 6 in *The New World of Microenterprise Finance: Building Healthy Financial Institutions for the Poor*, ed. by María Otero and Elisabeth Rhyne. West Hartford, CT: Kumarian Press.

Rossi, Peter H. and Howard E. Freeman. 1989. *Evaluation: A Systematic Approach*. Newbury Park, CA: Sage Publications.

Sebstad, Jennefer and Gregory Chen. 1996. *Overview of Studies on the Impact of Microenterprise Credit*. AIMS Project Report, USAID/G/EG/MD. Washington, D.C.: Management Systems International.

Zeller, Manfred, and Richard L. Meyer, eds. 2003. *The Triangle of Microfinance: Financial Sustainability, Outreach and Impact*. Baltimore: The Johns Hopkins University Press.

CHAPTER 14

Enterprise Level Impacts of Financial Sector Projects in Southeast Europe

Abenaa Addai* and Kristine Nienborg**

* Consultant, LFS Financial Systems GmbH, Berlin, Germany
** Former Consultant, LFS Financial Systems GmbH, Berlin, Germany

Why Impact Assessment?

The financial sector in developing and transition countries is heavily supported by donor assistance. Hundreds of millions of dollars are poured into the finance industry every year on the grounds that this public money fills holes left behind by the private financial sector. This assumption is supported by studies showing that specific target groups (such as the informal sector and small and medium sized enterprises (SMEs)) which are regarded as essential for economic and social development are not adequately served by banks and therefore lack the funds necessary for sustained development. The gap left by the private sector is filled by a wide range of programmes which focus, for example, on supporting existing banks in downscaling their operations in order to reach the "unbanked" or to better serve their corporate clientele, on greenfield operations or on upgrading non-governmental organisations (NGOs) and microfinance institutions (MFIs). All of these programmes aim to enhance economic and social development. In this sense, financial institutions are used as intermediaries to provide the target group (the economic actors in the real economy) with access to capital.

These credit programmes are financed by public funds. Although the degree of subsidies they contain is substantially lower than in many other development programmes, such programmes are justified only if the intervention generates social welfare benefits that spread beyond the enterprises receiving funds. Most credit programmes have a weighty agenda, and improving access to financial services and financing alternatives for a specific target group is only an intermediate objective. Their ultimate goals are to increase employment, contribute to private sector growth, and to improve household and thereby social wellbeing. Another main objective may also be to support the survival of entrepreneurs in the light of faltering social security systems. Therefore, the question is whether these programmes achieve their set objectives and what impact they have at the entrepreneurial, institutional and sectoral levels.

Methodological Issues

LFS Financial Systems GmbH was commissioned by KfW to conduct four impact analyses of their loan funds in Southeast Europe (Bosnia and Herzegovina (BiH), Kosovo, Montenegro and Romania[1]). The main analytical objective was to ascertain the funds' socio-economic, and micro- and macro-economic impacts. The analyses were designed along the lines of the best practices of the AIMS[2] tool sets, adapted to the circumstances of the funds and countries.

To construct a theoretical framework for analysis, LFS reviewed KfW programme documents to identify the following anticipated impacts of the funds at the enterprise level:

- private enterprise development

- job creation

- financial sector deepening (i.e. access to adequate financial services)

- social security

- poverty alleviation

- self-empowerment

Following discussions with KfW staff and consideration of the above-mentioned objectives as outlined in the programme documents, we concluded that the first three impacts were of primary importance and focused our analysis on these areas.

Plausible Association

We defined impact analysis as an inquiry to estimate the extent, pattern, or direction of change in the objectives that can be plausibly associated with the provision of credit. This is distinct from the more academic approach to impact research that seeks to measure change precisely and attribute it to an intervention with a high degree of confidence. The volatile nature of the financial sectors in Southeast Europe does not provide the necessary basis for academic impact research, as devel-

---

[1] Please refer to the Annex for descriptions of the four funds. "Fund" as used here refers to the fund in the respective country.

[2] AIMS: Assessing the Impact of Microenterprise Services, a project of USAID.

opment in this sector is often very fast and dramatic. Therefore, rather than proving impact within precise and statistically definable limits of probability, the findings are geared to help understand intervention processes and to identify and estimate the significance of impact that stands the test of plausible association.

Research Design

The impact analysis was carried out at the enterprise and institutional levels[3]. On the enterprise level, analysis compared two points in time, before and after the intervention, and used two sample groups (one recipient or client group, and one control or non-client group) to establish plausible association and to test the main research hypotheses, namely that the programme:

- serves its target group,

- increases the growth of assisted businesses as measured by income and employment,

- improves financing alternatives for the enterprise,

- increases household economic well-being as measured by increases in household income/expenditures, savings, etc.

We opted for an analysis which was small in size and scope, using easily measurable indicators and uncomplicated analytical techniques. A mixture of quantitative and qualitative approaches was used. To establish validity of the data and the reliability of the measures of change, the findings obtained through various methods were compared using triangulation techniques.

In each country we interviewed a sample group of 60 clients, which represent the following percentages of clients in the total outstanding portfolio of the partner banks financed by the relevant fund: Romania, 5%; Montenegro, 10%; Kosovo, 10%; and Bosnia and Herzegovina (BiH), 30%.

For comparison, an equally large non-client sample was surveyed. The enterprise survey was based on a standard questionnaire given to a selected sample of respondents as well as on a core set of case studies (around 10 in each country). These case studies helped to illuminate the impact process and the pathways of change, to test counterfactual reasons for changes in key variables and to investigate complex or unexplained phenomena. In each country, the survey was conducted jointly with a research institute or university.

To interpret results, it was necessary to determine the exogenous factors which might influence programme success and analyse the extent to which they affected

---

[3] Impact analysis at the institutional level was conducted in BiH and Montenegro. This part of the impact analysis however is not discussed further in this paper (see Wisniwski and Maurer in this book).

the programme. These factors included inflation, economic growth levels and patterns, the political situation, and the government regulations in the country concerned. It is not possible to measure precisely the contribution of each factor to the observed outcome, but it is useful to observe whether a particular hypothesised influence is present or absent and whether significant changes in these factors occurred during the period under review.

The impact analysis was designed both to provide feedback to KfW on the attainment of programme objectives and to serve as a market research study for the partner banks. The market research questions for the participating banks focused on the evaluation of existing products and new product development as a basis for analysing the changing situations of existing clients, the potential demand for new products, and the appropriateness of delivery systems.

The Characteristics of the Client Samples

The table below gives an overview of the characteristics of the 60 randomly sampled enterprises[4] in the four countries in which impact analyses were conducted. Whilst in Kosovo the majority of enterprises (61%) operate in the trade sector, the sample in BiH contains a comparatively high proportion of enterprises engaged in manufacturing (39%). The average number of employees per enterprise ranges from only 1.6 in Kosovo to 11 in BiH. An equally wide range of mean monthly turnover was revealed: from €6,000 in Romania and Montenegro to €37,000 in BiH. Entrepreneurs were asked to provide a rough estimate of investment[5] in the previous 12 months: enterprises in BiH had invested most with an average of €58,000; enterprises in Montenegro and Kosovo €26,000 and €27,000 respectively, and enterprises in Romania least with €15,000. Loan sizes were also substantially larger for the BiH sample (€32,000) than for the other three countries (€4,000 to €6,000).

Testing the Hypothesis: Loans Increase the Growth of Businesses

In the following, we focus on the research hypothesis that the fund increases the growth of assisted businesses with respect to two indicators: profit and employment. The complete results of our work, including a detailed impact analysis for each country, can be obtained from LFS Financial Systems GmbH, Berlin.

---

[4] In each country survey, the sample was stratified according to size and sector for further analysis.

[5] Investments are specified as financial inputs into the enterprise which are designed to increase output. Financial inputs are in this case defined as fixed assets and working capital.

Table 1. Characteristics of client enterprises

	Romania	Montenegro	Kosovo	BiH
% of (re)start-ups	n.a.	n.a.	n.a.	25%
Full-time employees (12 months ago)	4.5	3.8	1.6	11
Average monthly sales turnover (previous 12 months)	€6,000	€6,000	€10,000	€37,000
Average investment in previous 12 months	€15,000	€26,000	€27,000	c. €58,000*
Conditions of loan from fund				
Interest rate	12%-24% p.a.	21.6%-24% p.a.	15%-24 % p.a.	10%-16%p.a.
Average maturity (months)	19	8	10	36
Average loan size	€6,500	€4,000	€6,000	€32,000

* We asked entrepreneurs in BiH the amount they had invested in the past 3 years. The average figure was €174,000, giving an annual average of €58,000

To test the hypothesis that the loan increased the growth of the enterprise, respondents were asked about profit trends. In BiH and Romania, over 60% replied that their profits had increased during the previous 12 months, and the vast majority attributed this to an increase in their turnover. In Montenegro and Kosovo in contrast, only around 20% witnessed a positive trend, with the majority of enterprises reporting stagnant or decreasing profits.

The second indicator used to test the hypothesis that the loan assisted the business was the employment created within the previous 12 months. As shown in figure 2, the clients in BiH had the highest absolute increase in full-time positions at 57% (230 positions)[6] whilst clients in Kosovo had the lowest with 10% (15 new positions). In Romania 39 (12%) and in Montenegro 34 (19%) new positions were created by the sample group of clients.

The ratio of investment and loan-funded investment per incremental position shows that in Montenegro the most jobs were created for any given loan amount.

---

[6] In BiH incremental employment was compared to the period before loan investment, which in some cases was up to 36 months previously.

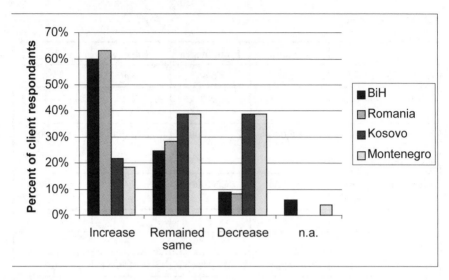

Figure 1.   Development of profit

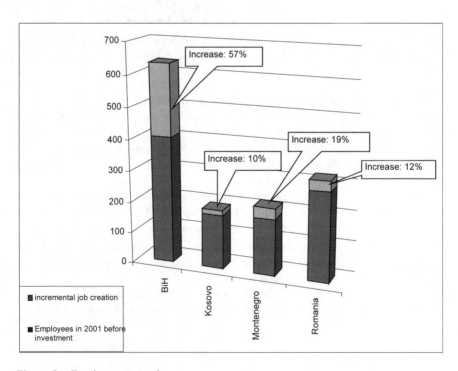

Figure 2.   Employment creation

Table 2. Investment per job

	BiH	Kosovo	Montenegro	Romania
Total invest-ment/job	€49,000	€94,000	€40,000	€23,000
Loan invest-ment/job	€8,000	€31,000	€7,000	€10,000

Interpreting the Results

A cross-country comparison of the development of the assisted businesses showed considerable variations: clients in BiH created the highest number of jobs, whilst job creation in Kosovo was rather low; clients in Romania and BiH achieved better profit results than those in Montenegro and Kosovo. The interpretation of differences in the above results is based on the most important, decisive factors:

- growth potential and enterprise size: we assume that the size of the enterprise is related to its growth potential.

- obstacles to enterprise growth: if access to finance is a major obstacle to enterprise growth, the loan should have a positive impact on business development.

- design of loan product: lending terms and conditions influence the type and duration of investments made by the client.

- impact direction: the loan might have other intended or unintended impacts outside the loan financed business.

- timing of impact analysis: loan programmes mature over time and client businesses may grow progressively. The earlier the impact analysis, the lower the measurable change in business indicators.

Romania

In Romania, 64% of the client entrepreneurs surveyed reported higher profits and an overall 12% increase in full-time employment. In order to establish a connection between this positive result and the loans received from the German Romanian Fund (GRF) via one of its partner banks, we tested whether the loans had influenced the clients' investment behaviour. Figure 3 below compares investments made by clients and non-clients in the previous 12 months.

Client enterprises invested an average of about €13,000, distinctly more than the non-client average of around €8,000. Whilst the amount of companies' own

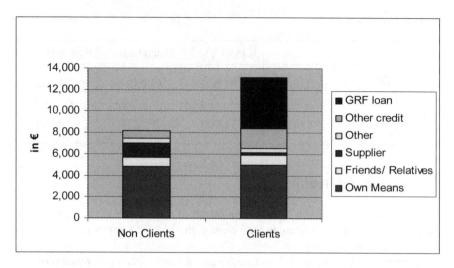

Figure 3. Average investment and financing structure

resources invested in the business remains equally high for both groups, the sur-plus invested by clients roughly equals the amount of the loan. We can therefore assume that the additional investment is related to access to credit.

As a result of client enterprises having invested more, one would expect their business development over the previous 12 months to differ from that of non-clients. Two out of three clients confirmed an increase in profits over the previous 12 months, compared to only one-fourth of non-clients. Increases in profits were in most cases attributed to higher turnover, but clients also often cited the intro-duction of new products, improved management and increases in productivity. Whereas one quarter of non-clients declared that profits had decreased, hardly any clients reported reduced profits. Falling profit levels were attributed to higher input costs and lower sales. Thus, clients were more likely than non-clients to strengthen their market position.

This positive client trend was also mirrored in employment creation: clients on average created twice as many jobs as non-clients; the former increased their work-force on average by 0.7 employees, the latter by 0.3. This translates into 39 addi-tional positions created by clients and 21 by non-clients. Enterprises that received a loan increased the number of employees by 23%, non-clients by only 9%.

Clients were more likely to increase profits and turnover, and they generated more employment. This positive trend for clients can be attributed to the receipt of a GRF loan.

The analysis shows that the tendency to increase investment with access to fi-nance is supported by the overall improvement in the investment climate in Ro-mania. Entrepreneurs tend to plan in longer time-horizons and therefore also make long-term investments.

Montenegro

As shown in figure 1 above, 80% of the client sample in Montenegro reported no growth in profits over the previous 12 months. A comparison of client and non-client investment during the previous 12 months reveals that clients invested slightly less (€ 11,000) than non-clients (€ 12,000). The figure below shows a change in the financing structure of clients: they seem to have used the loan for investment rather than investing their own funds.

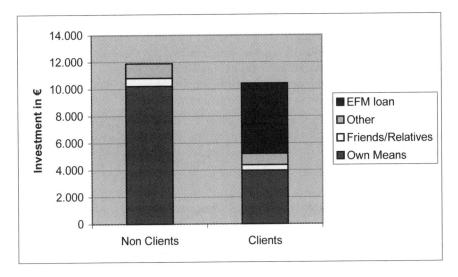

Figure 4. Average investment and financing structure

In contrast to Romania, loans did not induce additional investment. Moreover, the two groups invested in almost equal amounts and recorded similar changes in profit and employment. As such, there is no indication that access to finance led to business growth.

Presuming that loans replaced clients' own resources that would otherwise have been invested in the enterprise, the question arises: how did clients use their freed-up resources? This issue was explored by analysing the change in household income and savings, which are typically closely correlated in microenterprises.

The survey showed that clients were better off than non-clients with regard to changes in their household income and savings. One could therefore conclude that their own resources, which would otherwise have been invested in the business, were used instead to increase household expenditure and savings. The impact of the loan therefore had a greater impact on the household than on the enterprise.

The low measurable impact on the loan-financed enterprise must also be attributed to the very early timing of the impact analysis, as the programme was still in its pilot phase when the study was conducted. Furthermore, the enterprises targeted by the fund are typically microenterprises, and many of these serve as subsidiary activities (30%) that are not inclined to grow, but rather to generate enough income and a little profit to cover household expenses. We typically refer to these enterprises as " survivors". Last but not least, loans were short term with relatively high interest rates, which seems justified for the pilot phase of the programme, but which did not translate into significant enterprise growth or achieve overall impact.

Kosovo

As in the case of Montenegro, clients invested on average only as much as non-clients during the previous 12 months, which means that the loan did not induce additional investment but rather replaced other funding sources. To identify the role the loan plays in the development of their enterprise, clients were asked to specify the main obstacles to business development. These are listed below:

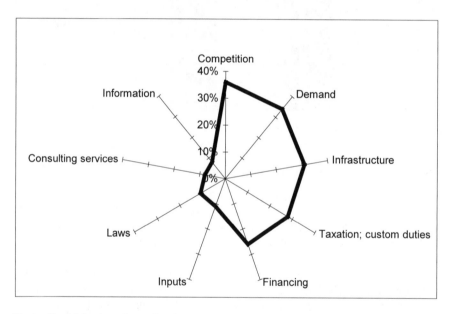

Figure 5.   Main obstacles to development

Their business activities are not diversified, and Figure 5 shows that clients find excessive or unfair competition and the lack of demand for their services to be the main obstacles to enterprise development. Even though Kosovo experienced GDP growth of 17% in 2001, nearly all clients who were interviewed complained of a decline in their businesses. Since they were mainly engaged in the trade, commerce and services sectors they felt the impact of reduced international assistance and presence directly: nearly 80% reported stagnant or declining profits during the previous 12 months. Inadequate infrastructure (mainly roads and electricity) is also named as an impediment, followed by high taxation and customs duties. Even though the banking system in Kosovo is extremely deficient, finance is ranked in fifth place amongst the primary barriers to enterprise development. On the other hand, it can be assumed that access to finance alone cannot bring about concrete improvements in the assisted business.

As shown above, clients experienced only modest growth in employment and profits. Nevertheless, as table 3 below illustrates, clients are better off than non-clients.

Table 3. Change in profit

	non-client	client
	%	%
Lower than 12 months ago	69.5%	39.0%
About the same as 12 months ago	25.4%	39.0%
Higher than 12 months ago	3.4%	22.0%
No answer	1.7%	0.0%

Our analysis led us to conclude that the client group invested their resources more profitably: more clients than non-clients increased their turnover, their profits were higher, and fewer clients than non-clients reported decreases. Furthermore, the growth rates experienced by loan recipients were either higher or the rates of decline lower than for the non-client group. One possible explanation is that the cost of external financing has sharpened client focus on profitable investment.

The increase in employment can be attributed almost entirely to the client group, who created 15 new full-time jobs in the previous 12 months. Non-clients employed only two new persons.

Summarising for the Kosovo sample: client businesses grew more rapidly than those of non-clients, but the overall impact on profits and employment remained low. The political and legal risks which reflect the situation then current in Kosovo – continuing ethnic conflicts and the inadequate legal framework – deter the foreign direct investment which Kosovo must attract to achieve sustainable economic growth. And sustainable economic growth is a precondition for a long-term increase in domestic purchasing power which will enable Kosovo's microenterprises and SMEs to drive development. Moreover, the targeted microenterprises are "survivors" with an average of 1.6 employees. Their potential to generate additional employment remains limited, although the loan was of vital importance for maintaining their current business levels.

Bosnia and Herzegovina (BiH)

In BiH, it was not possible to identify a control group, as all creditworthy enterprises which displayed the same characteristics as the client group had already received credits from formal sources. Client SMEs had also taken on sizeable loans with reasonable conditions from sources other than the fund, making it impossible to compare business development between the two groups .

Figure 6 below shows that the loans represented only 16% on average of the enterprises' financial resources. These resources mainly comprised reinvested profits and, to a lesser extent, savings. The relatively minor role played by credit in overall business investment makes it difficult to assess its impact. However, as the loan-financed enterprises are relatively large in comparison to those of the other three countries surveyed in Southeast Europe, their growth potential is higher: they invested on average € 58,000 per year, mostly through reinvestment from their own businesses.

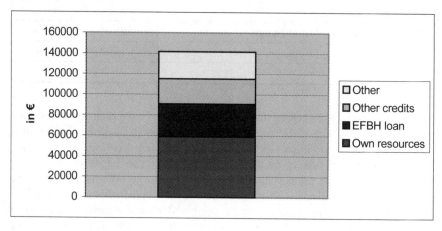

Figure 6. Average investment and financing structure

From the start of the programme, loan conditions were favourable for long-term investments. Interest rates were below 16% and loan maturities extended up to five years. The financial market and economic situation in BiH does not seem substantially better than in Romania, although BiH does have a stable currency due to its currency board. Lending risk is probably just as high in BiH as in Romania, but the banks grant longer terms for loans from the fund. This may imply that these positive lending conditions, which certainly support long-term investments, are "donor-influenced".

In early 2000, when most clients invested their loan proceeds, the overall economic situation was positive. The economy was still growing at around 10% per year, as BiH profited from high levels of external reconstruction aid. At that time, the majority of investment was used to replace broken, worn out or obsolete equipment (80% of the investment went into fixed assets), with a direct impact on turnover and employment. At the end of 2001, the growth rate dropped to 2.5%. We can therefore assume that if the analysis had been conducted in 2002, the measurable impact would have been substantially lower.

Relating Impact Results to Objectives of the Funds

The objectives of the funds as described in the project documents are broadly similar for all four countries: supporting the financial sector will enhance private enterprise; enterprises with access to credit will expand and contribute to the growth of the national economy.

The results of the impact analysis, however, varied from country to country, and varied substantially in terms of impact on employment and profits. The fund objectives should be detailed more specifically to define what exactly is to be achieved and to what extent. Some funds have objectives which cannot be fully realised because of the way the programme is implemented. For example, the European Fund for Kosovo includes "enhancing job opportunities" as one of its main objectives. Our results show that the enterprises currently targeted have little potential for job creation. Client enterprises were better off than non-client enterprises, suggesting that the loans helped to sustain their businesses and prevent them from declining. Therefore, we believe that it would be more appropriate to include objectives for these programmes which focus, for example, on maintaining employment or improving the welfare of households engaged in microenterprise. If job creation or fostering rapid economic development are the main objectives, why not alter the focus to support enterprises with larger growth potential?

Depending on the intended programme impact on the "real sector", the target group would range from larger enterprises to microenterprises, perhaps comprising the full range. The attempt to reach "survivors" or larger enterprises would imply different approaches and/or different "implementing partners" (e.g. partner institutions).

We also recommend adopting a more country-specific focus when designing loan programmes, adjusting the objectives to reflect the macroeconomic and social conditions in each country. There appears to be a substantial difference between what can be achieved in each country through the fund and what can be achieved through other loan programmes.

Once the assumptions underlying the objectives and the means of achieving them have been defined, the validity of these assumptions should be regularly assessed in surveys similar to the current impact analysis.

Even though all impact assessments are subject to methodological constraints such as respondent group sampling bias and budgetary restrictions that limit sample size, their results can help interpret whether objectives are being reached.

The funds managed by KfW are at a very early stage of their implementation in Kosovo and Montenegro – too early for a fully-fledged impact assessment. Lending to small and microenterprises is typically based on the graduation principle and repeated lending: most banks start by issuing working capital loans with short maturities. As time progresses and the bank-client relationship develops, maturities may lengthen and loan sizes increase. It would therefore be expedient to measure full impact after a few years have elapsed.

Annex: Short Descriptions of the Funds in Southeast Europe

The European Fund for Bosnia and Herzegovina

To support reconstruction and rehabilitation in Bosnia and Herzegovina (BiH), KfW established a revolving fund, the European Fund for Bosnia and Herzegovina (EFBH), having two components: the Housing Construction Loan Programme (HCLP) and the Small and Medium Sized Enterprise Fund (SMEF). Since April 1998, KfW has acted as agent in implementing the HCLP, which was established by the European Commission (EC) with €25 million (HCLP I: €15 million and HCLP II: €10 million). At the end of 1998, EFBH added a second window to promote small and medium-sized enterprises (SMEs) with funds from the governments of Austria (€2,5 million), Switzerland (approximately €0.65 million) and Germany (€0.5 million). In 1999, the EC also contributed €5 million to the SMEF.

Housing Construction Loan Programme

The HCLP was set up to make loans to individuals in order to finance housing (re)construction and rehabilitation and to improve living conditions and the social situation in Bosnia and Herzegovina. By mitigating the dramatic shortage of housing, the programme's priority aim was to encourage the return of refugees and to help displaced persons. HCLP's target group consists of Bosnian families currently residing in BiH. Within this target group, special attention was to be paid to refugees, returnees and displaced persons.

Medium and long-term loans for the repair, construction, extension or improvement of homes have been disbursed. The loans ranged from €1,250 to €17,500 and later to €25,000. Interest rates were set at 8% for mortgage loans and 10% for loans without a mortgage (up to €7,500) with maturities of up to 12 years.

Small and Medium-Sized Enterprise Programme

The objectives of the SMEF are to provide a stable and sustained supply of credit to private enterprises for expansion, (re)construction and the improvement of production capacity and for enhancing plant utilisation rates. It is intended to create long-term employment opportunities and income-generating activities in BiH which should also encourage refugees and displaced persons to return voluntarily.

SMEF may provide SMEs with a single loan at reasonable terms, but it also strives to establish companies' access to the Bosnian banking system and to financial resources over the long term.

The programme targets existing SMEs as well as start-ups with up to 50 employees in a variety of industries. The loans can be used to bolster working capital or for investments. It is the first programme in BiH to supply long-term loans of between €2,500 and €50,000 to SMEs. The maximum interest rates defined in the contracts with donors and agreed with the partner banks range from 12% to 16% per year, depending on the loan amount. The maturities of individual loans are adapted to the type of project to be financed and the capacity to repay, but may not exceed five years.

The European Fund for Kosovo

In 2000, KfW set up the European Fund for Kosovo, a refinancing fund to promote SME- and micro-lending activities by financial institutions in Kosovo. The donors currently participating in this fund are the European Union, represented by the European Agency for Reconstruction (EAR), and the German and Swiss governments.

In May 2000, EAR concluded a financing agreement with KfW to contribute to the European Fund for Kosovo. EAR granted €1 million for onlending to micro and small enterprises (MSEs) through the Micro Enterprise Bank of Kosovo (MEB).

In August 2000, the second financing agreement followed. EAR granted €3.63 million for onlending to small and micro enterprises through banks and non-bank financial institutions licensed in Kosovo. In autumn 2000, KfW started to negotiate a second EAR-refinanced loan for MEB for the purpose of onlending to MSEs.

Disbursement of the EAR funds to clients proceeded rapidly. By May 2001, the loan was disbursed in full to MEB. As of 31 March 2002, 630 loans amounting to €2,518,000 were outstanding to MEB clients under the EAR loan. On that date, the EAR credit line represented 20% of the total loan portfolio of MEB, which amounted to €12,365,000 with a total of 2218 sub-loans.

The European Fund for Montenegro

To support economic development in Montenegro, KfW started a pilot project in March 2000 in the form of a revolving fund for onlending to SMEs through Crnogorska Komercijalna Banka (CKB). KfW concluded an initial €0.4 million contract with CKB for refinancing micro loans and added a small grant for technical assistance. In September 2000, the Austrian government joined the project by contributing €0.2 million for onlending.

Based on the positive experience with the pilot project and in view of the continuously high demand for SME and micro loans, KfW set up the European Fund for Montenegro (EFM) to support the country's economic development by promoting the SME and micro lending activities of the financial sector. EFM is financed through contributions from the German government (via KfW), the Swiss government (represented by SDC), the European Union (represented by EAR) and the Austrian government which officially joined the EFM in June 2002.

By 2002, EFM's total funds amounted to € 8.76 million for onlending and € 1.1 million for technical assistance. With contributions from the German, Austrian and Montenegrin governments, the fund volume was further increased by € 2.05 million to provide a credit line for agriculture and rural areas (Rural Loan Programme – RLP). KfW acts as agent for the different donors and administers the refinancing funds for onlending to selected partner banks in Montenegro.

The KfW pilot programme and the EFM target private SMEs with fewer than 50 employees. In the pilot phase, start-ups were not eligible; the maximum loan amount was € 25,000 and maturity was limited to three years. The EFM target group has been broadened and now includes start-ups. The maximum loan amount has been increased to € 50,000 and the maturity to 5 years. Both in the programme pilot phase and in the context of the EFM, partner banks bear the full default risks and accept several types of collateral: mortgages, pledges, guarantees from individuals or legal entities, bank deposits and bills of exchange.

The German Romanian Fund

To support the transition process, the German government provided DM 10 million (€ 5.112 million) to Romania through KfW in 1998 to establish the German-Romanian Fund (GRF), a revolving apex fund. GRF finances micro and small enterprises, with a special focus on micro loans. The funds provided were split into an investment component of DM 8.5 million (€ 4.35 million) and a technical assistance component of DM 1.5 million (€ 777,000). The GRF received additional funding of DM 9 million (€ 4.6 million) in 2001 and € 9.6 million in 2002. The objective of the GRF is twofold: to provide credit to SMEs and improve the capacity of the Romanian financial sector to lend to the targeted enterprises.

The GRF refinances partner banks at market rates. The base rate for calculating the interest paid by the partner banks to GRF is the 6 months EURIBOR, plus a risk margin. The programme currently works with four partner banks: Banca Comerciala Carpatica (BCC), MCR/MIRO, Banca Romaneasca (BR), and Volksbank Romania. The partner banks' branch networks cover the whole of the country except for the eastern part. The sub-loans issued by the partner banks under the programme are offered at market rates in hard currencies. The partner banks are free to set interest rates and commissions on sub-loans in order to cover their intermediation expenses. In return, they bear the prime credit risk on sub-loans. The maximum loan amount in 2002 was € 60,000.

As of April 2002, the programme had disbursed more than 1,600 loans to the target group in Romania. No partner bank has ever defaulted on its repayment obligation to GRF. The repayment performance of the sub-borrowers is excellent: the arrears rate on sub-loans was less than 2% in April 2002. Only at one former partner bank, CEC, were four sub-loans written off. The maturity of the sub-loans is up to two years. The average maturity is 15 months, as most loans finance fixed assets.

CHAPTER 15:

Impact of Financial Sector Projects in Southeast Europe – Effects on Financial Institutions and the Financial Sector

Sylvia Wisniwski* and Klaus Maurer**

* Head of Bankakademie International, Frankfurt, Germany
** Consultant, Berlin, Germany

Introduction

This paper addresses the impact of KfW-managed programmes on partner banks and the financial sector at large in Southeast Europe. While impact analysis has traditionally focused on evaluating the impact of financial services at the household and enterprise level, this paper takes a different perspective by asking how such programmes affect both the institutional and financial sector level. Responding to these questions poses large methodological challenges since partner banks and financial sectors are rather complex organisational structures that are exposed to various internal and external factors. This paper therefore takes an eclectic approach and can be considered as work in process.

Since 1995, KfW has been responsible for a number of German financial cooperation programmes and has acted as fund manager on behalf of other bilateral and multilateral donor agencies. In these capacities, it has used two primary financial instruments to promote financial sector development in the region: first, refinancing lines to partner banks that on-lend these funds to specific target groups such as households, microenterprises and SMEs; second, technical assistance to partner banks in lending technology, credit risk management, information technology (IT) and management information systems (MIS).

In addition, various special instruments have been employed in selected countries. At the institutional level, these include stand-by credit lines, credit guarantee funds and equity participation in microbanks. At the financial sector level, technical assistance and funding have been provided to establish support institutions, ranging from a deposit insurance agency in Bosnia and Herzegovina to a credit reference bureau and a pledge registrar in Kosovo.

Finally, KfW has been a strong advocate of policy dialogue and donor coordination, facilitating the introduction and use of various financial instruments. By pooling funds from various donor sources the impact on the financial sector can be increased along with outreach. KfW has also contributed significantly to harmonising donor views and putting forward a joint strategy to strengthen financial sectors in the countries under consideration. In these capacities, KfW together with other donor agencies has played a catalytic role in sensitising local governments with a view to promoting conducive frameworks for microenterprise and SME finance.

Analytical Focus

This paper analyses KfW-managed programmes in four countries: Bosnia and Herzegovina, Romania, Kosovo and Albania. The table below provides an overview of these programmes.

Table 1. Overview of KfW-managed programmes (amounts in €million)

	Refinance	TA	Other instruments
BiH	31.8 (23.0 housing, 8.8 SME) (trust fund)	3.3	• Equity participation in MEB BiH (0.68) • Deposit insurance (5.0) • Guarantee Fund (10.0)
Romania	11.9	2.5	• Equity participation in MiroBank (2.0)
Kosovo	9.9 (8.6 SME, 1.3 housing)	1.2	• FEFAD equity participation in MEB Kosovo (1.2)
Albania	7.2	0.85	• Equity participation in FEFAD Bank (1.5) • Stand-by Credit Lines (1.0 m USD)
TOTAL	**60.8**	**7.85**	**21.5**

At the institutional level, two major approaches can be identified: a) down-scaling existing banks, and b) establishing greenfield financial institutions. In some countries, one or the other of these two approaches has been pursued, for example greenfield operations in Kosovo until mid-2002, while in other countries, for instance Bosnia and Herzegovina and Romania, the two approaches have been combined. FEFAD Bank in Albania is a hybrid form of greenfield financial institution since it emerged out of the FEFAD Foundation. However, to consider FEFAD Bank the result of an upgrading strategy would be misleading since FEFAD always operated as a commercially driven financial institution with the objective of obtaining a full license as a financial intermediary.

Depending upon the evolution of the country environment and the institutional capacity of the individual partner bank, a sequence of various financial assistance instruments has been employed. While the provision of long-term credit lines has always been among the first support instruments used and continues to be the major pillar of support programmes, these credit lines have been combined with special financial instruments. The credit guarantee fund for Bosnia and Herzegovina, for example, should facilitate local partner banks' access to international capital markets on more favourable conditions than the country risk rating would have warranted without a KfW guarantee. In Albania, the introduction of a stand-by credit line has made it possible for banks to use a larger proportion of locally mobilised, primarily short-term deposits for lending operations. The possibility of drawing on a credit line instantly to fund massive withdrawals of deposits has reduced the risk of the existing maturity mismatch.

Analytical Method

The methodological approach used here combines the collection of primary data with the analysis of existing reference material. In most cases, three-day on-site visits were made in the countries under consideration, except for Albania, where a desk study of project documentation was carried out. During these visits, interviews were held with representatives of the partner banks, including top and mid-level managers, and in some cases loan officers. In addition, information was obtained from key stakeholders of sector institutions such as central banks, supervisory authorities and bank associations. Finally, consultations took place with donor agencies engaged in financial sector programmes, including the European Bank for Reconstruction and Development (EBRD), the United States Agency for International Development (USAID), Deutsche Gesellschaft für Technische Zusammenarbeit (GTZ) and others. Various sources of secondary data were tapped: project documents and evaluations, central bank statistics, annual reports, and internal documents from partner banks and other financial institutions. The cut-off date for the quantitative information presented in this paper was 31 December 2001. Qualitative assessments draw on developments that occurred during 2002.

The degree of impact of KfW-managed programmes was found to depend on four factors:

- the framework conditions, including the structure of financial institutions and financial sectors, and the scale and depth of financial intermediation at the time KfW programmes began,

- the scope of the programme intervention as measured by the share of KfW-managed loans in the overall loan portfolio of each individual partner bank in determining impact on financial institutions, or the total volume of KfW-managed loans in relation to the scale of banking operations in each country in determining impact at the sector level,

- the duration of the intervention,

- the existence of other donor or government-sponsored programmes as well as the presence of commercial players that had an impact on partner banks and financial sectors generally.

As the following table indicates, the financial sectors of the four countries present very different profiles. KfW refinance facilities are limited compared to the total volume of bank assets and outstanding loan portfolios in the region. In terms of programme duration, activities in Albania and Bosnia and Herzegovina date back to 1998. In contrast, the small and medium (SME) credit line in Romania has been active since 2001, and in Kosovo the first loan contract with a partner bank in a downscaling exercise was signed in 2002.

In addition to the KfW-managed programmes, other donor and government agencies have provided massive support for the financial sectors in the countries under consideration. Foreign investors have also ventured into the region and operate with local subsidiaries such as Raiffeisenbank Austria in Bosnia and Herzegovina and in Romania, or participate in local banks such as Banca di Roma and the Banca Italo Albanese in Albania. Given these complex framework conditions and the limited empirical research carried out on site, this paper outlines preliminary conclusions. It develops a list of hypotheses relating to the impact of KfW-managed programmes at the institutional and sector levels.

Impact on Financial Institutions

This section analyses the impact of KfW-managed programmes on the participating financial institutions.

Terms, Methodology and Hypotheses

Methodologically, we distinguish between a) outputs and b) impact. *Outputs* are defined as the direct effects or results of an intervention. Results or outputs of the credit lines to partner banks are sub-loans to intended target groups such as SMEs. A major output related to technical assistance, for example, is the number of loan officers trained. *Impact* goes beyond the narrow project-related outputs and comprises more indirect, spill-over effects on the financial institution overall. The latter effects are of primary interest here.

We have limited the institutional impact analysis to the down-scaling approach and to financial institutions which existed before programme inception. This paper does not provide an impact assessment for greenfield institutions because outputs and impact cannot be discerned due to the dominance of external intervention.

Table 2. Country Profiles

	1998	1999	2000	2001
Bosnia and Herzegovina				
Macroeconomic Data				
– Population (million)	4.2	4.3	4.3	4.3
– GDP (€ million)	3,804	4,399	4,823	5,152
– Inflation (Federation of BiH)	5.2%	–0.7%	1.9%	1.7%
– Inflation (Republika Srpska)	–14.0%	14.1%	14.6%	8.0%
Financial Sector Data				
- Number of Banks	n/a	62	56	53
- Total Bank Assets (€ million)	1,993	1,996	2,181	2,750
- M2/GDP	21.1%	26.0%	26.9%	46.3%
- Total Credit to the Private Sector/GDP	38.3%	33.0%	32.4%	34.8%
Romania				
Macroeconomic Data				
– Population	22.5	22.5	22.4	22.4
– GDP (€ million)	29,026	29,424	33,027	41,395
– Inflation	40.6%	54.8%	40.7%	30.3%
Financial Sector Data				
– Number of Banks	45	45	45	n/a
– Total Bank Assets (€ million)	11,574	9,938	9,647	12,630
– M2/GDP	24.9%	24.9%	23.2%	23.4%
– Total Credit to the Private Sector/GDP	14.2%	15.9%	10.7%	9.4%
Albania				
Macroeconomic Data				
– Population	3.4	3.4	3.4	3.4
– GDP (€ million)	2,779	3,713	3,984	n/a
– Inflation	8.7%	-1.0%	4.2%	3.5%
Financial Sector Data				
– Number of Banks	10	13	13	13
– Total Bank Assets (€ million)	1,568	1,852	2,072	2,536
– M2/GDP	43.3%	47.3%	49.1%	n/a
– Total Credit to the Private Sector/GDP	3.2%	3.6%	4.1%	n/a

Table 2 (continued)

	2000	2001
Kosovo *		
Macroeconomic Data		
– Population	2.0	2.0
– GDP (€ million)	1,534	n/a
– Inflation	n/a	n/a
Financial Sector Data		
– Number of Banks	1	7
– Total Bank Assets (€ million)	103	502
– M2/GDP	n/ap	n/ap
– Total Credit to the Private Sector/GDP	0.1%	n/a

n/a: not available; n/ap: not applicable.

* Only the two years following the war in Kosovo have been taken into account.

Source: Own calculations based on central bank and IMF information for the respective countries.

The centrepiece of our analysis is the European Fund for Bosnia and Herzegovina (EFBH) and its six partner banks. The fund has been in operation since 1998. The analysis is complemented by more recent experience from Romania where the German-Romanian Fund (GRF) has entered into cooperation with four financial institutions. Table 3 presents an overview of the partner institutions by asset size, history of cooperation, and significance of programme loans.

Our analysis of institutional impact is essentially based on the hypothesis that KfW-managed programmes will have a positive impact on a partner bank if the programmes contribute to the partner banks' own objectives. The following section attempts to provide answers to the central question: To what extent have the programmes contributed to the partner banks' own objectives?

What are the partner banks' own objectives? All partner banks listed in Table 3, with the exception of the Romanian Savings Bank (CEC), are private commercial banks which presumably have two objectives: a) to strengthen their market position, customer base and sales, and b) profitability. These dual objectives are compatible with the development objectives of a) outreach and b) sustainability which govern donor-funded credit programmes and institutions. In the following we will look at the impact of the programmes on the partner banks' market position and profitability.

Table 3. Overview of participating financial institutions in BiH and Romania

Participating banks	Total Assets (€ million)	Start of cooperation	Programme loans/ Total loans
Bosnia and Herzegovina			
Raiffeisenbank	381	06/1998	7.4 %
Zagrebacka Banka	291	2000	3.6 %
Universal Banka	133	06/1998	5.7 %
UPI Banka	51	2000	5.6 %
Gospodarska Banka	38	06/1998	7.9 %
MEB Banka	34	06/1999	10.2 %
Romania			
Romanian Savings Bank (CEC)	1,068	03/1999	0.9%
Banka Romaneasca	90	03/2001	1.8%
Banca Commerciale Carpatica (BCC)	23	11/2000	12.3%
Microcredit Romania (MCR)	6	10/1999	64.4%

Impact on Partner Banks' Market Position, Customer Base and Sales

Market-making: The programmes have expanded the range of partner banks' financial services and products

Access to long-term refinance. Banks in Bosnia and Herzegovina (BiH), as in most other transition countries, have a fundamental bias in the term structure of their assets and liabilities. The bulk of their liabilities consists of short-term deposits, mainly demand and savings deposits, while the maturity of term or fixed deposits is rarely beyond three months. Through the KfW-managed programmes, banks gained access to long-term refinance which in turn enabled them to issue long-term loans. In fact, KfW-managed credit lines have become the major source of borrowing for most banks, as shown in Table 4 below.

There is no general evidence that international credit lines have crowded out local deposits. In all BiH partner banks, total deposits represent around 90% of overall liabilities with the exception of the greenfield MEB BiH with around 37%.[1] In Romania, the situation is different: borrowings by BCC and Banka Romaneasca

---

[1] Figures as of 30 June 2002.

Table 4. Programme credit lines as a share of total borrowings (31 December 2001)

Partner Bank	% of total borrowing	% of long-term borrowing
Bosnia and Herzegovina		
Universal Banka	73%	96%
Gospodarska Banka	70%	84%
Raiffeisenbank	48%	53%
UPI Banka	37%	n.a.
Zagrebacka Banka	36%	45%
MEB Banka	11%	12%
Romania		
Banka Romaneasca	5%	5%
Banca Commerciale Carpatica (BCC)	87%	89%
Microcredit Romania (MCR)	54%	84%
Romanian Savings Bank (CEC)	7%	n.a.

represent 25%-30% of their total liabilities.[2] However, scrutinising the structure of their borrowings more carefully, the only bank in which international credit lines account for a larger share is Banka Romaneasca: 17% of its total liabilities are financed by international development finance institutions or projects. Historically, Banka Romaneasca has had low levels of savings mobilisation. Whether this is due to the lack of incentives reflecting the availability of international credit lines or to other factors requires further study.

Introduction of long-term loan products. As banks struggle to match the maturity structure of their liabilities and assets, the bulk of lending is short-term. Among the BiH partner banks, fewer than 10% of their loans have a maturity of more than one year. Through participation in KfW-managed programmes, banks have introduced long-term loan products: loans to small and medium-sized enterprises for working capital and investment, and home mortgage loans to private households. In most partner banks, programme loans account for a major share of overall long-term loans, if not the largest share as is the case in Universal Banka in BiH, and Banca Commerciale Carpatica (BCC) and Microcredit Romania (MCR) in Romania (see Table 5).

---

[2] We exclude CEC and MCR from this analysis because they represent extreme cases. CEC is almost exclusively financed by local deposits. Borrowings represent less than 2% of total liabilities. MCR is not allowed to collect deposits from the public. It therefore finances its entire credit business out of its own funds and loans received from international lenders. Consequently, their borrowings/liabilities ratio was 92% at 30 June 2002 (IPC 2002).

Table 5. Programme loans as a proportion of total long-term loans (31 December 2001)

Participating banks	Programme loans/Long-term loans
Bosnia and Herzegovina	
Raiffeisenbank	17%
Zagrebacka Banka	8%
Universal Banka	48%
UPI Banka	n.a.
Gospodarska Banka	21%
MEB Banka	28%
Romania	
Romanian Savings Bank (CEC)	n.a.
Banka Romaneasca	5%
Banca Commerciale Carpatica (BCC)	83%
Microcredit Romania (MCR)	100%

Introduction of housing loans in BiH. The Housing Construction Loan Programme (HCLP) funded by the EU and managed by KfW introduced the banks to housing loans and mortgage lending. The programme demonstrated to the banks that the housing sector is an important area of business and a potential source of profits (EU Monitoring Report, March 2000, p. 11). Five out of six partner banks in BiH now also offer housing loans from their own resources (Glaubitt 2002, p. iii).

Sensitisation for SME lending. The SME programmes have created an awareness of the role and importance of private-sector small and medium-sized enterprises. SMEs have emerged as a new type of bank customer in transition economies, where the enterprise sector previously consisted of large corporate and mostly state-owned companies. In Romania, for example, the importance of SMEs for the country's economic development is reflected in the establishment of a separate ministry for SMEs. Some banks, such as Raiffeisenbank in BiH, have recently created a special department for SME lending. While these developments reflect the combined efforts of private, government and donor initiatives, KfW-managed programmes have contributed and reinforced these trends.

Sector diversification within the loan portfolio. New lending to SMEs helped diversify partner banks' loan portfolios. SME loan portfolios *per se* have a low concentration of risk because they comprise a large number of small individual loans. In BiH, loans to SMEs are spread across all sectors of the economy: 44% of approved loan amounts have been allocated to production, 21% to trade and commerce, 29% to services, and 4% to agriculture. In Romania, a higher share of loan volume (39%) went into trade and commerce and only 11% to production; 27% of loans were issued to mixed enterprises engaged in various activities, including trade and commerce, services and production. The higher share of the trade and commerce sector in the Romanian programme is due to the fact that the majority of loans (75%) are actually loans to microenterprises rather than SMEs.

Cross-selling. The credit programmes enabled the banks to sell additional products and services. For example, 36% of SME customers asked for additional services. These mainly comprised new short and long term loans, credit cards, money transfers and bank guarantees (LFS 2002, p. 36). Cross-selling becomes especially relevant as a cost-reduction mechanism in highly competitive situations when margins are squeezed; which is the case in the countries under consideration.

Market making: The programmes broadened the customer base of partner banks

Through participation in the programmes, the partner banks increased and broadened their customer base. In BiH, the housing and SME programmes attracted new clients. A recent survey among sub-borrowers found that 38% were new customers for the bank. Sixty percent of the housing loan customers interviewed said they had no previous contact with the bank (LFS 2002, p. 40).

The SME programmes led to the establishment of new enterprises. A considerable portion of the SME loans - 21% of all loans in BiH – were issued to start-ups or business restarts after the end of the war. The KfW-managed programmes provided incentives to the partner banks to tap new markets.

In BiH, the programmes facilitated Raiffeisenbank's market entry into Republika Srpska (RS). Taking over the customers and a high-quality loan portfolio from two ailing banks, Raiffeisenbank started operations in RS with a ready-made customer base and a significant scale of business.

The programmes improved customer service orientation

The newly introduced SME lending technology led to stronger client orientation at the loan officer level. In personal interviews with borrowers during household and enterprise visits, loan officers develop an in-depth understanding of the economic and personal situation of the borrowers and establish a close relationship with them. By obtaining comprehensive insights into the financial management of SMEs at both the household and enterprise levels, the partner banks are better able to offer credit and additional services.

The programmes facilitated partner banks' access to international capital markets

The KfW-managed programmes served as a reference point for international investors and potential strategic partners. Especially in the early years of programme implementation, association with KfW as an international financial institution gave the banks credibility in terms of trustworthiness and sustainability (EU Monitoring Report, March 2000). This enhanced the corporate image of a small bank such as BCC in Romania in its dealings with the national bank and with other international institutions.

A credit guarantee fund was set up in BiH by the German government and KfW specifically to create links and business relationships between West European commercial banks and banks in BiH. However, the fund came rather late and at a time when most banks in BiH had already entered into partnerships with strategic investors. Therefore, the role of the guarantee fund as a door-opener to the international capital markets for local banks did not materialise.

Impact on Partner Banks' Profitability

Assessing the impact of the credit programmes on the partner banks' profitability is rather difficult. Most partner banks still lack management accounting systems that treat different activities or products as distinct profit centres. While income and certain cost categories can be easily allocated to specific activities or products, the attribution of administrative costs poses a major challenge.

Acknowledging the methodological difficulties, a profit centre calculation was developed for the partner banks in BiH using the banks' financial statements.[3] Due to the underlying assumptions this does not present a fully accurate picture of the profitability situation but rather indicates the overall trend. Table 6 outlines the income and cost structure of the individual partner banks in BiH[5] and, in the last column of the table, the combined weighted average of the six banks.

The following observations can be made regarding the overall profitability of the banks:

- lending is a loss-making business for all banks. Increasing competition has reduced lending rates and has narrowed financial spreads while cost levels have remained high. The average administrative cost, at 9% of the average loan portfolio, plus the risk cost of more than 4% (measured by loan loss provisions) combine to produce an average operating cost of 13.4%.

- taking into account other banking activities, however, five out of six banks generated an overall profit. The profitability of banks in BiH largely depends on fee and commission income – primarily associated with payment and transfer services.

Table 7 compares the overall weighted average income and expense of the six partner banks (first column) to the income and cost structure of the SME and

---

[3] A similar calculation for Romania was premature as the more active partner institutions (MCR and BCC) had been engaged in the programme for only one or two years.

Table 6. Profitability of partner banks in BiH (2001)

	Raiff-eisen	Zagre-backa	Univer-sal	UPI	Gospo-darska	MEB	Weighted Average
Average loan portfolio (€ million)	102.1	92.0	67.1	21.6	16.0	14.6	52.2
Relative weight	33%	29%	21%	7%	5%	5%	100%
As % of average loan portfolio							
Interest income	12.4%	10.3%	12.8%	14.0%	9.9%	18.7%	12.2%
Interest expenses	2.8%	2.6%	4.2%	5.3%	2.8%	1.1%	3.1%
Financial spread	9.6%	7.7%	8.6%	8.7%	7.1%	17.6%	9.0%
Administrative cost	7.5%	8.2%	10.2%	8.8%	10.6%	20.6%	9.1%
Risk cost	3.5%	5.5%	5.0%	2.9%	1.5%	2.8%	4.3%
Operating cost	11.0%	13.7%	15.2%	11.7%	12.1%	23.4%	13.4%
Net income from lending	−1.4%	−6.0%	−6.6%	−3.0%	−3.5%	−5.8%	−4.4%
Placements with banks (net income)	−1.0%	0.6%	−1.1%	0.8%	−4.7%		−0.6%
Fees and commissions (net income)	5.6%	6.5%	5.0%	2.2%	8.9%	7.0%	5.7%
Foreign exchange gains and other income	1.7%	2.8%	1.0%	1.9%	0.2%	10.8%	2.3%
Net income (before tax)	4.9%	4.0%	−1.7%	1.9%	0.9%	12.1%	3.1%

Note: Universal Bank's risk cost of 5% excludes loses incurred from its takeover of Kommerzijalna Banka.

housing programmes. The cost estimate of the SME and housing credit programmes is based on two assumptions:

- administrative costs are assumed to be lower than the overall average, which includes the administrative cost of deposit mobilisation (estimated at 25% of total administrative cost) which are of course not incurred under the credit lines.[4]

- risk cost in the form of loan loss provisions was imputed at 50% of the portfolio at risk over 30 days.

---

[4] See an earlier study (Maurer 2001) for further details.

Table 7. Comparison of weighted average net income from lending of the six banks (% of average loan portfolio)

	Overall Average*	SME Programme	Housing Programme
Interest income	12.2%	12.0 %	9.0 %
Interest expenses	3.1%	2.0 %	3.0 %
Financial spread	9.0%	10.0 %	6.0 %
Administrative cost	9.1%	7.3 %	7.3 %
Risk cost (Loan loss provisions)	4.3%	4.8 %	0.5 %
Operating cost	13.4%	12.1 %	7.8 %
Net income from lending	–4.4 %	–2.1 %	–1.8 %

* Last column Table 6.

Based on these assumptions, lending under both programmes has not been profitable for the partner banks in absolute terms. In relative terms, however, the credit programmes have fared better than the overall lending operations of the partner banks.

Better loan portfolio quality and lower loan loss provision requirements have been a major contributory factor. This is especially true for the housing loan programme, which has risk costs of only 0.5%. The comparatively high risk costs under the SME programme are due to the deterioration of the SME loan portfolio at some banks in 2001 (Table 6). Monitoring and enforcement efforts were stepped up in order to improve SME portfolio quality.

Participation in the programmes, and especially with regard to the technical assistance provided, induced the banks to adopt improved credit risk management strategies and techniques. These included:

- cash flow based credit technology and appraisal techniques,

- strict borrower selection on the basis of repayment capacity and creditworthiness,

- the introduction of credit committees to ensure transparency and objective credit decisions,

- zero tolerance of delinquency, sending a strong signalling effect to borrowers,

- KfW's performance as a serious creditor, warming up "cold" donor money,

- the imposition of discipline on partner banks and clients,

- regular monitoring and close follow-up,

- strict enforcement where necessary.

These innovative lending techniques reduced administrative costs while keeping risk costs lower than average in the housing loan programme and roughly at the average in the SME loan programme. Given the increasing competition in the banking sector, partner banks face the challenge of striking an appropriate balance between efficiency (administrative costs) and portfolio quality (risk costs). The KfW loan programmes apparently have a better balance than the overall lending business. Several partner banks indicated that they have replicated features of the new SME lending technique in other loan products. Elements highlighted as adding most value to the banks' credit procedures were the use of credit committees and strict loan monitoring.

Impact on the Financial Sector

The impact of KfW-managed programmes on the financial sector depends on various factors, as noted in the introduction.

Let us first consider the framework conditions. The financial sectors of the four countries exhibit different levels of scale, breadth and depth of financial intermediation. Implementing financial services on virgin land in Kosovo obviously has better chances of creating a stronger impact than interventions in the more mature markets in the other countries under consideration.

KfW-managed interventions constitute only a limited portion of the total volume of bank assets and loans outstanding to the private sector. Kosovo, for obvious reasons, is the exception.[5]

Table 8. Relative share of programme loans in the 4 countries

As of 31.12.2001	BiH	Romania	Kosovo	Albania
Programme loans outstanding/ Total bank assets	0.9%	0.1%	1.0%	0.3%
Programme loans outstanding/ Total loans to private sector	1.6%	0.1%	20.6%	3.1%

Own calculations based on central bank statistics and data made available by bank supervisory agencies.

---

[5] Kosovo is a unique situation. MEB Kosovo was the first and only domestic retail bank in Kosovo in 2000.

This picture changes if we compare the number rather than the volume of outstanding loans. As of March 2002, for example, the outstanding loans of the partner banks participating in the German-Romanian Fund represented 2.2% of the total number of bank loan contracts. As of April 2002, the Microenterprise Bank of Kosovo (MEB Kosovo) held 65.6% of all outstanding loan contracts in the country's banking sector. In both cases, the market share in loan contracts is significantly higher than the market share of the bank's total assets or private sector loan portfolio. Unfortunately, information on the number of borrowers or loan contracts is not readily available in the countries in question, so there is little empirical evidence to sustain this argument. However, given the small size of individual loans, the KfW-managed programmes as a percentage of the total number of outstanding loans is larger than its percentage of the volume of loans outstanding.

Assessing the impact of the international credit lines only in terms of their direct effects as measured by market share, however, is too limited. The core question is to what degree these credit lines have created additional leverage effects within the partner banks, beyond the volume of funds borrowed. Did the partner banks show an active interest in penetrating the SME and housing markets? Did they start using their own funds to issue long-term loans to SMEs and the housing sector? The impact on the financial sector would be larger to the extent that the programme generates loans in addition to those refinanced through international credit lines.

Likewise, equity investments in microbanks may be judged by the demonstration effects generated by these greenfield banks in their respective financial markets. But, to create impact among other market participants, demonstration effects must be visible and "felt" in the market. Therefore, the size of the greenfield bank and its respective market share will be decisive in determining whether other commercial banks or nonbank financial institutions will adopt or adapt the business model of the greenfield microbanks. The table below shows a varied picture of the potential for generating demonstration effects through greenfield banks.[6]

Table 9. Relative market share of greenfield banks in selected countries

As of 31 December 2001	MEB BiH	MEB Kosovo	FEFAD Albania
Greenfield bank assets/Total banking assets	1.2%	73.4%	2.6%
Total outstanding loans in greenfield banks/Total loans to private sector	1.2%	42.1%	8.1%

Own calculations based on central bank statistics and data made available by bank supervisory agencies.

---

[6] Miro Bank in Romania is not included in the overview table. This greenfield bank was launched at the beginning of 2002, after the research cut-off date of 31 December 2001.

Given that MEB Kosovo is the leader in its market, its demonstration effects are the largest of the three greenfield banks under consideration. In comparison, FE-FAD has gained a significant share in the Albanian lending market, which suggests that it attracts the attention of other market players. In contrast, the Microenterprise Bank of Bosnia and Herzegovina (MEB BiH) is a rather small player and will find it difficult to create perceptible demonstration effects in the Bosnian banking system.

Finally, the KfW-managed programmes have not taken place in a vacuum. Given the importance of the financial sector for the economic recovery of the region, various donors, for instance EBRD and USAID, have defined financial sector strengthening as a core development goal since the 1990s. In addition, re-establishing political and economic stability in the Balkans has attracted commercially-driven investors to the region, providing additional funds and expertise. Austrian banks, including Raiffeisen, Volksbank and Hypo Alpe-Adria Bank, have ventured into Southeast Europe, making their mark especially prominently in Bosnia and Herzegovina and Romania. In contrast, in Kosovo, microfinance institutions (MFIs), largely NGOs, play a significant role in the credit business. As of April 2002, out of a total outstanding loan portfolio of € 80.4 million, 36.3% was administered by MFIs. The MFI share of the number of loan contracts amounted to 77.9%. NGOs are largely dependent on donor funding, which makes other donors' impact on the financial sector in Kosovo quite sizeable.

Against this background, the study defines the impact of KfW-managed programmes on the financial sector primarily in qualitative terms. In addition, impact is largely due to the combined effect of various activities undertaken by a variety of international and national organisations.

Partner Banks – "Picking the Winners"

By carefully selecting the soundest financial institutions and those with the greatest development potential on the basis of comprehensive due diligence examinations, programme credit lines leverage their funding and have an overall impact on the financial sector.

The European Fund for Bosnia and Herzegovina selected half a dozen partner banks out of a group of around 60 commercial banks during the late 1990s, and KfW as fund manager indirectly carried out a rating exercise, separating the high-potential banks from those with weak institutional capacity and little promise. However, not all partner banks chosen in Bosnia and Herzegovina became "winners". BH Banka and Komercijalna Banka had to be closed down and were required to exit the KfW-managed programme.

Qualifying for EFBH funds, which were among the first long-term resources available to commercial banks in Bosnia and Herzegovina, could be considered a quality seal for the partner banks. This produced a positive signal to other potential providers of funds and investors. It is not possible to prove that these institutions were led to the partner banks solely because of KfW's involvement. However, all partner banks cited the reputational gain and experience attained through access to EFBH credit lines as critical elements in their ability to establish relationships with other business partners.

The partner banks improved their growth prospects by engaging various funding sources. This, in turn, enhanced their ability to expand SME and housing lending beyond the limits of the credit line. The "KfW quality seal" may have been decisive in leveraging more funds for loans to the target population.

In addition, the success of the new loan products introduced by KfW-managed funds motivated several partner banks to use their own funds for lending to the target clientele. This fuelled the partner banks' expansion of private sector lending even further.

We expect that the existing partner banks will emerge as market leaders in the current consolidation of the banking sector in BiH. In late 2002, they already represented a considerable share of total bank assets (34%), loans (26%) and deposits (51%), with an upward trend. The sheer volume of operations of the group of partner banks will have a positive impact on the entire banking industry.

Greenfield Financial Institutions

The banking system in former Yugoslavia was characterised by centrally-planned credit allocation. Banks therefore had no experience in credit risk management as financial intermediation was not guided by market principles. After the dismantling of the former Yugoslav republic, this model was largely replaced by relationship lending. Only borrowers who had a strong personal relationship with the lending institution were able to borrow. The limitations of both models are obvious: While the former promotes politically driven credit rationing, the latter favours credit rationing based on personal contacts.

Greenfield institutions can produce demonstration effects in a specific environment

Against this background, one of the most important contributions of the greenfield banks is their approach to managing credit risk: anybody with sufficient capacity to repay and who is judged personally creditworthy can qualify for a loan, irrespective of their political or personal connections. At the same time, the greenfield banks promote strong repayment discipline. They follow up overdue loans immediately and execute collateral of willful defaulters.

The greenfield banks also place the individual customer at the centre of their banking activities. This contrasts sharply with banking in the former Yugoslav republic, where loans were "assigned" to socially-owned companies and deposits "belonged" to the state. Consequently, there has been a paradigm shift away from a supply-driven banking model that used banks as political instruments benefiting social ownership towards a demand-led banking model with individual client focus.

With the promotion of true credit risk management and client-centred banking, greenfield banks introduced new financial products and services. Whether these were microloans, as in the case of MEB BiH and FEFAD Albania, or the first loans ever disbursed to the private sector as in Kosovo, the greenfield banks have made a significant contribution to product innovation and market development.

Greenfield banks are also a model of customer service quality unknown in the former Yugoslav republics. Their customer approach incorporates a) large branch and automatic teller machine (ATM) networks operating close to the customer, b) rapid loan processing using simple procedures, c) very low entrance barriers, for example no minimum opening balances for savings accounts, and the acceptance of soft collateral.

Greenfield banks also operate as role models for transparency. Annual reports are now published regularly, introducing a new banking practice. FEFAD Albania, for example, discloses effective interest rates as one important mechanism to strengthen consumer rights (Kessler/Beck 2001, p. 5, 41). Greenfield banks also practise a zero-tolerance policy on fraud and corruption backed up by effective systems of internal and external controls.

In a virgin financial sector as existed in Kosovo, greenfield banks can take the lead in financial sector development. MEB Kosovo, for example, has become the benchmark for the Kosovar banking sector. MEB Kosovo was the first bank to enter the market, opening in January 2000. It had a monopoly position for about a year, and at the end of 2002 maintained a deposit market share of more than 70%. In such an exceptional environment, MEB Kosovo has been able to set the standards for banking operations, producing unique spill-over effects at the sector level:

- the presence of an international bank contributed significantly to instilling confidence in the new banking sector in Kosovo. Many Kosovars had lost their savings in the Yugoslav banks, so confidence was a prerequisite for attracting local resources for financial intermediation. The local banks that were subsequently opened benefited from the overall confidence in the banking industry.

- MEB Kosovo provided the first example of how to set up and run a commercial bank as a joint stock company, and brought international investors into the banking market.

- it was the first bank to move into Serbian enclaves and set up a multi-ethnic branch team.

- MEB Kosovo was the first bank to gain access to SWIFT (a global wire transfer system) and the MasterCard Europe system, facilitating noncash payments and consumer card transactions. Its pioneering efforts made it easier for other Kosovar banks to become members of these networks.

- MEB Kosovo is the only bank operating an ATM network in the country. Though the ATMs can be used only by MEB clients so far, it is envisaged that MEB will become the processing center for other banks.

The demonstration effect of MEB Kosovo as market leader and benchmark for the financial sector is widely recognised. However, these effects become more difficult to evaluate under different framework conditions. Empirical evidence suggests that the demonstration effects of greenfield institutions are reduced or even disappear when competition starts. Today's stiff banking competition in the region is primarily fuelled by two factors: a) markets are small and can accommodate only a few solid banks. b) foreign banks participate in the financial sector of all four countries either as minority or majority shareholders in local banks or through a local subsidiary. As a consequence, commercial banks venture into new, lower-end market segments in direct competition with greenfield banks. The market niche of greenfield banks is eroding, as demonstrated by reduced interest margins.

In response, greenfield banks originally set up as specialised microfinance or SME banks react by transforming into universal banks, broadening their product range and potential market coverage. This process has begun in Albania and in Bosnia and Herzegovina and is likely to evolve in Romania with the establishment of Miro Bank in 2002. At the same time, moving up market would be a logical response to reduced interest margins. Both trends, however, expose greenfield banks even more to competition from other commercial banks, with the following consequences:

On one hand, the unique or even monopoly position of the greenfield banks in the local financial market comes under attack. In such a situation, the greenfield banks' willingness to share information openly and serve as a role model is reduced. Information on the management, procedures and products of greenfield banks is no longer a public good, but a private good that must be protected.

On the other hand, greenfield banks can no longer pursue their self-centred approach of exclusive self-reliance. In the past they occupied a specific market niche and largely looked after themselves. Today, they are starting to look at the business and marketing strategies and product ranges of their direct competitors. MEB BiH, for example, monitors the consumer lending practices and leasing products of Raiffeisenbank.

MEB Kosovo is an exception in that it has operated as a universal bank from its inception. After having enjoyed a monopoly position for around a year, MEB Kosovo has now started facing serious price competition, particularly in international and national payments. However, being the largest bank in Kosovo, it has not yet had to make any changes to its own strategies in response to those of its competitors.

Greenfield institutions as a training ground for bank supervisors and central bankers

All greenfield banks have established close relationships with bank supervisory authorities and the domestic central bank in question. Consequently, the main stakeholders of the financial sector have been able to learn from the institutional experience of specialised microfinance or SME banks, drawing lessons for their financial sector policy. Greenfield banks, for example, prove that collateral substitutes can be equally or even more effective than traditional asset-based lending.

As the first bank in the market, MEB Kosovo automatically became the training ground for the new banking supervisory authority. Many local inspectors gained their first hands-on experience in licensing and on-site/off-site supervision with MEB Kosovo. This knowledge was then applied to banks established later. Several former bank inspectors obtained management positions in local banks. It can be assumed that they provide an additional indirect knowledge transfer from MEB Kosovo to other banks.

Greenfield institutions pilot-test new financial instruments

A major constraint that inhibits long-term lending in all the countries under consideration is the predominant share of sight deposits in banks' liability structures. Gaining access to sources of international long-term borrowing is one way to compensate for the lack of long-term funds. Another innovative instrument successfully tested by FEFAD Albania is international stand-by letters of credit issued by KfW. In contrast to international credit lines, these do not provide continuous long-term funding but rather stimulate and support the transformation of short-term deposits into long-term loans. The stand-by letter of credit serves as a stabilising device in case of massive withdrawals or other temporary liquidity short-falls. With a fall-back instrument that can generate liquidity quickly at any time, financial institutions should be willing to increase their maturity mismatch by using larger portions of short-term deposits for onlending.

This instrument is attractive for several reasons: it stimulates the mobilisation and use of local deposits, which are generally less costly than borrowing on the international markets, and this helps financial systems to become less reliant on the continuous supply of costly external funds. Successful pilot-testing at FEFAD Albania could lead to the wider use of stand-by letters of credit to promote financial intermediation in other commercial banks or non-bank financial institutions in the region.

Greenfield institutions can promote access through NGOs

MEB Kosovo has developed a unique model to link microcredit NGOs with the formal banking sector. This model enables NGO clients to use banking services such as deposit facilities and payment services that microcredit institutions such as NGOs cannot provide. In addition, by doing business with the formal banking sector, NGOs are likely to enhance their management skills and institutional capacities. This is particularly important in financial sectors where microcredit NGOs predominate in retail lending and serve a much larger number of borrowers than the commercial banks.

However, this should not be misinterpreted as another form of demonstration effect. Most microcredit NGOs started operating before MEB Kosovo came into existence. They also operate in a lower market segment and consider the MEB institutional model to be "too big to follow".

What are the features of the symbiotic relationship between MEB Kosovo and microcredit NGOs?

- in order to limit cash handling, almost all microcredit NGOs disburse loans by issuing cheques that must be cashed at MEB. Borrowers are also generally asked to repay the loan to an MEB account. Consequently, NGOs operate only in regions where MEB Kosovo has branches.

- MEB staff make weekly visits to several microcredit NGOs, offering deposit and payment services to NGO borrowers.

- MEB Kosovo has operated as a wholesale lender to one microcredit NGO.

- MEB Kosovo has installed an ATM in a minority region where only one microcredit NGO operates.

Consequently, MEB Kosovo and various microcredit NGOs operate in clear-cut markets and do not compete against each other. In fact, they rather complement each other and generate a win-win situation: microcredit NGOs specialise in microlending while MEB Kosovo provides deposit and payment facilities. This adds value to NGO services and serves customers more comprehensively. For MEB Kosovo, the attractiveness of the arrangement lies in easy access to a ready-made customer base for deposit and payment services. In addition, it creates potential for attracting borrowers that graduate from the scale of business funded by the NGO.

Efforts are already underway to establish a more formalised alliance between MEB Kosovo and selected microcredit NGOs. The latter would prepare the market and construct a loan portfolio that would be sold to MEB Kosovo, allowing the NGO to move to a new, untapped market. Whether designed as a formal alliance between the two or as an informal arrangement, the symbiotic relationship between MEB Kosovo and the microcredit NGOs makes a significant contribution to increasing the overall broadening and deepening of the financial sector.

Promotion of Sector Institutions

KfW has contributed to financial sector development through institutional initiatives that reduce transaction costs and improve risk management.

Deposit insurance enhances public confidence in depositories

The Deposit Insurance Agency of the Federation of Bosnia and Herzegovina (FBiH) started operations in February 2001. Since its inception, seven commercial banks have been accepted as members, representing more than half the total deposit base in FBiH. A similar agency was established for the Republik of Srpska (RS) in April 2001, but has not become operational due to lack of funds. Therefore, the RS banks do not offer any external deposit protection at present. However, a uniform deposit insurance mechanism incorporating both FBiH and RS banks is envisaged for the beginning of 2003.

Market research conducted by the FBiH Deposit Insurance Agency indicates that deposit insurance has enhanced the general public's confidence in depositories. According to a survey carried out in April 2002 (Müller 2002), 92% of the sample population in FBiH that knows about the existence of the Deposit Insurance Agency considers it to be important. The Deposit Insurance Agency instills confidence among 63% of respondents whereas 37% do not trust the insurance coverage. Around 19% of respondents would be willing to hold deposit balances in excess of the amount guaranteed in a bank that is member of the FBiH Deposit Insurance Agency. Compared to the results of a previous survey in June 2001, many more people now know about the deposit insurance mechanism, value its services and show increased trust in the banks associated with the Agency. In comparison, respondents from RS are much less well-informed and have stronger reservations concerning deposit protection. However, the survey reveals a clear tendency toward a more positive attitude during 2002.

Against this background, how has the deposit base evolved?

- as shown in table 10, the deposit base expanded significantly during 2001 (65%) compared to the relatively slow growth of less than 10% in the previous year.

- a positive structural effect occurred during 2001, when the proportion of long-term deposits in FBiH increased to almost 15%, facilitating long-term lending.

- deposits from individuals constituted 46% of the total deposit base in FBiH banks at the end of 2001. This is almost twice the figure for the previous year, which shows that the largest part of the newly mobilised savings during the year come from individuals. This reflects citizens' growing trust in the banking sector.

FBiH banks are clearly considered much more trustworthy than RS banks. The FBiH banks' lead position in the distribution of total savings in BiH has strengthened further. A particularly interesting feature is that the FBiH banks that entered the RS during 2001 captured a 16.2% share of total RS deposits within their first year of operations.

The introduction of deposit insurance strengthened confidence in depositories and facilitated a huge expansion of the deposit base as well as encouraging positive structural effects. However, these developments cannot be attributed primarily to the existence of the FBiH Deposit Insurance Agency. Only sound, large commercial banks qualified as members of the deposit insurance scheme. It is an open question whether the "quality seal" of the Deposit Insurance Agency attracted more savings to these banks or whether the same volume of savings could have been mobilised simply on the basis of the reputation and institutional strength of these banks.

Table 10.   Deposit mobilisation in BiH, 1999–2001

Year-end	1999	2000	2001
Total private sector deposits (€ million)	843.1	925.4	1,530.3
Short-term deposits up to 12 months (FBiH)	n/a	90.5%	85.3%
Long-term deposits over 12 months (FBiH)	n/a	9.5%	14.7%
Citizens' deposits (FBiH) as percent of total	24.3%	27.4%	46.0%
FBiH share of total deposits	82.7%	86.5%	88.2%
RS share of total deposits	17.3%	13.5%	11.8%
FBiH banks' share in RS deposit market	0.0%	0.1%	16.2%

Source: Own calculations based on information provided by the Banking Agency of BiH. Information on the banking system in FBiH as of December 31, 2001.

Another factor to be taken into account when analysing the evolution of the deposit base in 2001 is the conversion from the deutschmark to the euro, which virtually forced the general public to use deposit facilities. However, the continuously high level of deposit balances maintained during the first quarter of 2002 indicates that the banking sector was able to hang on to deposits. This experience contrasts sharply with other countries in the region. In Kosovo, for example, the banking sector experienced an equally massive mobilisation of deposits by the end of 2001 but faced a significant drop of the deposit base during the first quarter of 2002. These different trends could indicate a greater degree of trust in the Bosnian depositories, to which the deposit insurance scheme might have contributed.

Other sector support institutions enhance financial infrastructure

As market leader in the Kosovar banking sector, MEB Kosovo was the most interested party and also the best qualified financial institution to take the lead in developing sector support institutions. In 2001 and 2002, MEB Kosovo actively promoted the creation of the Kosovo Credit Information Service (KCIS), and the office of pledge registrar for moveable assets and, to a lesser degree, the Kosovar bank association.

KCIS identifies borrowers with bad credit histories; the pledge registrar is tasked with facilitating the legal enforcement of moveable assets as innovative collateral. These two instruments should enhance overall access to loans and reduce transaction costs for lenders and borrowers. While both instruments have been well received within the microcredit NGO community, only a few commercial banks have shown interest in the initiative. This might be attributed to the very strong commitment and operational involvement of MEB Kosovo in setting up the two schemes, which could have created scepticism about the neutrality of the instrument. Also, commercial banks' lending operations still rely primarily on traditional collateral so that a pledge registrar for moveable assets is of little relevance. However, this might change with the diversification of loan collateral in the future.

MEB Kosovo participated in the conceptual development of these initiatives and covered the start-up costs. MEB Kosovo provided staff time to establish KCIS, and KCIS marketing activities were handled by MEB staff until they reached a critical mass. KCIS was housed in the MEB building before finding its own premises.

Conclusions

From the experience gained with KfW-managed programmes in four Southeast European countries, we can draw several conclusions and derive lessons with regard to a) their impact on the financial institutions involved and b) their impact on the financial sector.

- The impact on financial institutions using the downscaling approach has been largely positive. KfW-managed credit programmes provide long-term funding that is currently not otherwise available in the market and facilitate medium and long-term lending.

- The programmes' combination of credit lines and technical assistance has expanded the range of financial services and products, broadened the customer base, raised customer service orientation and facilitated partner banks' access to international capital markets.

- The programmes have supported the partner banks on their paths toward profitability, which is a prerequisite for the sustainability of financial services. The programmes have fared better than overall lending operations, primarily as a result of the improved credit risk management techniques they introduced. Further increases in operational efficiency and improvements in the banks' cost structures remain major challenges.

- The impact of different financial instruments still is sensitive to appropriate timing under given framework conditions. Credit guarantee funds can have a powerful impact if they open doors to international capital in markets where few banks have such access. In more developed financial systems where the local banks' large deposit bases are mostly short-term, stand-by credit lines could be used at an early stage of cooperation to stimulate local fund mobilisation.

- Institutional impact varies across partner banks. Generally speaking, the programmes have had the strongest effect a) on private rather than state-owned banks, b) on small to medium-sized banks where programme loans account for more than 5% or even 10% of the loan portfolio, c) on banks which have participated in the programme for some time. It requires a minimum of two to three years for impact to materialise.

- The impact of KfW-managed credit programmes on the financial sector is limited in quantitative terms. The programmes generally account for less than 1% of banks' assets and less than 2% of loans to the private sector, except in Kosovo. However, when considering the number of borrowers reached, the respective market share increases. KfW-managed programmes create an impact beyond the nominal value of the funds employed by generating leverage effects in partner banks and through the demonstration effects of greenfield institutions.

- Leverage effects, i.e. mobilising additional funds to expand lending in the target markets, depend on the partner bank. "Picking the winners" refers to the selection of partner banks that combine an active interest in the target market with significant growth potential.

- The demonstration effects of greenfield institutions are particularly strong in virgin financial sectors such as in Kosovo. However, the demonstration effects actively pursued by greenfield institutions end where competition begins.

- Greenfield institutions have successfully helped central banks and supervisory authorities to become familiar with microfinance best practices.

- Greenfield institutions can expand the financial sector and enhance financial intermediation by establishing close ties with microcredit NGOs. By refinancing microcredit NGOs and providing complementary financial services to NGO clients, greenfield institutions increase their outreach. However, this symbiotic relationship works only when the greenfield institutions and the microcredit NGO serve different market segments.

- The creation of institutions such as deposit insurance agencies, credit reference bureaux or pledge registrars has a strong impact on the financial sector. In contrast, target-group oriented measures, such as SME and housing credit lines, can generate only indirect sector impact, which is a function of the market share of the respective partner banks.

- KfW-managed programmes had the greatest impact in countries where the scale and depth of financial intermediation was relatively limited when support activities started. This is certainly true for Kosovo, where KfW was among the first development finance institutions to enter a virgin financial market, and to a lesser degree for Albania and Bosnia and Herzegovina. In contrast, the Romanian financial sector was five times as big as the respective financial sectors in Albania and BiH alone, making it more difficult for financial support instruments to achieve a sizeable impact. The original plan to select a "big player" in the Romanian financial sector as the first partner bank (the Romanian Savings Bank - CEC) did not produce the desired results, and cooperation was discontinued by 2002. Incorporating small to medium-sized banks as partner institutions proved to be more effective, but has not yet generated a measurable impact in the Romanian financial sector.

- The largest variety of financial instruments in the four countries under consideration were employed in Bosnia and Herzegovina. Furthermore, the funding for EFBH considerably exceeded the other country programmes in both absolute and relative terms. This comprehensive approach produced considerable impact, particularly at the institutional level. However, given that KfW also supported the Deposit Insurance Agency and that large volumes of savings were mobilised in Bosnia and Herzegovina, the introduction of stand-by credit lines would further complement efforts to stimulate local fund mobilisation.

- KfW-supported activities started almost at the same time in Albania, Bosnia and Herzegovina, and Romania. However, the German-Romanian Fund made a fresh start in 2000 with the incorporation of new partner banks. The Kosovo programme, which started in 2000, is relatively new. The duration of the intervention seems to have a smaller effect on impact than the overall framework conditions and the scope of intervention.

References

Bank of Albania 2002: Commercial Bank Register.

Bank of Albania: Annual Report 1998, 1999, 2000.

Banking and Payments Authority of Kosovo (BPK) 2001: Annual Report 2000. Prishtina, May 2001.

EU Monitoring Report 2000: Monitoring Support for EC Assistance to Bosnia and Herzegovina, March.

Glaubitt, Klaus 2002: Institutionalizing the European Refinancing Fund in Southeast Europe. *The European Fund for Bosnia and Herzegovina (EFBH), Kosovo (EFK), Montenegro (EFM) and Serbia (EFS). Third EFBH/First Regional Donor Workshop. 10-11 June 2002, Mlini.*

IMF 2002: Bosnia and Herzegovina. Staff Report for the 2001 Article IV Consultation. Washington, DC, February.

IPC 2002: Promotion of the SME Sector in Romania. BMZ No. 98 05 011. Half-Yearly Report. January-June 2002.

Kessler, Katharina and Monika Beck 2001: Republik Albanien. FEFAD II. Schlußprüfungsbericht und BMZ-Teilevaluierung zur "Wirksamkeit der EZ in Tranformationsländern". Frankfurt a.M.

LFS (Abenaa Addai) 2002: The European Fund for Bosnia and Herzegovina: Impact Analysis - Survey Results.

Maurer, Klaus 2001: Assessment and Review of the Terms and Conditions of the Housing and SME Credit Programmes.

Müller, Rainer 2002: Public Opinion on Deposit Insurance in BiH. Internal Paper. Sarajevo, April.

National Bank of Romania 2002: Statistical Section.

National Bank of Romania 2002: Romanian Banking System, March.

Treichel, Volker 2002: Stabilization Policies and Structural Reforms in Albania since 1997 – Achievements and Remaining Challenges. IMF, Washington, DC, February.

PART V:

Summary and Conclusion

CHAPTER 16:

Summary and Conclusion

Ingrid Matthäus-Maier* and J. D. von Pischke**

* Member of the Board of Managing Directors, KfW, Frankfurt, Germany
** President of Frontier Finance International, Inc., Washington DC, USA

Introduction

This book explores three themes related to financial sector development in Southeast Europe (SEE). One is the very positive impact that well-designed development assistance can have on the financial sectors of transition economies, including those that until recently were engaged in armed conflict. Another is the contribution that financial sector development can have on economic recovery and development. The third is the effectiveness of KfW's perspective and strategies that work with and through the financial sectors in SEE.

The results achieved through these approaches demonstrate what donor finance can do in transition economies. Impact in the form of enhanced institutional capacity can be achieved through technical assistance and cooperation and through the provision of funds to retail financial institutions that in turn on-lend to micro and small businesses and to private households for home improvement. KfW plays two roles in this process: it acts as an agent for the German government and other European donors, namely the European Union and development agencies of the governments of Austria, the Netherlands and Switzerland; in addition to that, KfW contributes additional funds mobilised on the international capital markets.

Stability was not yet guaranteed in Southeast Europe in 2002. However, the analyses and observations in this book suggest that cautious optimism is justified, both with regard to the overall situation and to the three points listed above. It is entirely reasonable to conclude, with some satisfaction, that KfW-managed projects in the financial sectors of Southeast Europe are providing a dynamic base for the development of social market economies in the region.

This dynamism is due in large part to KfW's emphasis on fostering sound financial institutions with the specific objective of providing financial services to micro and small enterprises (MSEs) and to private households. The primary strategic objective is to create more efficient financial sectors, because finance integrates all monetised markets, producing gains that benefit society as a whole. To achieve this efficiency objective, we must simultaneously promote and reconcile the complementary goals of competition and sustainability. Success is measured in terms of how well the systems serve the small end of the market, where poor people and others of modest means conduct business. This test relates to the overall objective of development cooperation, which is to improve the living conditions of people in partner countries.

Such improvements are essentially dependent on innovation. The financial innovations developed and employed in Southeast Europe could also benefit other volatile countries and regions. Examples include the introduction of new financial products, the provision of credit lines, the opening of economies formerly closed to foreign investment in the financial sector, and the launching of private banks specialised in serving the small end of the market. Innovations in the public sector include financial market regulation and its application, and deposit insurance, which have chequered performance histories but are essential in modern financial sectors.

The support provided by KfW and its partners has an immediacy and takes on greater importance because of the opportunities and imperatives of EU accession, which will permit much better management of all varieties of risks for transition economies. Further work is necessary to prepare the financial sectors in Southeast Europe for eventual EU accession and to reach agreement on realistic target dates.

The experiences featured in this book demonstrate the three ways in which financial innovation occurs. The first is by lengthening the term structure, making it possible to offer longer loan maturities and to attract longer term deposits, or to build core deposit bases that are stable over the long term and can be used to lend on longer terms. The second form of financial innovation is the reduction of transaction costs. These are the non-interest costs that are required to operate financial institutions, and the non-interest costs that the clients of financial institutions pay to gain access to financial services. Transaction costs create barriers, in terms of time, money and inconvenience.

Finally and most importantly, the third form of innovation is the refinement of valuation processes. The valuation process may be roughly defined as what lenders think they are lending against, including collateral, a borrower's reputation, and whatever else provides confidence and comfort to lenders. Changes in these perceptions can create massive leaps toward sustainability, outreach and impact, as exemplified by a shift from asset-based lending, in which the size of the loan is a function of the value of the physical collateral pledged, to cash flow lending in which loan size is a function of the borrower's projected cash flow.

The following synopsis of the chapters in Parts I through IV highlights how the various policies and initiatives interact to produce developmental results.

Financial Sector and Economic Development in Southeast Europe

Mehl and Winkler of the European Central Bank (chapter 2) demonstrate that financial sector reforms in the second half of the 1990s laid the basis for the financial sectors in Southeast Europe to contribute to economic growth and development. These reforms focused on a) harder public-sector budget constraints in efforts to secure economic stability and efficiency, b) tighter supervision of financial institutions and markets to ensure financial stability, and c) opening the financial sector to foreign investors in order to tap the benefits of competition and modern practices and thereby broaden outreach. Significant progress has been achieved, and the importance of continued efforts in financial sector development is indicated by the lag between SEE and EU accession countries in monetisation and intermediation: SEE financial sectors basically perform mechanical functions such as payment operations and safekeeping. Their potential to contribute to growth-creating intermediation of financial resources is only beginning to be realised.

Approaches to Building Financial Sectors in Southeast Europe

Following the introductory paper on the economies of SEE by Mehl and Winkler, the following two papers lay out the approach applied by KfW in its efforts to promote development in a manner that reduces economic distortions while promoting social wellbeing. The first of these, by Köhn and Erhardt (chapter 3) illustrates how KfW operates in the financial sectors of transition and developing countries, and specifically in Southeast Europe. The approach is based on the realisation that a public-sector investment institution can take risks and pursue strategies which may be considered too risky by private investors, while at the same time being accountable for the responsible use of taxpayers' funds.

KfW's approach to financial sector development is based on four important principles:

First, project design is adapted to local conditions within a broader and robust structural framework that is oriented toward the sustainability of the activity it promotes.

Second, target-group orientation, which in this context emphasises micro, small and medium-sized enterprises because of their capacity to create employment, survive crises and alleviate poverty.

Third, competition and market orientation: KfW carefully selects financial institutions, such as partner banks, that have the potential to operate according to market principles and whose commercial operations are conducive to social progress. Dealing with several institutions simultaneously in a single market creates competition, as demonstrated by the downscaling and greenfield microfinance efforts in SEE. Competition is intended to set in motion processes that will wring the inefficiencies out of nascent markets and ultimately lead to consolidation in the banking industry. Market orientation includes the provision of funds by KfW at rates and with maturities more favourable than those prevailing in the distorted SEE markets in order to facilitate the achievement of clear development objectives. Rational pricing, for example, is achieved by building competitive markets.

Fourth, donor coordination and policy dialogue, which are essential and ongoing elements in the context of SEE financial market promotion.

One important example of donor coordination and policy dialogue is KfW's proposal, outlined by Glaubitt and Schütte (chapter 4), to institutionalise the European funds that support SME programmes and housing finance activities. KfW manages these funds on behalf of the European Commission and the governments of Austria, Germany, the Netherlands (FMO) and Switzerland. Since 1998, these programmes have stimulated the small end of financial markets in Bosnia and Herzegovina, Kosovo, Montenegro and Serbia. Each fund was independently established for a fixed period in each recipient country. Their innovative technical feature is that they lengthen the term structure, thereby enabling local commercial and microfinance banks to offer term loans to clients for investment in productive fixed assets and housing.

One option KfW is currently exploring is institutionalisation by establishing a foundation, preferably permanent and with a regional focus. Institutionalisation involves pooling the funds and managing them in a manner that would continue to encourage private financial institutions to target clients currently regarded too risky and costly to accommodate. This could be achieved by launching innovative services and techniques that reduce transaction costs, lengthen term structures and refine valuation processes.

Ahmed of the International Finance Corporation and Wallace of the European Bank for Reconstruction and Development (chapters 5 and 6) agree that transition unavoidably leads to unemployment. Thus, employment creation in transition economies is imperative, but by its nature a sluggish process. The micro and small enterprise (MSE) sector is most immediately responsive to the opportunities created by liberalisation. The firms in this sector provide the bulk of nonfarm employment and income in Southeast Europe. Judicious financing of MSEs creates leverage that leads to improved social outcomes. Such financing has often been regarded as risky. However, innovations undertaken by financial institutions specialised in serving these target groups have produced sustainable results without continued injections of subsidies – and the methods employed are consistent with good financial practice generally.

Two means of creating the capacity to provide financial services at the small end of the market have been used. First, product development by local commercial banks has been fostered through long-term refinancing and technical assistance that has induced the banks to provide financial services to SMEs. Second, capacity has been created through specialised greenfield institutions ("microfinance banks"). Wallace notes that the provision of long-term funding to and through these banks has helped fill a large gap in the financial system.

A fortuitous feature of MSE portfolios is that they are particularly resilient to crisis, be it in South America as described by Rhyne of ACCION International (chapter 7) or Eastern Europe as noted by Wallace. This feature of MSEs is a function of their flexibility and of their position in the economy, usually at or close to the basic consumption level, which exhibits some immunity to economic shocks.

Neuschütz of the Deutsche Investitions- und Entwicklungsgesellschaft (DEG) (chapter 8) argues for equity investment, the ultimate form of long-term funding, as a tool that permits banks to realise their potential as a source of growth and development. International financial institutions (IFIs), private financiers and strategic investors perform a bridging function by committing venture capital and expert know-how to banks in transition economies. This nurturing makes these banks attractive candidates for a takeover that would present opportunities for increased efficiency, outreach and effectiveness. An increasingly important element in this process is a strategy that allows IFIs and donor agencies and their contractors to exit their role as shareholder, technical assistance provider or lender of long-term funds. A graceful and rewarding exit by those performing any of these bridging functions requires a vision, strategy and long-term planning. This is a continuing challenge in a volatile environment.

All of the roles Neuschütz cites above are designed to foster sound institutions, which requires patience and commitment by management, owners and also by donors and promotional investors and their agents.

Pioneering Banks and Bankers in Southeast Europe

Southeast Europe has attracted pioneering banks and bankers since the second half of the 1990s when foreign investors began to enter the region's financial sectors. The foreign investors brought innovations with them. Foreign commercial banks, especially Austrian banks such as Raiffeisen Zentral Bank (RZB), have vigorously expanded their presence in Southeast Europe in order to exploit their first-mover advantage by acquiring existing banks or by setting up wholly owned subsidiaries. Witte of Raiffeisenbanka Jugoslavija (chapter 9) identifies the incentives for taking a long term view in the region's relatively untapped markets. These include large volumes of savings held outside banks, term structures that are short but which can be lengthened at the network level by international commercial banks, and high interest rates.

Microfinance banks are a new form of financial institution that have been particularly successful in Southeast Europe, as noted above by Wallace of EBRD and by Zeitinger of Internationale Projekt Consult (chapter 10). Success is attributed to a clear governance structure, technical assistance in the start-up phase, international funding and strong management. An innovative and not uncontroversial feature, described by Ahmed as an efficient means of structuring incentives and aligning interests, is that the management services provider is a co-owner of the banks.

Of great importance for MSEs was the establishment of microfinance banks by a core group of like-minded donor institutions consisting primarily of EBRD,

FMO, IFC, and KfW, and DOEN Foundation as a social investor. These organisations collaborated with IPC, which played a dual role, first as the technical partner, and secondly by providing funds through its investment arm IMI The success of these microfinance banks is described by various contributors to this book. Key performance features include strong portfolio development, high portfolio quality, and a commitment to MSEs, exemplified by the fact that the overwhelming majority of loans issued are for amounts of less than € 10,000. As described by Zeitinger, these banks are increasingly becoming universal banks with a diversified range of financial services geared to MSEs.

Providing a range of services to MSE clients was greatly assisted by Commerzbank, which became a shareholder in several of the microfinance banks discussed above. Its participation in this field was a milestone: possibly the first arm's length transaction in which a commercial bank became an equity holder in microfinance institutions for the purpose of concentrating on international trade and payment transactions. Through these banks Commerzbank develops new business with SMEs in Southeast Europe while at the same time facilitating transactions between these new clients and its existing client base in Germany and elsewhere. Baechle of Commerzbank (chapter 11) outlines the bank's strategic view that participation is an attractive alternative to setting up its own branches or agencies.

Research and Impact Analysis

The innovations described in this book have been fostered by an intensive exchange between research and practice, as documented by Heidhues of the University of Hohenheim, Stuttgart (chapter 12). The widely recognised importance of sustainability and institution building is based in part on earlier research on the provision of farm credit in development assistance projects. The precise role that finance can play in improving the welfare of poor households has been documented through massive research on household behaviour in rural and agrarian economies. The work carried out by researchers has led to an understanding of the overlap and complementarity among savings, credit and insurance. Likewise, the careful consideration of incentives is now a standard element in financial project design as a result of innovations in economic analysis.

Research has also led to the introduction of impact analysis as a means of evaluating the effectiveness of donor interventions in financial markets. The overview by Dunn of the University of Missouri (chapter 13) of the use and methods of impact analysis indicates that significant progress has been made in addressing the motivational and technical design challenges of impact assessment. Social scientists and practitioners are defining best practice principles, although some controversial features remain. Microfinance impact assessments have concentrated primarily on the micro level, i.e. the enterprise and the household level. Work on impact assessments at the meso (financial institutions) and macro (financial sector) levels is not so advanced.

Through surveys incorporating interviews with samples of clients and nonclients, Addai and Nienborg of LFS Financial Systems (chapter 14) found that the impact of KfW-sponsored financial sector investments has been mixed but largely positive on enterprise growth and household income. Enterprises using new financial services tend to develop new products, increase their productivity and improve their management. Results differ among the countries surveyed and the client groups served. Generally, impact needs time to materialise.

Wisniwski and Maurer of Bankakademie International (chapter 15) note that the analysis of impact on the financial sector is novel and innovative in its own right. They conclude that the impact of KfW-sponsored financial sector investments on financial institutions and the financial sector is positive. The depth and breath of impact varies depending on the framework conditions, the scope of the programmes, the duration of the intervention and the existence and nature of other donor and government programmes.

Wisniwski and Maurer also conclude that the investments made by donors have helped banks improve their market position, customer base and sales, thereby expanding their outreach to MSEs. These authors note that lending on its own is loss-making for the banks surveyed in some markets because of highly competitive net interest margins between borrowing and lending rates; but that fee income can make these banks profitable overall. The KfW-managed portfolios fared better than overall lending activity due to better loan portfolio quality and lower loan loss provisions. New products and new clients led to cross-selling effects that compensated for lending losses.

The selection of partner banks by KfW, based on its strategy of "picking the winners", was identified by Wisniwski and Maurer as having another impact on the financial sector. The microfinance banks supported by KfW had strong demonstration effects. They also provided a training ground for bank supervisors and central banks, and collaborated with NGOs in ways that promoted access to microfinance offered by these NGOs. In addition, KfW programmes geared towards sector institutions, such as deposit insurance funds and stand-by liquidity guarantees for banks, were evaluated as having a strong positive impact.

Conclusions and Emerging Best Practices

Several general conclusions about SEE financial sector development can be drawn with a high degree of confidence. First, the impact of donor-sponsored financial sector investments can be very positive. Donor intervention has been an essential ingredient in accelerating development. Of greatest importance is that donor interventions have *expanded access* to financial services. The primary beneficiaries are the target groups, such as MSEs, not previously served by formal financial institutions. Donors can help to ensure that these gains will continue to be available to low-income groups by using a financial system approach that provides equity capital, loan funding for rapid outreach, and technical assistance for institution building. Experience in Southeast Europe also demonstrates the importance for financial system development of best practice principles governing institutional behaviour. These include compliance with regulations and industry standards, funding terms oriented to market conditions, and working with, rather than against, market forces and private enterprise.

At this early stage of financial sector development in transition economies, new microfinance banks with foreign ownership occupy critical market niches. These specialised institutions serve MSEs as a means of generating growth and employment. They also offer housing loans for reconstruction purposes. These institutions appear to be essential if the aim is to achieve rapid results, and their market niches, in general, remain relatively robust.

Downscaling, which consists of financing local commercial banks for on-lending to MSEs and providing technical assistance for this purpose, holds promise and has demonstrated a positive impact in Southeast Europe. However, downscaling is often more costly than setting up new institutions due to the time required to reform and strengthen local commercial banks. Adopting innovative strategies such as unconventional lending technologies, new products and a clear business focus on MSE clients requires significant institutional changes in existing banks. The potential for outreach is great, especially when large banks are willing to downscale. The downscaling of local banks also provides a competitive balance to the formation of new microfinance banks.

However, experience indicates that microfinance banks may be a more cost-effective way for donors and investors to reach out to MSEs. Microfinance banks' expenditure on technical assistance per loan is generally lower, and portfolio growth is generally higher, than in downscaling projects. Microfinance banks as greenfield institutions start without any inherited institutional disadvantages and rely on the know-how, expertise and financial resources of their international owners.

The second general conclusion is that donor intervention has positively affected the *market structure* of the financial sector in Southeast Europe by promoting competition among financial institutions and efficiency in financial intermediation. These results affirm KfW's comprehensive approach as featured in this book. This strategy is to provide assistance to new microfinance banks while at the same time refinancing commercial banks and supporting sector level institutions in order to accelerate financial system development.

A third area where donor intervention has played an important role is *governance*. Donors have been instrumental in improving the regulation and supervision of banks in Southeast Europe. Microbanks have set an example in disclosure and transparency, providing clear information on their quantitative performance and development. Transparency is also valuable when dealing with clients: expectations are clear and contractual performance requirements understood. Donor intervention has led to a significantly improved ownership structure in the region's banks, both through equity investments and indirectly through "picking winners." This in turn has attracted investments and, through restructuring, led to acquisitions by private foreign banks.

Nevertheless, the Bolivian case described by Rhyne highlights the fragility and vulnerability of financial systems. National economic factors such as an economic downturn and the impacts of political instability, regulatory barriers facing MSEs, and market factors such as a surge in consumer lending and credit market saturation can lead to over-indebtedness, placing severe financial strains on financial institutions serving the small end of the market. The Bolivian example also highlights the importance of institutional safeguards to prevent as well as cope with crises. Possible safeguards include a) the use of credit bureaus, which can provide the credit histories of loan applicants and indicate the number of lenders to which a borrower is currently indebted, b) strengthening the specialised knowledge of financial regulators so that microfinance is well understood, and c) diversifying the client base served and products offered.

Last but not least, the role of donors is changing as private sector institutions and investors expand their presence. Donor assistance is increasingly complementary and catalytic, and often functions indirectly. This role change is welcomed. Support to sector level institutions holds much promise. Experience indicates that with comparatively limited investments in financial institutions and in funding for sector level institutions, donors can trigger significant developmental impulses.

Outlook and Future Directions

Innovations need time and patience to come to fruition. Full impact seldom materialises quickly, especially in complex settings, as is the case with financial sector reform in Southeast Europe.

Weak macroeconomic conditions, for example a persistently negative balance of payments and sluggish foreign direct investment, reveal the importance of supporting domestic enterprises. Despite significant progress, SEE financial sectors still lag behind those of EU accession countries in terms of monetisation and intermediation, and therefore their contribution to financing the economy is limited. Bottlenecks in lending to MSEs need to be further reduced in order to improve the conditions required to boost economic growth.

However, bottlenecks are likely to remain for some time. For both the microfinance banks and commercial banks, long-term refinancing continues to be highly restricted because of the country risk premia that the international capital market places on Southeast Europe. Basle II requirements are likely to restrict international commercial long-term lending to the region even further. IFIs will therefore continue to play a very substantial and important role as suppliers of funds.

Despite their rapid and sound development, the nascent microfinance banks are prime candidates for continued assistance that will permit them to lengthen the term structures of their assets and thus facilitate longer term investment by MSEs. This can be achieved by linking these banks to the local commercial banking debt markets through appropriate risk sharing mechanisms as well as by developing synergies among the networks of these microfinance banks. This may be pursued through the establishment of a holding structure.

Commercial banks require further financial assistance to enable them to target customers at the lower end in a sustainable manner. In many traditional banks, key barriers to MSE lending remain.

These bottlenecks could be reduced by the institutionalisation of the European Funds in Southeast Europe. Their amalgamation would provide an additional source of funding for MSEs as well as for infrastructure, which could push the financial frontier outward through financial sector innovation. The focus is shifting toward developing the capital market and insurance markets. This would provide banks and enterprises with more sources of long-term financing alternatives. Mutually beneficial public-private partnerships between development finance institutions and private banks are likely to be formed as a basis for leading the financial sectors in Southeast Europe through their next phase of innovations. While the financial sector reform process in the late 1990s provided the basis for the innovations described in this book, these initiatives have been largely driven by the international donor community. In the future, however, the private sector will be expected to take the lead in shaping the banking sector in Southeast Europe.

Opportunities are likely to arise along the region's path towards EU accession that will address the shortcomings and bottlenecks analysed here. However, these opportunities and challenges have so far not been examined in depth. Appropriate policy decisions remain to be developed and implemented.

Index of Names

Index of Countries

Index of Banks and Organisations

Index of Terms

stabilisation and Association
  Process VI
state-owned enterprises 2, 52, 153
sustainability VIII, 47, 53, 55, 56,
  75, 76, 111, 150, 154, 159, 161,
  164, 177, 200, 205, 218, 226, 227,
  230

T

target group 2, 3, 5, 47, 54, 56, 57,
  58, 59, 75, 77, 80, 81, 82, 84, 85,
  87, 109, 116, 126, 144, 145, 151,
  179, 181, 191, 192, 194, 195, 198,
  228, 231
technical assistance (TA) 45, 47,
  56, 57, 64, 66, 72, 73, 76, 80, 82,
  85, 103, 110, 116, 125, 138, 145,
  193, 194, 195, 198, 207, 218, 225,
  228, 229, 231, 232
technical cooperation (TC) 85
term structure 46, 201, 226, 228,
  229, 233

transaction costs 46, 53, 56, 117,
  150, 215, 217, 226, 228
transition countries VIII, 4, 31, 33,
  36, 38, 40, 46, 52, 67, 71, 72, 73,
  75, 77, 79, 101, 103, 104, 105,
  107, 111, 134, 136, 138, 152, 154,
  179, 201
transition economies 2, 16, 34, 38,
  45, 72, 73, 76, 135, 153, 155, 203,
  225, 226, 228, 229, 232

U

upgrading 66, 74, 138, 179, 196

V

valuation 22, 46, 143, 226, 228

Cooperation with Developing and Transition Countries: The KfW Group

The KfW Group gives impetus to economic, political and social development on a global scale. As bankers we work efficiently every day. As promoters we stand for the sense and sustainability of our actions. The proceeds of our work flow back into our promotional activities and help to secure our promotional potential in the long term. The brand names KfW Promotional Bank, KfW SME Bank, KfW Development Bank, DEG and also Export and Project Finance come together under the umbrella of the KfW Group.

On behalf of the German federal government KfW Development Bank finances the expansion of the economic and social infrastructure and enables the introduction of protective measures for natural resources and the environment. DEG supports the private sector through its investments. Their common goal is the sustainable development of the partner countries.

Financial Cooperation (FC) improves the economic and social situation of the people in developing and transition countries and contributes to poverty alleviation, resource conservation and the preservation of peace worldwide.

On behalf of the German federal government KfW Development Bank grants loans at favorable interest rates with long terms and also financial contributions. To complement the funds provided from the federal budget, the KfW Group raises funds on the capital market. It grants the funds it raises either in combination with budget funds as low-interest loans or in the form of promotional loans at market conditions.

KfW Development Bank finances investments in the economic and social infrastructure and also reform programmes. It supports the buildup of efficient financial systems that provide microfinance and supply small and medium-sized enterprises with loans. It also contributes to improving agricultural production. The activities of KfW Development Bank look to the future: the aim is to go beyond the impacts of individual projects and to dismantle structural obstacles to development in the partner countries. KfW is currently financing some 1,400 projects in 109 countries.

The projects promoted via FC funds are selected jointly by the German federal government and the partner country according to development policy criteria. The local partners are responsible for the preparation, implementation and operation of the projects. KfW Development Bank gives them professional advice in planning and implementing and also in monitoring the projects. At the same time, it supervises the proper use of the funds.

Within the KfW Group DEG improves private-sector structures in developing and transition countries, thereby making room for private business initiatives. These initiatives form the basis for sustainable economic growth and a lasting improvement in people's living conditions.

As a specialist for long-term project and corporate finance, DEG advises private enterprises, structures and finances their investments in Africa, Asia and Latin America as well as in Central, Eastern and Southeastern Europe, and in this way mobilises long-term investment capital, technical expertise, and management and marketing experience.

Together with its clients it develops solutions that are adapted to the individual project and the specific risk situation of the relevant country. Additional factors that determine the success of DEG's activities are long-term financings and intensive, lasting support through partnership.

DEG invests in profitable, environmentally and socially sustainable projects in all economic sectors opening up to private entrepreneurial activity.

Another main focus of its work is the development of the financial and capital markets. Local financing institutions are given reinforcement and the spectrum of financial services on offer is being expanded. It is through these financing institutions that small and medium-sized private enterprises gain access to capital.